THEORY OF WOMEN IN RELIGIONS

WOMEN IN RELIGIONS

Series Editor: Catherine Wessinger

Theory of Women in Religions

Catherine Wessinger

NEW YORK UNIVERSITY PRESS
New York

NEW YORK UNIVERSITY PRESS
New York
www.nyupress.org

References to Internet websites (URLs) were accurate at the time of writing. Neither the author nor New York University Press is responsible for URLs that may have expired or changed since the manuscript was prepared.

Library of Congress Cataloging-in-Publication Data
Names: Wessinger, Catherine, 1952–   author.
Title: Theory of women in religions / Catherine Wessinger.
Description: New York : New York University Press, 2020. | Series: Women in religions |
Includes bibliographical references and index.
Identifiers: LCCN 2020016805 (print) | LCCN 2020016806 (ebook) |
ISBN 9781479899197 (cloth) | ISBN 9781479809462 (paperback) |
ISBN 9781479831395 (ebook) | ISBN 9781479860814 (ebook)
Subjects: LCSH: Women and religion.
Classification: LCC BL458 .W44 2020 (print) | LCC BL458 (ebook) | DDC 200.82—dc23
LC record available at https://lccn.loc.gov/2020016805
LC ebook record available at https://lccn.loc.gov/2020016806

New York University Press books are printed on acid-free paper, and their binding materials are chosen for strength and durability. We strive to use environmentally responsible suppliers and materials to the greatest extent possible in publishing our books.

Manufactured in the United States of America

10 9 8 7 6 5 4 3 2 1

For Clinton and Ken, to Robert S. Ellwood with appreciation for his encouragement to write this book, and in memory of Sister Fara Impastato, O.P. (1920–2014), who pioneered Women's Studies at Loyola University New Orleans.

CONTENTS

ACKNOWLEDGMENTS

This book has benefited from input from many colleagues, friends, and supporters. I am grateful to Rebecca Moore and Laura Vance for reading all or portions of the manuscript and providing very helpful feedback. The book has benefited enormously from comments provided by anonymous reviewers of the manuscript, and I appreciate the time and effort they put into providing me with feedback to improve the book. I thank Jennifer Hammer of New York University Press for her expert editorial guidance.

I thank Henrietta Stockel for input on the book's discussions of the Chiricahua and Mescalero Apache, and Linda E. Olds for sending me her comments on the psychology chapter. I thank Karma Lekshe Tsomo for her advice on the section on the ordination of Buddhist nuns; Kecia Ali for feedback on issues involving Muslim women and for making me aware of the work of Amina Wadud; Deborah Halter for guidance on Catholic doctrines, documents published by the Vatican, and assistance locating photos; Bishop Jane Via and Bishop Suzanne Thiel of Roman Catholic Womenpriests-USA for information on the Roman Catholic Women Priests movement and its history; Sister Terri Bednarz, R.S.M., for information on the Sisters of Mercy of the Americas and for sharing her New Testament studies expertise with me; and Sister Annmarie Sanders, I.H.M., associate director for communications of the Leadership Conference of Women Religious, for checking the paragraphs that I wrote about the LCWR and tensions with the Vatican. Thanks go to Scott Lowe for answering my questions relating to Chinese language matters and to Robert Pearson Flaherty for his assistance with romanization of Korean names.

I thank Chengpang Lee and Ling Han for publishing their insightful article, "Mothers and Moral Activists: Two Models of Women's Social Engagement in Contemporary Taiwanese Buddhism," in the journal I co-edit, *Nova Religio: The Journal of Alternative and Emergent Religions.*

I have cited their article in this book, and I appreciate their reading and correcting the section in which I discuss Dharma Master Cheng Yen and SHIH Chao-hwei and their respective expressions of social activism. Lee and Han's insightful article illustrates a strategy I have noted in the movement of women living in conservative religious societies beyond the patriarchal gender role of wife and mother to social activist.

Through my years at Loyola University New Orleans, I have had fruitful conversations with colleagues Tiina Allik and Elizabeth Goodine about feminism and the study of women in religions, and I appreciate their sharing their views with me.

I am grateful to Henry John Drewal, Denis Vejas, the Episcopal Diocese of Massachusetts, Shih Chao-hwei and the Hongshi Buddhist Theological School, Jorge Mañes Rubio, Melissa Hammer and Sonia Epstein, and the photographers who have contributed images to Wikimedia Commons for permission to publish the photographs included in this book.

I thank my students at Loyola University New Orleans for the questions, discoveries, and analyses they expressed in my "Women in World Religions" course, which I have taught since the early 1990s. I continue to learn from my students and their explorations into women in religions. One insightful student, Jaime Elizabeth Johnston, is quoted in the conclusion.

I appreciate Robert S. Ellwood's encouragement of my writing this book many years ago before I was sidetracked by another important research project. I am grateful to have known and been inspired by Sister Fara Impastato, O.P. (1920–2014), the first women professor in the Religious Studies Department at Loyola University New Orleans, who pioneered women's studies at the university. Lastly, my son, Clinton, and husband, Ken, have lived with me during the various periods I was writing this book and attempting to live out the lessons learned in my studies of women in societies and religions; I am glad to have them in my life. This book is dedicated in gratitude to Sister Fara Impastato, Robert S. Ellwood, Clinton Wessinger, and Ken Richards.

Introduction

Why Study Women in Religions?

In the previous two centuries, economic, educational, and social changes have permitted some women to make gains toward greater equality in their religious traditions as well as in diverse new religious movements. However, equality for women in many religions and societies remains contested throughout the world. Religious beliefs and worldviews have been used to justify the subordination and abuse of girls and women. Religious beliefs and worldviews have also been used to support the equality of girls and women.

In order to illuminate the factors impacting women in religions in the present and future, we need to explore the social and religious dynamics of the past. Is patriarchy in religion and society inevitable? Is subordination of women in society caused by religion? Are sexist aspects of religion developed in response to sexism in society? Is it possible to create families, societies, and religions in which females and males are equal? If so, what are the factors that promote equality?

This book provides an overview of socioeconomic and psychological factors and dynamics supporting patriarchy in the past and in the present. It shows how religion is often used to promote sexism and enforce patriarchy and, conversely, how women and men are utilizing and shaping religions to support women's equality. *Patriarchy* is defined here as male dominance in family, society, and institutions, including organized religious activities. This book puts forward a theory concerning the socioeconomic factors that supported the development of patriarchy through various patterns of societies, as well as the factors supporting the transition toward increasing equality of girls and women in societies and their religions. It draws on relevant data and theories in several disciplines—anthropology, archaeology, history, sociology, psychology, and gender studies—and integrates them into a history of religions approach to the study of women in religions.[1]

Religious worldviews and gender roles interact with each other in complex ways. The nature of a society's economy, which is shaped by the technologies that humans use to feed themselves and their families, influences family and political structures beginning with a division of labor by sex. Early full-time specialization and division of labor by sex allotted public religious, political, and other roles to men, which resulted over time in less flexibility in roles for women. Religion is a key arena for the promulgation of gender ideals, roles, and relationships that reinforce economic and gender inequalities in families and society.

Religion is one of the most important sites for social and individual construction of gendered roles and meaning. Religious myths, scriptures, theologies, ethical norms, and religious law codes reinforce unequal gender arrangements, class hierarchies, and other social inequalities such as those based on ethnicity or race. However, even in highly patriarchal religious traditions, women develop and maintain their own religious expressions and interpretations. Moreover, religious representations of gender and inequalities are contested, not fixed, and may change over time.

Every religious tradition is internally diverse and contains resources that can be used to support gender equality, as well as other resources that can be used to support the subordination of women.[2] (The same is true in relation to contested class and ethnic hierarchies.) These resources include myths, scriptural passages, theological or philosophical concepts, ritual activities, and recollections of significant foremothers. Which religious resources are utilized and become predominant is dependent to a great extent on the economic structures of the culture, which influence the degree to which there is widespread social expectation for the subordination of women or for gender equality.

When technological and economic changes cause the division of labor by sex to begin breaking down, and women gain increasing access to education and economic earning power, they and members of other disadvantaged groups will seek equal access to positions of religious leadership, reinterpret or reject myths that have been used to justify subordination, and revise previously oppressive theology. Advocates of gender equity will mine the resources of their religious traditions to locate empowering teachings, scriptures, and role models for women active in religion and society. This is increasingly happening in the world's religions. At the same time, some women will depart from the religious traditions in which they were raised to move to more affirming religions, or to shape or discover new religions they find empowering, or to abandon religious belief altogether.

Struggles for Equality

Women's equality in religions and societies continues to be highly challenged. Some of the cases that we learn about from the news and other sources relate to women's struggles for equality within their religious institutions and cultures, while other cases are literally matters of life and death. All of the instances of subordination and oppression are caused by sexist attitudes that devalue girls and women so that they are seen to varying degrees as being less than human.[3] Consider the following examples of women struggling for their equality and their religious and human rights.

The Vatican versus American Sisters

In 2012, toward the end of the tenure of Pope Benedict XVI (papacy 2005–2013), the Vatican's Congregation for the Doctrine of the Faith (CDF) issued a "doctrinal assessment" of the Leadership Conference of Women Religious (LCWR), an organization consisting of the heads of 80 percent of the orders of Catholic sisters in the United States. The doctrinal assessment charged the sisters affiliated with the LCWR of being concerned primarily with social justice issues, not supporting the Vatican's prohibition of the ordination of women to the Catholic priesthood, protesting the Vatican's approach to pastoral ministry to homosexuals,[4] taking positions contradicting the Vatican's teachings on human sexuality, and not being sufficiently active against abortion and euthanasia.[5] The doctrinal assessment alleged that speakers at annual LCWR assemblies made "radical feminist" statements inconsistent with Catholic teachings promoted by the *magisterium* (the teaching authority of bishops headed by the pope). Most importantly it found that the LCWR was not sufficiently obedient to Catholic bishops, "especially the Roman Pontiff." To rectify the many errors the CDF saw being promoted by the LCWR, it appointed Archbishop J. Peter Sartain of Seattle as "Archbishop Delegate" along with two other bishop delegates to oversee the implementation of a mandate for the revision of the LCWR's governing statutes and the content of its conferences and instructional materials and ensure that the Mass would "have place of priority in LCWR events and programs."[6] The Eucharist, necessarily celebrated by a priest, would be a central part of LCWR gatherings.[7] (In the Catholic Church, the priesthood and all other ordained positions are reserved for men.)[8]

In April 2015, the CDF and the LCWR issued a joint statement that the mandate was completed, and the LCWR officers met with Pope Francis (papacy 2013 to present) for one hour. One month later, the LCWR issued a statement saying that "the sanctions called for in the CDF mandate were disproportionate to the concerns raised." It revealed that the LCWR officers and members "felt publicly humiliated as the false accusations [in the doctrinal assessment] were re-published repeatedly in the press." Despite experiencing the pain of unjust criticism of the LCWR, the sisters concluded that the "communal contemplative prayer," listening, and dialogue "processes in which we engaged as a conference became a profound source of personal growth for each of us and deepened and strengthened the bonds that exist among us as women religious."[9]

Mormon Women Request the Priesthood

Priesthood in the Church of Jesus Christ of Latter-day Saints (LDS Church, or Mormon Church) is available to every Mormon male who is deemed worthy. Boys may be ordained into the Aaronic priesthood at age twelve, and young men may be ordained into the Melchizedek priesthood at age eighteen. The priesthood is necessary to hold leadership positions in the LDS Church. All girls and women are excluded from being ordained in any form of the LDS priesthood. Mormon women are expected to support priesthood holders and be active in a women's international philanthropic organization called the Relief Society.

On October 5, 2013, about two hundred Mormon women affiliated with Ordain Women, a group that advocates that girls and women

Sister Simone Campbell, Executive Director of Network: A National Social Justice Lobby, speaks in lower Manhattan on September 24, 2012 as part of the Nuns on the Bus tour against a Republican-proposed budget that the sisters argued would be detrimental to the poor. This was the first of a series of annual Nuns on the Bus tours on behalf of social justice issues. Courtesy of Thomas Altfather Good, Wiki Commons.

receive the same ordinations in the LDS Church priesthood as boys and men, gathered outside the Tabernacle on Temple Square in Salt Lake City, Utah. As they watched boys and men enter the Tabernacle to attend a meeting termed the "priesthood session," each woman politely asked the LDS Church representative for an admission ticket and each was told she could not enter. Danielle Mooney of Boston, Massachusetts, asked if all the boys and men entering the Tabernacle were priests, and she was told that not all of them held the priesthood. Mooney replied, "Well, I'm not a priesthood holder, but I am a member of the church." Husbands supportive of Ordain Women told the church representative, "I'd like to attend the priesthood session with my wife, because the church says that families are so important,"[10] but they were told they would have to enter the session without their wives.

On June 22, 2014, Kate Kelly (b. 1980), the founder of Ordain Women, was excommunicated for her ongoing public work on behalf of the ordination of girls and women in the LDS Church.[11] After her appeal of the excommunication was rejected by the president of her stake (a region containing several LDS congregations), and then by the LDS Church First Presidency (consisting of the president of the church plus two counselors), Kate Kelly moved on to work as a human rights lawyer at Equality Now in New York City.[12] Nevertheless Ordain Women continues to advocate for ordination of girls and women in the Church of Jesus Christ of Latter-day Saints.[13]

"Gendercide" in India

Many Indians—the majority of whom are Hindu—utilize medical technology to determine the sex of an unborn child and then abort female fetuses in the hope that a subsequent pregnancy will produce a son.[14] Female feticide, female infanticide, and murder of young wives so the husband's family may acquire dowry wealth from another bride's family have economic motivations in a society in which sons are preferred, having daughters poses significant economic costs, and the country is modernizing but material resources remain scarce.

The frequent manner of killing wives by setting them on fire has resonance with Hindu myths in which the goddess Sati burned herself to death in response to her father's insult to her husband, Śiva. In certain parts of India, a woman who committed *sati* by being burned (allegedly voluntarily) on the funeral pyre of her deceased husband is venerated as a goddess, a *sati* (literally, "good woman"). Strict legislation against aiding and abetting *sati* was passed after the 1987 *sati* of eighteen-year-old Roop Kanwar, but occasional cases of *sati* have persisted through the early 2000s. A rough idea of the magnitude of the problem of murder of women by fire can be seen in the results of a study that was published in the medical journal *The Lancet*, which reported that out of over 163,000 fire-related deaths in India in 2001, about 106,000 were women between the ages of fifteen and thirty-four.[15] Some wives survive an attempted dowry murder by fire or acid and spend the remainder of their lives in great suffering; other desperate wives commit or attempt suicide to escape abuse by their husbands and their husbands' family members who are demanding additional dowry.[16] In response, the website of the 50 Million Missing

Campaign, founded by Rita Banerji, includes a page offering advice to young women and their parents about how to spot warning signs during marriage negotiations and after the wedding that indicate that the groom's family may be planning to demand exorbitant dowry and endanger the young wife's life.[17]

Muslim Girls' Education in Afghanistan and Pakistan

On November 12, 2008, eleven girls and four female teachers walking to school in Kandahar, Afghanistan, were assaulted by men, probably Taliban, who pulled their *burqa*s from their heads and sprayed or threw acid into their faces. Some of the 1,300 students attending Mirwais School for Girls were in their late teens and early twenties who had not had the opportunity to attend school earlier. The Taliban government in Afghanistan, which was toppled by the American military invasion in 2001, had banned the education of girls and women, as well as women's activities and work outside the home. Two weeks after the acid attacks, the female teachers and the male principal, supported by fathers and mothers who wanted their daughters to gain education, reopened the school, and brave Afghan girls and young women resumed attending.[18]

The Taliban in neighboring Pakistan also wanted to prevent girls from being educated. The most high profile case in Pakistan of a Taliban attack against a girl attending school involved Malala Yousafzai (b. 1997), who was living in the Swat District of Pakistan and who began blogging on the need for girls' education when she was eleven. Subsequently she appeared in a *New York Times* documentary and gave numerous print and television interviews advocating for the right of girls to attend school. On October 9, 2012, she and two other girls were shot as they rode in a school bus that was invaded by two Taliban, young men in their twenties. A bullet struck Malala in the head and passed through her neck. Malala was ultimately taken to Birmingham, United Kingdom, for medical treatment, and she and her parents and brothers were given asylum.[19] In 2013 she was nominated for the Nobel Peace Prize. In 2014 she was co-winner of the Nobel Peace Prize. Meanwhile teachers in parts of Pakistan where the Taliban are active continue to risk their lives to teach girls, and girls risk their lives by attending school.

Malala Yousafzai speaks at Women of the World Festival at the Southbank Centre in London on March 8, 2014. Courtesy of Southbank Centre, in Wikimedia Commons.

Subordination of Buddhist Nuns

Women wishing to become fully ordained Buddhist nuns (Sanskrit, *bhikṣuṇī*; Pali, *bhikkhunī*) have more stringent rules applied to their ordinations than men who become fully ordained monks (Sanskrit, *bhikṣu*; Pali, *bhikkhu*). Women have a two-year probationary status before full ordination, which men do not have. Whereas full ordination of a man as a *bhikṣu* is conferred by ten *bhikṣus*, full ordination of a woman as a *bhikṣuṇī* must be conferred by ten *bhikṣuṇīs* and then by ten *bhikṣus*. These rules are recorded in the *vinaya* (code of monastic discipline) as coming from Gautama Buddha (ca. 563 B.C.E.–ca. 483 B.C.E.)—referred to informally by many as simply the Buddha; hence, many fully ordained monks believe that they cannot be revised. The *vinaya* states that the Buddha gave eight *gurudharmas* (weighty rules) to *bhikṣuṇīs*, which have the effect of subordinating all *bhikṣuṇīs* to all *bhikṣus*. One of the weighty rules states that a *bhikṣuṇī*, even if she has been ordained one hundred years, must bow down to a *bhikṣu*, even if he has been ordained only one day.[20] Though contemporary nuns in

Mahāyāna Buddhist areas such as China, Taiwan, Vietnam, and South Korea, as well as Chinese populations outside the People's Republic of China, have full ordination as *bhikṣuṇī*s and are respected religious leaders, for centuries in Southeast Asia and Tibet, nuns have not had access to full ordination and have been less respected and not fully included in Buddhist education.

Since 1987 Buddhist women have participated in an international organization named Sakyadhita (Daughters of the Buddha), which works for the improved status of Buddhist women including nuns.[21] In 2001 SHIH Chao-hwei (b. 1957), a Mahāyāna Buddhist *bhikṣuṇī*, scholar, teacher, and activist in Taiwan, supported by male and female scholars of Buddhism attending a conference, publicly rejected the eight weighty rules.[22]

The work of educated lay nuns called *mae chii*s (who keep eight, nine, or ten precepts) in Thailand such as Khunmae Prathin Kwanon (b. 1944), an educator and social activist on behalf of women and children, and Khunying Kanitha (1922–2002), an attorney and also social activist on behalf of women and children, contributed significantly to the establishment of two institutions for the education of *mae chii*s, the Institute of Thai Maechees founded in 1969 and the Mahapajapati Theri College founded in 1999.[23] In recent decades, nuns in Theravada Buddhist traditions in Sri Lanka and Thailand have worked for and obtained full ordination, thus reestablishing the *bhikkhunī sangha* (community of fully ordained nuns) in Sri Lanka,[24] and establishing it for the first time in Thailand, where the ordination of *bhikkhunī*s continues to be illegal. Nevertheless, led by Dhammananda Bhikkhunī (formerly Dr. Chatsumarn Kabilsingh, b. 1944), a retired university professor of Buddhist philosophy who received full ordination in Sri Lanka, the nearly one hundred Thai *bhikkhunī*s are becoming accepted by laypersons if not by Thai monks and the government.[25]

Tibetan nuns living outside Tibet, now part of the People's Republic of China, who like virtually all ethnic Tibetan nuns have novice status, are studying to obtain the highest degree in Tibetan Buddhist philosophy and are becoming leaders in the Tibetan diaspora community. The first twenty *geshema* degrees earned by Tibetan nuns were awarded in October 2016 by Tenzin Gyatso (b. 1935), the Fourteenth Dalai Lama, who has encouraged the nuns' studies.[26] Ogyen Trinley Dorje (b. 1985),

the Seventeenth Karmapa, has promised to fulfill his vow to administer *bhikshunī* ordination to nuns in the Karma Kagyü order of Tibetan
Buddhism.

Disputed Gender Roles for Women in the Southern Baptist Convention

Although the Southern Baptist Convention in the United States has a
democratic polity in which congregations vote to ordain ministers, and
may, if they choose, ordain women, discrimination in this Christian
denomination has persisted. The Baptist religion holds that every person is free to interpret the Bible for herself or himself and that each
person can have his or her own direct, unmediated relationship with
God. Yet, currently in the Southern Baptist Convention, Baptist funda-
mentalism, which takes a literalist approach to interpreting the Bible, is
weighted strongly against the ordination of women, the hiring of women
as pastors, and women teaching men theology in any capacity including
as seminary professors. "Literalist" here refers to the *belief* that scripture
is being interpreted literally, even as literalists read translated biblical
passages through the lens of a theological faith position. That is, scriptural literalists do not actually interpret the meaning of passages in their
original languages and in light of the social contexts in which they were
composed. Based on literalist readings of New Testament passages, the
elected delegates to the annual Southern Baptist Convention have twice
passed resolutions (in 1984 and 2000) stating that women should not
teach theology to men and should not be pastors. During the period
of the "fundamentalist takeover" of the Southern Baptist Convention
from the late 1970s through the early 1990s, women and "moderate" (as
opposed to "conservative") professors were purged from Southern Baptist seminaries.

A high-profile case involved the forced resignation in 1994 of Professor Molly T. Marshall from the theological faculty at the Southern
Baptist Theological Seminary in Louisville, Kentucky. Marshall was
accused of heresy by fundamentalist Southern Baptists. This episode
was painful to Marshall, as well as to her female and male feminist
students whose support for Marshall was not heeded by the seminary
president and the board members. Marshall is currently president of

Central Baptist Theological Seminary in Shawnee, Kansas, which serves students—including female students—in seven locations in the world and has female and male faculty.[27] In 2018, Marshall published an essay denouncing the use of "selective" biblical inerrancy (the belief that the Bible contains no errors) in order to "preserve male privilege."[28]

Controversy over Orthodox Jewish Women as Rabbis

Although women are ordained rabbis in Reform Judaism, Reconstructionist Judaism, and Conservative Judaism, until recently women have not been ordained rabbis in Orthodox Judaism, and female rabbis remain controversial. A rabbi is someone whose education in Torah—the Hebrew Bible and Talmud—and *halakha* (Jewish religious law) is officially recognized. A rabbi instructs other Jews in how to live and worship as Jews according to Torah. In today's Judaism, a rabbi may be hired by a congregation to perform pastoral care functions as well as teaching. While more women in Orthodox Jewish groups have been studying Torah, and some women have become experts, many Orthodox congregations continue to maintain distinct gender roles, practice sex segregation during worship, and do not ordain women as rabbis. In an Orthodox synagogue the public worship and Torah study space generally belongs to men, and women sit out of the men's sight and pray silently so as not to distract the male worshippers.

Nevertheless, since 2009 a small number of women have been ordained *maharat* (a qualified legal, spiritual, and Talmudic leader), or *rabba* (female rabbi) or *rabbanit*. The term *rabbanit* is "another way to render rabbi in the feminine, but one that historically has designated the wife of a rabbi. However, these women proudly use this honorific to show that they are masters of Jewish law."[29] The first of the ordained Orthodox women was Sara Hurwitz (b. 1977), who was ordained *maharat* by Rabbi Avi Weiss (b. 1944) and Rabbi Daniel Sperber (b. 1940). After Weiss changed her title to *rabba*, other Orthodox rabbis protested. Subsequently, in 2009, Rabba Sara Hurwitz became dean of the newly founded Yeshivat Maharat in the Bronx, in New York City. The school permits its graduates to choose their titles—*maharat, rabba,* or *rabbanit*. Yeshivat Maharat's graduates are being hired by Orthodox congregations. In 2016 Lila Kagedan became the first graduate of Yeshivat

Maharat with the title *rabbi* and she was hired to serve at the Mount Freedom Jewish Center in Randolph, New Jersey. In 2017, the Orthodox Union, whose membership includes more than four hundred Orthodox synagogues in North America, "adopted a policy prohibiting its synagogues from hiring female clergy," so the employment prospects of future graduates of Yeshivat Maharat remain to be seen. At the present time, most are hired in synagogues "under the direction of a senior male rabbi."[30]

Muslim Women Giving Sermons and Leading Congregational Prayers

A number of Muslim cultures promote sex segregation, which means that men and women who are not related or married should not interact with each other. In such Islamic societies men generally have dominance in public spaces, while women are supposed to remain at home, or if they go out they must be covered and accompanied by a male relative. Although during the lifetime of Muhammad (571–632 C.E.) Muslim women and men prayed together in the mosque (*masjid*) in Medina, Islamic sex segregation has been extended to occasions of public prayer, especially in a mosque. The day and hour for weekly congregational prayer in a mosque is Friday after 12:00 noon. The sermon given at Friday midday worship is called *khutbat al-juma* (narration at the time of congregational prayer), and the person giving the sermon is termed a *khatib*. The *khatib* usually serves as *imam* (leader), the one who leads the congregation in prayer, but the role of *khatib* and *imam* may be performed by two different people. In Islam there are no ordained clergy. Respected members of the community are asked to serve as *khatib* and *imam*. Since the mosque is a public space, women frequently pray at home, or if they go to the mosque for Friday prayer, they pray in an area separate from the men. Customarily only a man may serve as *khatib* and *imam*. Until recently a woman was able to serve as *khatib* and *imam* only in groups consisting of women.

In 1994 Amina Wadud (b. 1952), an African American woman who converted to Islam when she was twenty and is a professor of Qur'anic studies, became the first woman in contemporary times to give a sermon to a congregation of men and women, which she did in the mosque of the Muslim Youth Movement of South Africa in Capetown. In March 2005 she gave a sermon and led the prayer in a Muslim congregation of both sexes gathered in a room in the annex of the (Episcopalian) Cathedral of St. John the Divine in New York City, with tight security because of bomb threats. Due to international media attention to the event, many Muslim religious scholars responded by issuing *fatwas* (legal opinions) against women leading prayers in congregations consisting of men and women, although a few scholars issued *fatwas* in support of the practice.[31] Wadud, and now other women, continue to lead prayers in mixed congregations.

Inspired by women's mosques in other countries, the Women's Mosque of America was founded in 2014, in Los Angeles, California. In its once-monthly Friday congregational prayer gatherings, women give the sermons and lead the prayers. Women and children, including boys age twelve and younger, may attend the Friday service.[32] The women's mosque movement is spreading in various countries.

Study of Women in Religions

Discrimination against women as illustrated in these examples is rooted in a binary view of gender, which alleges differences in the humanity of males and females. This viewpoint frequently moves toward the perspective that males are good and females are weak-willed and inclined toward evil and must be controlled by men. Gender dualism in society may be expressed in religion in oral and written myths, customs, theologies, and law codes.

Supported by socioeconomic factors relating to women's increased earning power and education, and therefore increasing social expectations of equality—all of which exist unevenly in societies today—women across the globe are resisting patriarchy and working to achieve equality of girls and women with boys and men. Some religious traditions are responding by making changes to include females on an equal basis, while some individuals and religious institutions and cultures are resisting calls for equality.

Education can often be a means by which women become knowledgeable about their rights within their religious traditions. Yet religious education may also be a means to teach women to accept subordination in families, communities, and religions. Secular education can enable women to gain skills leading to economic earning power, which tends to improve women's status in families and society. But the improvement process is not simple or direct. As women become more knowledgeable about their rights in society and religion and begin to speak up, they face sexism and backlash. Education in itself does not immediately empower women, but it does create conditions in which more women may seek to speak and act on behalf of themselves and other women.

This book introduces relevant methodologies, terms, and concepts to aid in understanding women and their roles, representations, and challenges within religious traditions. It discusses theories relating to the emergence of patriarchy, debunks an invasion theory of the origin of patriarchy that was popular among feminists in the 1970s and 1980s and continues to have a following, and draws on archaeology, anthropology, history, sociology, psychology, and history of religions to articulate a theory of economic and psychological factors that shape gender roles and thereby impact women's place and treatment in religions. It shows how technological and related economic and social factors influence gender roles and the extent to which there is equality or subordination of women. And it discusses how the myths, theologies, and law codes in religious traditions reinforce socially accepted gender roles.

Economic empowerment and education are keys to improving the status of girls and women throughout the world. When women are educated and economically self-sufficient, they are more likely to undertake the work of implementing changes toward equality in their religious traditions and cultures, although, as noted, they face the resistance of sexist men and women. If the resistance to women's equality is too entrenched, some women may choose to join or found other religious groups or leave religion altogether.

The theoretical discussion in this book relates what historian of religions Rita M. Gross termed "developmental patterns of societies"[33] and their gender roles as delineated by anthropologists and archaeologists to the study of women in religions. Scholars in the fields of anthropology and archaeology discuss gender roles associated with *foraging* (hunting and gathering), *pastoralism* (keeping herds of domesticated animals either by sedentary or nomadic peoples), *horticulture* (planting seeds with digging sticks or hoes), *intensive agriculture* (tilling the ground with a plow pulled by draft animals), and *complex societies* (class-stratified state societies in which there is craft specialization and which has an intensive agricultural base). In recent centuries we have seen the development of *industrialized societies*, and very recently, *postindustrial societies* in the digital, information age, which nevertheless continue to rely on industrial production.

This book argues that the available technologies for subsistence (physical survival and well-being) shape the economy in which women and men make decisions about division of labor, which then become customary and reinforced by gender ideologies and religious traditions. The gender customs and values of a society influence the psychology of girls and boys, women and men, who may draw on religious expressions to reinforce their culturally defined roles and identities or to broaden those gender expectations to some degree. The book argues further that in contemporary societies, due to economic, educational, social, and also psychological factors, the division of labor by sex is breaking down. This is resulting in changes in gender roles and women beginning to demand and work for equality within their respective religious cultures.

Chapter 1 describes the beginning of the academic study of women in religions and its relationship to waves of feminist movements. It discusses how the intersectionality of racism, sexism, homophobia, class disparities and class domination, and prejudice and discrimination directed toward members of particular cultures and religions is relevant to the study of situations of females in various parts of the world.[34] This type of study is necessary to discern constructive efforts that may be exerted on behalf of girls and women.

This chapter also elaborates the interdisciplinary methodology used in the book, and defines terms that are relevant to the study of women in religions. It offers the term *classical patriarchy*[35] to refer to class-stratified, hierarchical societies in which inheritance is patrilineal, residence of married couples is patrilocal, sons are valued over daughters, women of well-to-do classes do not have direct access to economic productivity and therefore have their work devalued, and a double standard of morality is applied to women of particular classes in order to control their sexuality. In classical patriarchy, family "honor" is based on the sexual "purity" of women, and a woman whose sexual purity is regarded as compromised is seen as disposable. Women in classical patriarchy collude with men to perpetuate women's subordination in order to receive the benefits they perceive as accruing to themselves in these social systems. The chapter points out that matrilineal and matrilocal societies are *not* matriarchal; at the same time, it shows that women in these societies have advantages that women do not have in classically patriarchal societies. The types of technology and economy that are usually associated with matrilineal and matrilocal societies and classical patriarchy societies are described.

Chapter 2 outlines the book's primary economic theory that relates developmental patterns of societies and their respective gender roles to the study of women in religions. The "invasion theory" of the origin of patriarchy promoted by archaeologist Marija Gimbutas, which was strongly influential on the views of feminists in the late twentieth century and which continues to be a popular theory in some quarters, is demonstrated to lack supporting evidence. The invasion theory provides a mythic explanation of women's "fall" into patriarchy and implies that women will again be great in the future. This chapter discusses the economic theory of the emergence, continuation, and transformation of patriarchies based on the work of anthropologist Ernestine Friedl and historian Gerda Lerner and describes a range of prehistoric, historical, and ethnographic examples.

Chapter 3 considers several psychological theories of how male dominance, patriarchal family and social structures, and gender roles affect the psychologies of women and men and the self-esteem of girls and women. Psychological theories compatible with the economic theory are presented in this chapter, including the thesis of psychoanalytic sociologist Nancy Chodorow and psychoanalytic psychologist Dorothy Dinnerstein that psychological resistance to women in positions of authority is caused by children's rebellion against their primary nurturers in patriarchal societies—their mothers; professor of psychology Linda E. Olds's thesis that patriarchy is supported by dichotomous thinking, and her description of "feminine-identified women," "masculine-identified men," and "androgynous women and men" as a means to reflect on gender roles adopted and performed by individuals; and feminist author Gloria Steinem's thesis that for a feminist revolution to occur in society, there first has to be a "revolution from within" by women engaging in various means of increasing personal self-esteem, which has been eroded and torn down by forces of sexism and patriarchy.

Chapter 4 describes issues that are significant to the study of women in religions and gives a variety of illustrative examples. These issues include gender roles; marriage and divorce; property rights for women; myths and doctrines about the cause of the limitations of the human condition; views of women's bodies; violence against women; women as religious specialists based on charisma and shamanism and women as religious specialists based on credentials possibly combined with charisma; goddesses and other concepts of the divine; inclusion of women in rituals, women's rituals, and rituals that affirm women; whether or not the religious tradition and religious persons extend equality to LGBTQ persons; and whether or not there is movement beyond patriarchy in the religion. An examination of these issues indicates the degree to which women are equal or subordinated in a religious and cultural tradition.

The conclusion considers where we are going in cultures and religions as women begin to gain equality and gender roles change. With technological and economic changes, the division of labor between women and men is slowly starting to break down, at least in some families. When parents play equal roles in nurturing their children, childhood and youthful rebellion is directed toward both fathers and mothers, so the dread of women in positions of religious and secular authority theoretically will start to diminish. When distinct gender roles break down due to women and men doing similar types of work, children may take either or both parents as role models. Same-sex couples who are rearing children illuminate the limitations of the binary conceptualization of gender roles in parenting, and studies are demonstrating that their children thrive due to the increased attention they generally receive from both their parents.

As the social expectation of equality in society increases, women begin to expect and demand changes in their traditionally patriarchal religions. Some religious traditions are moving women into positions of authority and are using inclusive language for God and human be-ings in rituals and scriptures, while other religious traditions continue to resist these changes. Some women move on to create or participate in new religious movements that express and support women's equality. Other women leave organized religion altogether, which is the increas-ing trend today.

1

Foundations, Methodology, and Key Terms

In the mid-1960s women who were newly admitted to graduate programs in theology and religious studies began asking why women were missing from the content of courses and curricula. They started to undertake their own research on women in religious traditions. Female graduate students pursued these questions and studies of women in religions and theology often in spite of a lack of encouragement or in the face of active discouragement from their male professors.[1] By the early 1970s, there was an explosion of scholarly literature on women in religions, and there is no sign that this expansion of knowledge is slowing. This important and vast new body of knowledge is being produced because a sufficient number of feminist women and men are active researchers and authors in academia. They ask questions about women in history, societies, and religious traditions and pursue the acquisition and analysis of this data.

Prior to this period, men dominated the academic disciplines. To this day male-dominated disciplines and university programs remain in all parts of the world. Feminist scholars in all disciplines have pointed out that male-dominated scholarship has been *androcentric* (male-focused). The androcentric perspective assumes that women are included in the study of "man," but women are largely invisible to this outlook. In the history of religions, the androcentric perspective blinded male academics from seeing the study of women's religious lives as being important.[2] It prevented them from seeing the presence of women and of female metaphors for God in scriptures. And it also prevented them from seeing the implications of passages in scriptures and theological writings that disparage women, sanction the subordination of women, and sometimes sanction physical violence to control women.

Rita M. Gross, a pioneer in the academic study of women and religions, points out that a "quadruple androcentrism" affected knowledge of religious traditions:

First, in most religious traditions, those who kept that tradition's records chose to record men's experiences and thinking much more frequently than women's. Second, even when information about women was recorded, later commentators often neglected to keep those records alive in communal consciousness and memory. Third, when contemporary academic scholars study the history of a religious tradition, they usually focus on what the tradition itself has emphasized—the records of its male heroes. Finally, many, if not most, contemporary practitioners within that tradition are ignorant of the history of women in their tradition and, perhaps relatedly, are hostile to feminist scholarship about the tradition.[3]

Whereas the androcentric study of religions resulted in the marginalization of women in religion textbooks and courses, the *gynocentric* (female-focused) study of religions illuminates not only women, but also the ways in which women and men relate to each other in families, societies, and religions. The study of women in religions describes gender roles that have been promoted by religious cultures.[4] It reveals a great deal about both women and men. The in-depth study of women and gender in religions and societies rounds out and makes more complete our exploration of human beings in the cultures and religions they create.

This book is grounded in the academic field of the history of religions. History of religions draws on a variety of specialized disciplines, including textual translation and interpretation, history, theology, anthropology, psychology, sociology, and archaeology. History of religions methodology is thus interdisciplinary, although individual scholars usually specialize in particular approaches. The interdisciplinary nature of the history of religions is nicely compatible with the interdisciplinary nature of women's studies and gender studies. The tools of multiple academic disciplines are necessary to increase knowledge and understanding of humans and their religious expressions and enable deeper understanding of gender and women's experiences in religious cultures.

As its name suggests, the history of religions seeks to delineate the history of a religious tradition and the people within it, its emergence and sources, influences, changes over time, beliefs and practices, scriptures, and artistic and social expressions. Since the history of religions as an area of research developed out of theology, particular attention is usually paid to what people believe—their ideas and worldviews—along with accompanying practices, modes of worship, and social organizations. As we will see, by paying particular attention to women's roles and experiences as well as concepts of gender within religions, we can build a fuller and more accurate picture and understanding of humanity.

There are two rules of thumb that the student of religions should keep in mind.

First, *always expect diversity* in practice and belief within any given religious tradition. Cumulative religious traditions—the collective body of related beliefs and practices as they exist through time—are large, diverse, and ambiguous enough to permit individuals within traditions to select what they want and ignore the rest. For every religious tradition, there are always dissenters, exceptions, and variations.

Second, *there is always more that can be learned to enhance understanding.* Keep in mind that it is impossible in any treatment to present everything there is to know about women in a religious tradition. In fact, it is impossible to know everything there is to know about a religion. Learning is a continuous process.

Key Terms

Key terms are used in the interdisciplinary study of women in religions, and as they relate to the emergence, expressions, and increasing transformation of patriarchy. Therefore, some definitions are needed. There is some variation in definition, and other scholars may stipulate somewhat different definitions. The following discussion articulates how specific terms will be employed in this book.

Religion

Scholars of religions do not all agree on one definition of *religion.* Historian of religions Robert D. Baird has taken theologian Paul Tillich's phrase *ultimate concern* and stipulated that this phrase refers to "a concern which is more important than anything else in the universe for the person involved."[5] Rita Gross explains, "Religious beliefs and behaviors typically answer people's questions regarding matters of significant, overriding importance to them."[6] A religion is focused on the achievement of a *goal* (the ultimate concern), and it will prescribe particular *methods* to achieve the goal. People's understanding of the ultimate concern is determined by views about the universe, reality, and human beings; in other words, religion involves a *cosmology* and a *view of human nature*. The cosmology and view of human nature constitute a worldview. According to Gross, "Any belief that functions as the most significant arbiter for decisions and actions and any behaviors whose value is unlimited to the actor are religious beliefs and behaviors whatever their content."[7]

The comparative study of the world's religions reveals that ultimate concerns are always focused on achieving well-being. Ultimate concerns address the human discomfort with finitude—the limitations of existence.[8] All religions address what humans view as the problem of suffering and death. The experience of suffering caused by other human beings or by apparently natural causes are identified in many of the world's religions as "evil," caused by evil forces or beings.

The human religious impulse is geared to attempting to overcome suffering and finitude. Most religions involve prayers and various types of sacrifices to achieve well-being here in earthly existence (e.g. health, long life, wealth, progeny). These types of desires—and in many religions they are the ultimate concern—can be said to constitute "this-worldly" goals. Even when a religious tradition has an ultimate goal relating to life after death, it still addresses the concerns that people have to achieve well-being in their daily lives. Many religions teach that finitude will be overcome completely in an existence after death, either by achieving immortal salvation in heaven or by attaining states such as *mokṣa* in Hinduism and *nirvāṇa* in Buddhism, both involving liberation from the cycle of rebirth. These types of ultimate goals accomplished in after-death experiences can be said to be "other-worldly." Some religions teach that the ultimate concern can be achieved only individually through the exertion of self-effort. Other religions are focused on the accomplishment of individual salvation through divine grace. Many religious movements are based on the belief that the ultimate goal is collective salvation of humanity or of a particular group of people, either through collective effort or through divine intervention, or by a combination of the two. Scholars have termed this type of religious movement *millennialism*.[9]

If religion expresses ultimate concerns, then in the study of women in religions it is fruitful to explore the ways in which ultimate concerns are gendered. How is the divine, the sacred, gendered in theologies and religious philosophies? How are symbols of the ultimate reality gendered, and what are the social implications of this symbolism for real women and men? Are women in a religious tradition believed to have access to the means to achieve the ultimate concern? Are women regarded as being capable of achieving the goal as defined by the religion? Does the society permit women to be educated in the religion's scriptures and to practice the methods to achieve the ultimate concern? If women are regarded as able to achieve the ultimate goal equally with men, how does this relate to women's roles in society? Does the religion promote equality for women, or the subordination of women? Do women exercise religious leadership equally with men, or are women subordinated and marginalized in religious institutions? If a religious tradition restricts women from achieving the ultimate concern and enforces the subordination of women, what are the beliefs and practices upon which women rely to nurture themselves and provide meaning for their lives? Do women who are subordinated in a religious tradition develop their own ultimate goals and the means to attain them? What sorts of organizations, rituals, and beliefs are created by women as alternatives to patriarchal religious traditions? What kinds of religions do women create in a culture in which there is growing social expectation for equality? What are the characteristics of a religion in which women and men are equal?

Religions—their ultimate concerns and their supporting worldviews and social customs, artistic productions, and organizations—are expressed in human cultures. Religion can be defined as being "a cultural system integrating teachings, practices, modes of experience, institutions, and artistic expressions that relates people to what they perceive to be [ultimate]."[10] In the United States, people are generally accustomed to regarding religion as separate from everyday life, but most religious people—people with ultimate goals and related worldviews—regard religion as pervading every aspect of their daily lives. Religion provides interpretations and explanations for our experiences. Religion tells us the proper way to act in daily life. Contemporary people who identify "religion" with "organized religion," which they perceive as being stale and dogmatic, may prefer to use the term *spirituality* instead.

Culture

Culture is defined here as consisting of all the products and constructs of human beings: their social organizations and institutions; family structures; stories, myths, and scriptures; artwork, drama, dance, and music; forms of worship; and social constructions of gender. If an ultimate concern is the "most important thing" for a person or a group, then it will certainly be expressed in the products of human creativity.

Feminism

The backlash against the feminists working in the late 1960s and 1970s for women's equality and challenging patriarchal gender roles perpetuated a negative stereotype that demonized feminist women. To clarify their feminist perspective, many women's studies programs from that time to the present have distributed T-shirts that state: "Feminism is the radical proposition that women are human beings."[11]

It may appear obvious today that women are human beings, but the history of religions demonstrates that often women have been defined as being less than human. For example, the thirteenth-century Catholic theologian Thomas Aquinas (1225–1274) wrote in his *Summa Theologiae* that women are *deficiens et occasionatus*, "unfinished and caused accidentally" (often translated as "misbegotten"). His view of women was based on the understanding of human biology articulated by the Greek philosopher Aristotle (384 B.C.E.–322 B.C.E.), who in turn was reflecting the view often found in agricultural societies that the embryo comes from the man and is planted in the woman's womb, where it is incubated until the child is born. According to Aquinas,

> the active force in the male seed tends to the production of a perfect likeness in the masculine sex; while the production of woman comes

from defect in the active force or from some material indisposition, or even from some external influence; such as that of a south wind, which is moist.[12]

This Aristotelian biology prompted Aquinas and other Catholic priests and theologians to conclude that women are defective in body and mind and to act accordingly. Although Aquinas did not take the perspective to its extreme conclusion, it was a short step from the Thomistic view of women as "misbegotten males" to the perspective articulated in the *Malleus Maleficarum* ("Hammer of Witches") written in 1486 as a manual for identifying witches. The *Malleus Maleficarum* was written by a German Catholic priest and inquisitor, Heinrich Kramer, perhaps with the assistance of Jacob Sprenger, whose name was listed as co-author. *Malleus Maleficarum* argues that women predominate as witches because women are defective in their human nature. As deficient human beings, women are drawn to copulating with devils due to their insatiable lust. The *Malleus* argues that even the Latin word for woman indicates her weak nature: "And all this is indicated by the etymology of the word; for *Femina* comes from *Fe* and *Minus*, since she is ever weaker to hold and preserve the faith." The conclusion in the *Malleus Maleficarum*, "Therefore a wicked woman is by her nature quicker to waver in her faith, and consequently quicker to abjure the faith, which is the root of witchcraft,"[13] was used to justify the torture and execution of thousands of women as witches from the fifteenth to the mid-eighteenth centuries in a period in Europe that has been called "the Burning Times" by contemporary feminist witches.

The perspective that women are defective in their human nature and are therefore to be kept under the control of and subordinated to men is what feminism seeks to counter. There are many types of feminist perspectives on the problems that affect women and the best way to address them.[14] In this book, *feminism* is defined as the point of view that women are fully human and have the same range of talents and capacities as men, and that therefore women should have the freedom to develop and use their talents as they choose. This definition of feminism is compatible with the view that men are fully human and have the same range of talents and capacities as women, and that therefore men should have the freedom to develop and use their talents as they choose.[15] Rita

Gross articulates the goal of feminism as "freedom from gender roles,"[16] meaning a social context in which woman and men are free to choose the roles and activities that fit their inclinations and talents.

In patriarchal cultures, males are socialized to suppress certain portions of their personalities, which are deemed "feminine" and are devalued and considered inappropriate for "real men" to express.[17] The human characteristics that men are forbidden to manifest in a patriarchal culture are usually qualities of nurturing, caring, and empathy. Thus, patriarchy's rigid gender boundaries are damaging to boys as well as girls, men as well as women.

Gross points out that "feminism can be understood as both an academic method and as a social vision," and it grows out of the "realization that women *are* human beings."[18] Feminism as an academic method applies critical scholarship to studying women, men, and gender roles in societies. It also provides information and analysis that is often utilized in the struggles for the equality of girls and women. This book, written from the perspective of feminism as an academic method, seeks to convey understandings of women in religions and cultures.

Feminist social activism has been classified by scholars into three initial broad historical movements, or "waves." Due to economic, social, and educational factors these movements were first initiated in the industrialized countries of North America and Europe, but work today for women's well-being and equality is global and has many expressions. Religion played important roles in each wave and continues to do so today.

What is termed the "first wave" of feminism consisted of women's struggle for the right to vote and other rights in Canada, the United States, the United Kingdom, and European countries from the mid-nineteenth through the early twentieth centuries. In the United States middle-class white women, prevented from entering Christian seminaries and ministerial leadership and other professions, had nonetheless gained organizational skills while working in Christian women's voluntary associations that promoted the abolition of slavery, eradication of prostitution, and prohibition of alcohol. Although some women, such as the sisters Sarah Grimké (1792–1893) and Angelina Grimké (1805–1879), believed that the Christian gospel was empowering to women, other activists for women's rights, such as Elizabeth

Cady Stanton (1815–1902), argued that patriarchal Christianity was being used to oppress women and that the contents of the Bible needed to be reinterpreted by women. Stanton organized a committee of twenty-six women to write feminist critiques of biblical passages, which were published in the two-part *Woman's Bible* in 1895 and 1898. Former slave Sojourner Truth (1797–1883) gave an incisive critique of the female gender roles of the day, based on her Christian faith, in her famous "Ain't I a Woman?" speech in 1851 at a women's rights conference,[19] but she was not accepted by many white women in the movement. In the United States, the struggle for women's right to vote continued past the lifetimes of the women who initiated it and was carried to a successful conclusion through the leadership of Alice Paul (1885–1977), who was a Quaker, with the addition of the Nineteenth Amendment to the Constitution in 1920.[20]

During the mid-1960s and early 1970s what is termed the "second wave" of feminism gained momentum in North America and Europe as women became conscious of "the feminine mystique."[21] The title of the 1963 book by Betty Friedan (1921–2006), the phrase referred to the notion that women found fulfillment as stay-at-home wives and mothers, when in fact many women were deeply unhappy with the constrictions on their lives. At the same time, increasing numbers of women began attending colleges and universities, the sexual revolution was being spurred by the invention of the birth control pill and other types of easily available contraception, and the countercultural movement began questioning old assumptions and ways of doing things. Feminist theologians and historians began to recover the lost and suppressed history of women's participation in the world's religions, particularly Judaism and Christianity.

During the second wave of feminism and afterward, however, a backlash of public opinion against women working for women's equality gained strength. The word *feminist* became imbued with the negative—and inaccurate—connotation that feminists are women who do not like men and who are attempting to establish the rule of women over men. In the United States this stereotype was concisely and emphatically conveyed by radio talk show host Rush Limbaugh's expression "feminazi." The effect of this pejorative stereotype is seen in the fact that today many woman and men who say they believe in women's equality hasten to add that they are not feminists.

Second-wave feminism was dominated by middle-class and upper middle-class white women and their concerns. Feminist women of color critiqued white feminists for assuming that white women's experiences of discrimination due to sexism were equivalent to the complex experiences of discrimination that affect women of color.

The third wave of feminism, beginning roughly in the 1980s, is sensitive to the diversity of women in nationality, ethnicity, color, sexual orientation, and gender status. Third-wave feminists share opposition to all forms of oppression, including colonialism and environmental harm.[22] In this wave of feminism, women of color observed that white feminist Christian women's attempt to speak for all women denied the reality of differences among women. Identifying themselves by the term "womanist," which was coined by poet and author Alice Walker (b. 1944) in *In Search of Our Mother's Gardens: Womanist Prose* (1983),[23] African American womanists stress their concern for the survival of their cultural communities while asserting their capability, strength, and equality in the face of sexism, racism, and classism. They address the historical liabilities of slavery, segregation, poverty, and restricted access to education.[24] American theologians who call themselves *mujeristas* work for Latina liberation as integral to their struggle for justice and peace for Latina/o communities;[25] their counterparts in Latin America, who identify themselves as Latina theologians, also advocate for basic human dignity for Latina women living in Central and South America.[26]

As the third wave of feminism continues, some feminists argue that a fourth wave of feminism began around 2012 with increased use of social media. Author Kristen Sollee describes the characteristics of fourth-wave feminism as "the queering of gender and sexuality based binaries," sex positivity, body positivity, trans inclusiveness, anti-misandry (against the hatred of men), and digitally driven.[27]

Women in cultures and religious traditions around the globe are working today to achieve equality and to eliminate the abuse of girls and women. They are carrying out the struggle on terms that are congruent with their own religious and cultural values and are not relying on the values of white, western feminists.[28] Feminist Muslimas work for Muslim women's equality based on the Qur'an and *hadith* (reports of the sayings of the Prophet Muhammad) and the values of their Muslim traditions.[29] Feminist African Christians work for African women's equality based on their Christian faith and its sources as well as indigenous African values.[30] Asian feminists of diverse religious persuasions work for women's equality based on their respective religions and cultures while they simultaneously challenge those cultures to become supportive of women's rights.[31]

Intersectionality

In an article published in 1991, African American law professor Kimberlé W. Crenshaw highlights the *intersectionality* of race, gender, and class in women of color's experiences of subordination and devaluation in patriarchal and white-dominant cultures, in contrast to white feminists' initial concern solely with the problem of sexism. Crenshaw points out that multiple factors involving race, gender, and class can result in the "intersectional disempowerment" of women.[32] By attending to the intersectionality of factors of racism, sexism, homophobia, income disparities and class domination, and discrimination and prejudice directed toward members of particular cultures and religions, we can better understand the situations of women in various societies and religious traditions in order to discern constructive efforts to improve their situations.

Women of faith around the world are keenly aware of the intersectionality of colonialism and patriarchal religious traditions. They are also aware that the access of girls and women to education and economic earning power is key to building increasing social and religious expectations of equality.

Sex, Gender, and Sexualities

Early feminist scholarship defined *sex* as the physiological given of either maleness or femaleness and pointed out that *gender*—the roles of males and females—is socially constructed. Gender studies has complicated the binary understanding of sex by pointing out that some persons are born with a combination of male and female characteristics, and some persons do not have the usual male (xy) and female (xx) chromosomes; some, for instance, possess xxy chromosomes.[33] Some cultures offer special roles for visibly *intersex* individuals (persons with characteristics of both female and male). In the west, physicians have traditionally assigned a sex to intersex infants by making a surgical change, and then instructing parents to raise the child as a boy or girl according to that change. The field of gender studies has demonstrated that there are a number of societies that are unlike western societies in that more than two sexes are defined and assigned gender roles.

Anthropologist Serena Nanda defines *sex* as "the biologically differentiated status of male or female. It includes anatomic sex, particularly the genitals, and also secondary and invisible characteristics such as genes and hormones." She defines *gender* as "the social, cultural, and psychological constructions that are imposed upon the biological differences of sex." Nanda points out that sex and gender are culturally constructed. She notes that in many societies "anatomical sex is not the dominant factor in constructing gender roles and gender identity." Nanda uses the term *sexuality* to refer to "erotic desires, sexual practices, or sexual orientation."[34]

Sociologists Candace West and Don H. Zimmerman distinguish between *sex*, *sex category*, and *gender*. They define *sex* as "a determination made through the application of socially agreed upon biological criteria for classifying persons as females or males. The criteria for classification can be genitalia at birth or chromosomal typing before birth, and they do not necessarily agree with one another." According to West and Zimmerman, placement in a *sex category*

> is achieved through application of sex criteria, but in everyday life, categorization is established and sustained by the socially required identificatory displays that proclaim one's membership in one or the other category. In this sense, one's sex category presumes one's sex and stands as proxy for it in many situations, but sex and sex category can vary independently; that is, it is possible to claim membership in a sex category even when the sex criteria are lacking.

They define *gender* as "the activity of managing situated conduct in light of normative conceptions of attitudes and activities appropriate for one's sex category. Gender activities emerge from and bolster claims to membership in a sex category."[35] West and Zimmerman contend that gender "is not a set of traits, nor a variable, nor a role, but the product of social doings." Gender is "exhibited or portrayed through interaction." West and Zimmerman use the phrase "doing gender" to refer to the performance of gender in everyday interactions.

"Doing gender means creating differences between girls and boys and women and men, differences that are not natural, essential, or biological. Once the differences have been constructed, they are used to reinforce the 'essentialness' of gender."[36]

West and Zimmerman describe how small children are subjected to *sex role socialization*. From the moment they are born, girls and boys are taught and molded, physically and mentally, into a culturally defined sex category for their sex. Female infants and male infants are dressed in particular ways and treated in particular ways, and their births are celebrated or not celebrated in certain ways, depending on their assigned sex. West and Zimmerman describe how little boys in patriarchal cultures are socialized to the gender ideal of efficaciousness, "being able to affect the physical and social environment through the exercise of physical strength or appropriate skills," while little girls are socialized to value their appearance, "managing themselves as ornamental objects." Both boys and girls "learn that the recognition and use of sex categorization in interaction are not optional, but mandatory."[37] Children learn to regulate themselves to enact the gender identities that have been assigned to them. Children and adults who find that their personal characteristics and behaviors do not fit into the designated gender or sex category have difficulty.

As part of sex category or gender designations, it may be that particular types of work are assigned to women in one culture, while the same types of work might be assigned to men in a different culture. In some cultures women and men perform the same or similar types of work. The same is true of particular types of behavior and modes of being religious. What are considered to be socially acceptable behaviors for women and men vary from culture to culture, and religion to religion, depending on that culture's definitions of gender.

The social constructions of sex category and "doing gender" by individuals are not static. They change in response to developments in technology, economy, family and social organization, historical events, and the life choices and trajectories of individuals. According to West and Zimmerman, social change "must be pursued both at the institutional and cultural level of sex category and at the interactional level of gender."[38]

An initial step toward changing female gender roles and ways of doing gender in a patriarchal religious society is likely to be the assertion that pious mothers should be active outside the home to reform society. One example is the "cult of true womanhood" that was influential in the United States in the nineteenth century and that, in conjunction with Protestant revivalism, had the effect of motivating Christian women to become active outside the home in women's voluntary associations to address social problems, thus doing gender as pious mothers as social activists.[39]

In Taiwan in the twentieth century, the Mahāyāna Buddhist nun Dharma Master Cheng Yen (b. 1937) founded the Buddhist Compassion Relief Tzu Chi Foundation in 1966 to which housewives donated small amounts of household money to provide assistance to the needy. The organization has since grown to 10 million members. Tzu Chi has provided assistance to victims of disasters such as Hurricane Katrina in New Orleans and the American Gulf Coast (2005), Hurricane Sandy in the American Northeast (2012), Typhoon Haiyan in the Philippines (2013), and the 7.8-magnitude earthquake in Nepal (2015). Tzu Chi provides meals and other items to enhance the lives of the needy and provide education and healthcare, and its work includes efforts to protect the environment. The Buddhist nun Cheng Yen is a model of the active compassionate mother that housewives may emulate in doing gender in their compassionate work outside the home. Tzu Chi's membership includes women and men of all ages in forty-seven countries.

Sociologists Chengpang LEE and Ling HAN point out that a younger and more educated generation of Buddhist women in Taiwan, inspired by the example of Mahāyāna Buddhist nun SHIH Chao-hwei (b. 1957) and their own commitment to feminist values, self-consciously take on the role of moral activists in advocating social justice causes, including gender equality for gay men and lesbians.

Dharma Master Cheng Yen led housewives to perform charitable activities outside the home by extending the gender role of the mother in traditional Taiwanese families. Shih Chao-hwei and moral activists inspired by her move beyond patriarchal gender roles to assert equality of all persons in society.[40]

Patriarchy, Classical Patriarchy, Male Dominance, Paternalism, Sexism, Misogyny

The English word *patriarchy* ("rule of the father") is derived from Greek and Latin words that referred to the father (patriarch) as the head of the family who owned his wives and children as well as his slaves and made decisions about their lives. Patriarchy is now a term that refers to the general dominance of men within the family and in society. Feminist historian Gerda Lerner defines *patriarchy* as

> the manifestation and institutionalization of male dominance over women and children in the family and the extension of male dominance over women in society in general. It implies that men hold power in all the important institutions of society and that women are deprived of access to such power. It does not imply that women are either totally powerless or totally deprived of rights, influence, and resources.[41]

Anthropologist Ernestine Friedl defines *male dominance* as "a situation in which men have highly preferential access, although not always exclusive rights, to those activities to which the society accords the greatest value, and the exercise of which permits a measure of control over others."[42] Dominance over others is determined by differential access to economic resources.

The degree of men's dominance and women's empowerment or powerlessness varies in different types of societies. As we will see, roles of women and men are strongly influenced by a society's economy: women's status is based on the extent to which women have access to economic resources and are perceived as being economically productive.

Classical patriarchy is found where descent and inheritance are patrilineal, and residence of spouses is patrilocal, with brides leaving their natal families and becoming members of their husbands' families. It often develops in societies based on intensive agriculture in which the earth is tilled using a plow pulled by large draft animals. Land is owned by some men and/or their patrilineal extended families (which include grandparents, sons and their wives, and grandchildren, and in which inheritance of land is through the male line). These men control, first, the farming, and subsequently, other means of production, including the labor of men and women of lower status. The economic power of men of privileged classes translates readily into political power. If economic resources are scarce in a classical patriarchal society, then health care and nutritional and educational resources are provided primarily to sons. While women in a patrilineage may work hard to process agricultural products into secondary products used by the family, bear children, care for the children and other members of the husband's family, cook, and do the washing and the general housework, women in the family and society are not regarded as being economically productive by the men because they are dependent on their husbands for access to the primary products (earlier, agricultural products, or today, money) needed for subsistence. Women's lack of access to primary economic activity, which yields the products needed for survival, combined with their physical removal from their natal families upon marriage, ensure their subordination and increase the likelihood of their oppression in classically patriarchal cultures. Women in such families have little or no protection from abuse or even murder at the hands of their husbands and in-laws.

Male economic and political dominance is paralleled with male dominance in religious institutions. Often a male deity is invoked as sanctioning patriarchy as right and good, but this does not preclude female deities from being utilized to support patriarchy. Female deities such as Amaterasu, the Sun Goddess and ancestor of the Japanese imperial family, and Durgā, a Hindu warrior goddess, are just two examples of goddesses who have been conceptualized and worshipped to support the rulership of men.[43]

Lerner points out that women in patriarchal cultures often collude in their subordination, because they have been socialized to do so and because they perceive themselves as deriving benefits from the patriarchal family and social structures. She terms this situation *paternalistic dominance* and defines it as "the relationship of a dominant group, considered superior, to a subordinate group, considered inferior, in which the dominance is mitigated by mutual obligations and reciprocal rights." According to Lerner, paternalistic dominance is the exchange of "economic support and protection given by the male for subordination in all matters, sexual service and unpaid domestic service given by the female."[44]

In the optimum paternalistic heterosexual marriage, the husband loves and cherishes his wife, and the wife loves her husband and is happy to serve him in return for his protection and economic support.

Likewise, the father loves and cherishes his daughters, and the daughters love and take pride in their father who protects and financially supports them. But in the most oppressive patriarchal or paternalistic hetero-sexual family situation, although the wife gains prestige and wealth by being married to an important man, she is little more than an orna-ment to enhance his status: she may be her husband's sexual slave, the mother of his children, and the household drudge. Similarly, daughters may be regarded by their father as economic burdens to be married off as quickly as possible, or used as their father's pawns in marriage alli-ances; they may even be commodified and sold into prostitution/sexual slavery. Women in an oppressive patriarchal family have little protection from physical and sexual abuse.

Lerner defines *sexism* as the concept that one sex (in this case, the male) is superior to the other sex.[45] According to Lerner, an ideology of the inferiority of the dominated group justifies their continued subordi-nation and exploitation. But in a situation of paternalistic dominance, the dominated are not without some rights and privileges. When women col-lude in their subordination by indoctrinating their daughters to be sub-missive and obedient to men and by applying social pressure on women who do not conform to patriarchal expectations, they do so in order to gain privileges and rights—economic support, love, status—to which they are entitled in the patriarchal society. Religion functions to teach and enforce patriarchal gender roles, to provide meaningful religious ex-periences to women, to heal women damaged by patriarchy, and to help them negotiate and improve their status in the patriarchal social order.

Misogyny means hatred of women. The *Malleus Maleficarum* is a clas-sic misogynistic text that inspired grotesque violence against women in the Burning Times. As is the case with hatred directed toward various ethnic groups, and non-gender-conforming persons, intense fear and hatred of women are deeply ingrained in cultural assumptions and in-culcated in each generation, which, in turn, make the hate appear to be normal, right, and rational.

There Is No Matriarchy

There are no matriarchal—woman-dominated ("rule of the mother")—cultures at present, and there is no evidence to indicate that matriarchal cultures ever existed in the past.[46] Since the popular meaning of the word *matriarchal* when applied to society is that of a society in which women dominate men, and no such society has been known to exist, the term *matrifocal*—focused on the mother—is preferred in this book. Matrifocal and matrilineal societies, with or without matrilocal residence of husbands with their wives' families, do not subordinate men. In these societies women and men work together to support and raise children and to perpetuate their religion and culture.

Anthropologists have demonstrated that women have advantages when they live in societies in which inheritance of land and other wealth is matrilineal, and residence of married, or otherwise paired, hetero-sexual couples is matrilocal. Children belong to the matrilineage, the extended family consisting of several generations in which inheritance and kinship are traced through the mothers. Matrilineal and matrilocal societies are not matriarchal, because men exercise political and religious leadership, and men take leadership roles in their natal families. The authoritative head of the matrilineal extended family of an adult woman will not be her husband or father; it may be her brother. In rare cases, such as the Mosuo in Yunnan and Sichuan provinces in China who do not marry, the head of the family may be her mother or grandmother. When women in matrilineal and matrilocal societies have significant access to direct economic productivity, for example in foraging or horticultural societies, or now in jobs and businesses that produce income, this contributes to women's status.

After conducting ethnographic research from 1981 to 1999 among the Minangkabau—a population in West Sumatra in Indonesia numbering approximately 4 million, with an additional approximately 3 million living elsewhere in Indonesia and Malaysia—anthropologist Peggy Reeves Sanday has argued for a new definition of "matriarchy" to designate matrilineal peoples with women at the center of the family and who have significant roles in religious expressions and a say in political matters. But the Minangkabau studied by Sanday, like other matrilineal and sometimes matrilocal peoples, do not subordinate men; they have created a society that values girls and women but also values boys and men and allots them significant roles in religious and political leadership. The

Minangkabau preserve their traditional religious culture and customs known as *adat* and combine them with Islam.[47]

German feminist philosopher Heide Goettner-Abendroth has defined "matriarchy" as being when "mothers are at the center of society, as manifested by matrilinearity and by mothers' (or women's) power of economic distribution, both in the context of gender equality." Based on case studies, she states that matrilocal residence of a husband or male partner may or may not be present in a "matriarchal" family.[48] However, the majority of anthropologists eschew "matriarchy" as an adequately descriptive term for matrilineal family structures. By alleging that such families are necessarily "matriarchal," Goettner-Abendroth overlooks the male dominance that can existence in families in which the eldest mother's brother—the uncle—is the family head and controls the management and distribution of economic resources.[49] Therefore, in this book the term *matriarchal* is not used, since it is unnecessary and misleading when studying women in families, societies, and religions. Importantly, anthropologists have demonstrated that whether or not women produce and distribute economic resources is important to their status in a society.

Matrilineal and matrilocal cultures are typically found in foraging or horticultural societies, although the largest number of foraging and horticultural societies are patrilineal and patrilocal, or they may practice other complex forms of residence of spouses and inheritance. If women in a foraging society provide the bulk of the family's diet, the society is more likely to be matrilineal and matrilocal, and the religion is more likely to promote the value of women to society in its myths and rituals. Horticulture, the most rudimentary form of agriculture, relies on the hoe, a variation of the foraging woman's digging stick,[50] and in a number of horticultural societies the farming is done primarily by women. Women's concrete economic contributions to survival, combined with matrilineal inheritance, and perhaps matrilocal residence of spouses, result in societies in which women have significant status and authority. Women's contributions to family and group survival are valued, and this is typically reflected in their religion, but it does not mean that men are devalued or subordinated. Women's authority in matrilineal and matrilocal families does not match the dominance of men in patriarchal families.

The Development of Male Dominance and Patriarchy

Tracing the processes by which societies become patriarchal is relevant to the study of women in religions, because most of the dominant historical world's religious traditions are patriarchal. Understanding the characteristics of egalitarian religious cultures and patriarchal religious cultures assists in ascertaining the dynamics that characterize social movement away from male dominance.

From the 1970s on, numerous feminists looked to prehistory for religious expressions they thought were pre-patriarchal. These so-called Goddess feminists were searching for usable resources for feminist spirituality in the present. An "invasion theory" of the origin of patriarchy became popular among feminist women and men. As we will see in the following chapter, there are shortcomings to the invasion theory. Chapter 2 also describes why the economic theory provides more convincing explanations about social changes that affect the status of women in societies and religions.

2

The Economic Theory of the Emergence and Transformation of Patriarchy

In the search for factors that support egalitarian and also patriarchal societies and their religions, much light has been shed on different types of cultures by the discipline of anthropology.[1] Today's societies are very complex and include people whose lives are impacted by a combination of some, or all, of earlier technological/economic social patterns and their respective gender roles with later technological/economic social patterns and their gender roles. The earlier developmental patterns of society include *foraging, horticulture, intensive agriculture, pastoralism*, and *complex societies*. Pastoralism overlaps with horticulture and intensive agriculture, because it is often practiced by sedentary farmers who move their herds periodically to fresh pastures, and because pastoralists who are nomadic live interdependently with nearby farming populations.

Gender roles, religious doctrines, and values formulated in earlier socioeconomic patterns continue to be influential in the lives of women and men living in *industrialized societies* today. A religious tradition can act as a conservative force in continuing to promote patriarchal gender roles even when women are increasingly gaining access to education and earning power in a society that is changing due to technology and therefore economy. On the other hand, innovations within an old religious tradition can promote equality in gender roles in religious institutions and society. Advocates of both the subordination of women and the equality of women mine their respective religious traditions for resources to utilize in support of their points of view.

Ethnographic and historical evidence indicate great variability in the organization of families, societies, and gendered relationships in all stages of economic development. Depending on environmental factors and personal choices, foraging and horticultural societies may be organized with various combinations of patrilocal, matrilocal, avunculocal (young married couples living with the wife's uncle), neolocal (married couples setting up residence in a new location), or multilocal residence, and patrilineal, matrilineal, or bilineal inheritance. There are also extended families consisting of parents, their adult children, and their children's spouses and the grandchildren, as well as nuclear families. Anthropologist David F. Aberle noted that out of the 564 societies included in the 1957 *World Ethnographic Sample*, 84 (15 percent) were matrilineal. Arguing that matrilineal descent likely developed within the social context of women's work groups doing the majority of the agricultural labor, Aberle found that the heaviest concentration of matrilineal societies was found in "dominant horticulture" societies, with small domesticated animals and no great importance placed on large domesticated animals. There were 47 matrilineal societies out of the 188 dominant horticultural societies, making up 56 percent of the 84 matrilineal societies in the entire *Sample*. What Aberle termed "African horticulture" societies placed importance on small and large domesticated animals (usually cattle) in addition to horticulture, and they were more likely to be patrilineal. Of the 46 African horticultural societies in the *Sample*, there were 32 patrilineal societies and only 5 matrilineal societies. Aberle concluded that patrilineal descent is strongly correlated with the importance placed on factors such as large domesticated animals, large-scale irrigation of crops, and/or plow agriculture or wet rice agriculture, all of which generally involve the coordinated labor of men either in caring for large domesticated animals, or in farming, or both. Out of the 66 pastoralist societies in the *Sample*, 51 were patrilineal, while only 3 were matrilineal. Of the 117 societies with intensive agriculture involving use of the plow, 69 were patrilineal, and only 9 were matrilineal. Out of the 84 matrilineal societies in the *Sample*, less than half (41) had matrilocal or dominantly matrilocal residence of married couples.[2] The arrangements between women and men and their families change as climate, technology, and the corresponding economy and division of labor between men and women change. Gender roles in families and society also change in response to warfare, colonialism, and globalized social and economic forces.

Women and men in general have more egalitarian roles in foraging and horticultural societies that are matrilineal and matrilocal, and this is reflected in their religious traditions. Women have restricted means of independent economic productivity in classical patriarchy based on intensive agriculture. In classical patriarchy women are subordinated, and may be abused, in extended families that are patrilineal and patrilocal, and patriarchal gender values are reflected in the religious traditions. This tends to remain true for a long time after portions of the society become industrialized and urbanized.

Friedl argues, "It is the right to distribute and exchange valued goods and services to those not in a person's own domestic unit . . . which confers power and prestige in all societies."[3] In early developmental patterns of society, the sources for the valued goods and services included hunting, raiding and warfare, horticulture, pastoralism, and trading. Friedl points out that men have had preferential access to the goods and services most valued by societies from foraging societies to many horticultural societies and that this led to the greater likelihood of men becoming political leaders. Since in foraging societies men gain access to valued goods by long-range travel for hunting, trading, and raiding, and women do not engage in such long-distance travel because of pregnancy, nursing, and care of small children, men have an advantage over women in gaining social prestige and having the products of their labor most admired by group members.[4]

While the trend in human society toward increasing male dominance has its origins in foraging societies, and it increases as societies become sedentary, specialized in occupations, hierarchical, and class stratified, nevertheless gender roles are the products of complex and interactive processes. In the archaeological record, ethnographic accounts, and historical records, there is no straight line from egalitarianism to subordination of women, and in contemporary times there is no straight line from subordination to equality, but significant factors and dynamics may be discerned along the way.

In this chapter we will consider some prehistoric and historic societies to illustrate how technologies, economies, and social dynamics influence gender roles and religious traditions. Religions reflect the gender and class roles within a society and frequently reinforce these as being proper. In today's diverse and globalized world, there is lack of consensus about gender roles and how they should be supported in society by religions. There is competition between individuals, groups, and religions that promote gender equality and those that strive to enforce traditional patriarchal gender roles.

The economic theory describes factors supporting particular gender roles in cultures and their respective religions based on empirical evidence. It is therefore more plausible than the "invasion theory" of the origin of patriarchy articulated by archaeologist Marija Gimbutas, which was popular in the 1970s and 1980s among educated feminist women and men and continues to have advocates. Because there are numerous publications promoting the invasion theory of the origin of patriarchy, we will consider it briefly and indicate its shortcomings and why the economic theory has greater explanatory power.

Archaeology, Gender Roles, and the Inadequacies of the Invasion Theory of the Origin of Patriarchy

The Aryan Invasion Theory in Linguistics

The Eurocentric invasion theory of the origin of patriarchy popularized by Marija Gimbutas rests on a thesis formulated by linguists in the nineteenth century to account for the dispersal of Indo-European languages in the Indian subcontinent (South Asia), Central and Western Asia, and Europe. Nineteenth-century linguists found that the ancient Indian language of Sanskrit and the equally ancient Old Iranian language have strong affinities with Greek and Latin and with the European Romance languages derived from Latin. They found that Celtic and Germanic languages belong to this vast Indo-European language family, as do Baltic and Slavic languages.

Linguists posited the prehistoric movement of Indo-European speakers westward from the Russian steppe (grassland) through Europe and another movement eastward into the Indian subcontinent as occurring in waves of invasions undertaken by nomadic warrior pastoralists riding in chariots.[5] Utilizing the term by which the Iranian and Indian Indo-European speakers identified themselves—*arya*, "noble/cultured ones"—nineteenth-century linguists dubbed these peoples "Aryans." The invasion theory became an assumption not only for linguists, but also for archaeologists, even though at that time there was no concrete evidence indicating that invasions took place immediately prior to the first historical writings.

V. Gordon Childe, a linguist and archaeologist, published an influential book in 1926 entitled *The Aryans: A Study of Indo-European Origins*, in which he identified the southern Russian steppe north of the Black Sea as the Aryan homeland. In his 1950 book, *Prehistoric Migrations in Europe*, Childe concluded that the Aryans migrated into Europe during the late Bronze Age. (The Bronze Age in Europe spans from ca. 3300 B.C.E. to ca. 300 B.C.E.) Childe postulated that these invading Aryan warriors drove horse-drawn chariots, thereby having a military advantage over sedentary European farming communities, which was a mistaken assumption.[6]

During World War II (1939–1945), Adolf Hitler turned the linguists' and archaeologists' invasion theory of the origin of the Indo-European language family into a theory of racial superiority to undergird his project of German expansion, conquest, and extermination of Jews, Roma, and members of other groups. Childe repudiated *The Aryans*, even though it had not advocated for "the delusion of racial superiority" of the Aryans.[7] After World War II Childe continued his work, and in his later writings he concluded that the original Aryan homeland was the Anatolia region in Turkey, part of Western Asia.

Marija Gimbutas and the Invasion Theory of the Origin of Patriarchy

Beginning in the early 1970s, the Aryan invasion theory was elaborated upon by Lithuanian American feminist archaeologist Marija Gimbutas. Gimbutas and other feminist authors have utilized the invasion theory to explain the origin of patriarchy in Western Asia and Europe. Gimbutas identified the area in Anatolia and southeastern Europe just west of the Black Sea and including Greece, Italy, and the islands in the eastern Mediterranean as being a unified Neolithic culture (ca. 7000 B.C.E. to ca. 3000 B.C.E.) based on sedentary agriculture. She termed this area "Old Europe." Gimbutas interpreted archaeological artifacts as indicating that the Old European society was a peaceful, matrilineal, goddess-worshipping society, in which women had high status due to their roles as priestesses and the religious celebration of women's life-giving powers. Gimbutas described the Old Europeans as art-lovers, whose aesthetic appreciation was expressed in beautiful objects made of gold, copper, ceramic, shells, and marble.

Gimbutas interpreted Upper Paleolithic (ca. 35,000 to ca. 10,000 B.P. [before the present])[8] female figurines and Neolithic female figurines as representing the widespread and unified worship of not many goddesses, but of a single Great Goddess having many manifestations. In *The Language of the Goddess* (1989) and *The Civilization of the Goddess* (1991), Gimbutas claimed that she had deciphered the meaning of the symbols and markings of Old European works of art. Spirals, zigzags, meandering and parallel lines, cross-hatching, all had specific meanings in the Old European culture of the Goddess. Depictions of birds, frogs, snakes, fish, bees, butterflies, caterpillars, eggs, and animals, as well as the ubiquitous female figurines likewise conveyed very specific, life-affirming meanings in the Old European civilization. According to Gimbutas, Old European Goddess symbolism also included death, depicted in representations of vultures and owls.[9]

Gimbutas asserted that Old European culture ended due to repeated invasions of armed nomadic pastoralists from the south Russian steppe, whom she termed "Kurgans" after the name for the burial mounds found in that area. Gimbutas described the Kurgans as being patriarchal, armed, and violent. According to Gimbutas, the low state of Kurgan civilization was even reflected in their inability to create beautiful works of art to leave in the archaeological record. Gimbutas believed the patriarchal Kurgans were "indifferent to art."[10] According to Gimbutas, the Kurgan invasions took place in the fourth and third millennia B.C.E. The language used by Gimbutas to describe the Kurgan invasions makes it clear that she equated these Aryan "penetrations" or "thrusts" with the rape of Goddess-loving Old Europe.[11]

Gimbutas's theory of the origin of patriarchy and her celebration of the peaceful, egalitarian and Goddess-worshipping Old European culture strongly influenced numerous religious feminists who were seeking spiritual alternatives to patriarchal religions. Gimbutas's scenario of the Old European civilization in which men and women lived and cooperated together, which was destroyed by armed invaders who imposed patriarchy, has been presented in numerous popular Goddess spirituality books, including *The Chalice and the Blade* (1988) by author Riane Eisler,[12] who asserts that humanity is currently at a point where we can consciously direct the evolution of society and can make the choice between the partnership and the dominator models.

In the history of religions, "myth" may be defined as a narrative that conveys the values of a people, as well as provides explanations about why the world is the way it is and its meaning.[13] The origin of patriarchy narrative of invasions by armed outsiders functions as a myth, a "sacred history,"[14] for some feminists. It provides an explanation of how women came to be subordinated: in other words, it explains the "Fall" of women. It places the blame for the Fall squarely on the shoulders of violent men, the patriarchs. This sacred history also promises that the fallenness of the human condition will be overcome by women and men working in partnership, but particularly through the efforts of women now conscious of their identification with the life-giving Goddess. This myth serves to raise the self-esteem of women who believe in it by asserting that women were not always oppressed, that in prehistory women were formerly great, and that they created a peaceful and beautiful civilization. For believers in this myth, the Old European civilization is a model for future partnership societies. If partnership of women and men was achieved in the past, it can be reestablished. This myth does in reverse what feminists say patriarchal myths of humanity's "Fall" (for example, see the myth of Adam, Eve, and the Serpent in Genesis 2–3) do: it blames the limitations of the human condition on the opposite sex—in this case, men.

Critiques of Gimbutas' Theory

Archaeologist Lynn Meskell points out that Gimbutas failed to take into account the many figurines of males and of humans with no sexually distinguishing marks found in the archaeological record in Western Asia and Europe. Gimbutas instead focused on female figurines or artifacts that she interpreted as being representations of females, thereby "shaping the vision of a single, omnipresent female deity."[15] While Gimbutas's insights about some particular artifacts may be valid, it is unlikely that she deciphered and interpreted the symbolic "language of the Goddess" in the multitude of artifacts and works of art from the Upper Paleolithic through the Neolithic to the early Bronze Age—a period of time encompassing approximately 32,000 years. Nor can it be assumed that diverse Upper Paleolithic and Neolithic female figurines in Europe all referred to a single Great Goddess, or if they all had reference to any goddesses at all.

According to archaeologists Ruth Tringham and Margaret Conkey, Gimbutas perpetuated the "modern myth" that all pastoralists "are patriarchal and warlike."[16] As we will see, descriptions by archaeologist Jeannine Davis-Kimball of evidence from Bronze Age *kurgans* and her own ethnographic observations of Kazakh nomads show that Gimbutas misrepresented the cultures of Eurasian Steppe nomadic pastoralists. The archaeological evidence from *kurgans* indicates that the steppe peoples were more egalitarian, as well as artistic, than Gimbutas claimed, and Davis-Kimball felt that this conclusion was supported by what she observed of Kazakh nomadic pastoralist life.

Whereas recent DNA studies indicate that there were migrations into Europe of peoples from the steppe, it is not clear that these were violent invasions. Archaeologist Colin Renfrew notes that there is no archaeological evidence for warrior horsemen before 1200 B.C.E.[17] Renfrew also points out that nomadic pastoralists do not drive chariots, although warriors who lived in intensive agricultural societies engaged in the process of kingdom- and empire-building did.[18]

Renfrew has accounted for the dispersal of Indo-European languages by what he terms the *wave of advance model*. According to this theory, the spread of Indo-European languages occurred with the spread of sedentary agriculture that developed in Anatolia. From Anatolia, some farmers transported their families, seeds and plants, and domesticated animals in boats to what is now Greece and other Mediterranean islands. The earliest evidence of farming in Europe dating to approximately 6000 B.C.E. is found in Greece and Crete. Farming settlements are always correlated with increased population. Renfrew suggests that agriculture was spread by the offspring of farmers moving a little distance, perhaps twenty to thirty miles, from their natal farms to establish their own farms. The gradual increase of population and the spread of farming thus could account for the initial dispersal of Indo-European languages. The increasing distance in time and space from the original farming area would account for the divergences in the Indo-European languages and the development of subfamily trees of languages. The wave of advance associated with farming would have occurred in different parts of the world with accompanying social changes.

There is no evidence of invasions westward into Europe of chariot-driving pastoralists (an oxymoron) during the fourth millennium B.C.E., as posited by Gimbutas, although recent genetic studies suggest that there were migrations of steppe pastoralists into Europe in the third millennium B.C.E. In 2015 the "steppe hypothesis" (minus the chariots) of the introduction of Indo-European languages in Europe received support from genetic studies that demonstrated that beginning about 2500 B.C.E. there was a large movement of people (who buried their dead in *kurgan*s) from the Eurasian Steppe into Central Europe.[19] It is not inconceivable that both the steppe migration theory and Renfrew's theory of the gradual spread of agricultural peoples, also possibly speaking Indo-European languages, thousands of years earlier from Anatolia into and throughout Europe describe movements of peoples that contributed to the development of European peoples, their languages, and cultures. Renfrew believes that genetic studies of prehistoric Anatolian peoples may indicate that there were two waves of movement of Indo-European language-speakers into Europe, with the migration of farmers from Anatolia being earlier than the migration from the steppe.[20] Renfrew's theory stressing developmental changes within societies that produce class hierarchy and male dominance remains highly pertinent, despite the geneticists' confirmation of a westward migration of people, termed the Yamnaya, associated with *kurgan* burials.

According to Renfrew, contemporary archaeologists are more likely to interpret changes in the archaeological record as reflecting changes internal to a preexisting culture, and not as necessarily reflecting the imposition of a new culture on an earlier one.[21] The archaeological evidence in Western Asia and Europe supports what in this book is termed the *economic theory*, derived from anthropology, which asserts that internal social changes led to increasing male dominance as sedentary farming increased and in some areas developed into intensive agriculture. Intensive agriculture involving farming with a plow, and increased class stratification was accompanied by what archaeologist

Andrew Sherratt has termed the *secondary products revolution*, in which the primary products of domesticated animals, such as milk and wool, were processed into secondary products, such as cheese, yogurt, thread, and cloth.[22] In the evolution of human societies, women were the ones who processed primary products into secondary products, as they were increasingly removed from the production of primary products of herds of animals and crops grown on land owned and farmed by men, who also supervised their male and female laborers.[23]

Sedentary agriculture is associated with increased populations and ultimately produces conflicts over land ownership, as well as the rise of urban centers, kingdoms, and later empires. Tringham and Conkey note that

> an equally compelling argument can be made that the supposed devaluation and disempowerment of women did not occur until several thousands of years *after* the Goddess movement's postulated "end" of Old Europe. We can postulate that it is the processes of urbanization—not the processes of pastoralism—that instigate marked re-negotiations of gender (including the restriction of women's social action and the marginalization of women's labour and household production). Such processes did not become part of continental European life until Romanization (in the late first millennium BC).[24]

In various parts of the world and in different eras, there have been invasions of peoples possessing technological advantage over indigenous inhabitants, and such cultural dominance impacts the gender roles, as well as the religion, of the colonized subjects. But invasions alone cannot account for the origination of patriarchy in all times and places in the world where it has existed. As articulated by archaeologists, social changes also occur within societies due to the development of new technologies related to agriculture, urbanization, and warfare; these cause changes in social organization and division of labor by sex, which are expressed in religions. An economic theory that traces the origins of patriarchy, as well as its ultimate transformation, in the different developmental patterns of society has greater explanatory value than the invasion theory of the origin of patriarchy.

Gender, Religion, and Developmental Patterns of Societies

The economic theory, which is based on analysis of societies by anthropologists and archaeologists, delineates the factors that shape gender roles in what historian of religions Rita Gross has termed developmental patterns of societies.[25] These gender roles are expressed in religions and theologies, and religions contribute to enforcing what are deemed to be proper gender roles. Changes in the technologies and resulting economies that influence division of labor by sex, and therefore gender roles, also produce religious changes. Examination of the technologies, economies, gender roles, and religions in different developmental patterns of societies is therefore fruitful in the study of women in religions.

Egalitarian Foraging Societies

Archaeologist Margaret Ehrenberg speculates that about 100,000 years ago the invention of technology to hunt large animals—spears and bows and arrows—and other technologies such as slings and baskets to carry babies and gathered food, encouraged early women and men to divide the labor needed for their survival and that of their offspring.[26] Archaeologists J. M. Adovasio and Olga Soffer point out that women were probably the persons who first manufactured strings and lines from plant fibers and began using them to make knotted nets and weaving them to make fabrics and clothing articles as far back as the Paleolithic This technological breakthrough has been called the "String Revolution," but Adovasio and Soffer prefer to call it the *Fiber Revolution*. Although anthropological studies have shown that men may be weavers, Adovasio and Soffer point out that in most tribal societies women make baskets and women virtually exclusively do loom or frame weaving, having also gathered the plant items used in the process. In addition, they point out that ethnography reveals that women frequently make pottery. They posit that the Fiber Revolution as well as pottery-making contributed to the sexual division of labor as much as the invention of spears and bows and arrows.[27]

According to anthropological literature about foragers summarized by archaeologist Robert L. Kelly,[28] in environments with large game and available plant foods, men range widely tracking and killing large animals and bringing meat back to the band to be shared with its members. Women also walk significant distances as they gather plant foods, hunt small animals, and—depending on the environment—collect shellfish and fish with lines and nets. Women may leave their young children at a base camp to be watched by other women, older men, or older children while they leave to do their gathering. Sometimes women and men hunt together, as well as gathering and fishing with nets. In general, women do not travel as far as men, nor are they separated from their children for periods of several days, as are the men.

When the environment permits, the products of women's subsistence activities may provide 60 to 80 percent of the band's food, with women sharing gathered foodstuffs with their immediate relatives and mates. Foraging women process the gathered foods so that they can be consumed. Food produced by women for their families is the mainstay of the band's nutrition. According to Ernestine Friedl, the meat brought back by men is likely accorded higher value, because success in hunting is sporadic and less dependable than gathering. When hunters return with meat, there is excitement among the members of the band who anticipate receiving a share. It seems that even at the foraging stage of human society, women's work is not valued as much as men's work. According to Friedl, "The person who gives [food] to others creates the obligations and alliances that are at the center of all political relations. The greater the male monopoly on the distribution of scarce items, the stronger their control of women seems to be."[29]

Thus, from the beginning of human societies, the products of men's labor were likely regarded as more valuable than the reliable products of women's labor. Since large game hunting was more dangerous than gathering, it imparted greater prestige to men who hunted. The long-distance travel involved in men's hunting also contributed to men assuming public roles in interactions with other groupings of people and ultimately established men in positions of political leadership. The greater possibilities that foraging men had for trading items with members of other bands and/or residents of agricultural settlements and for bringing back to their own band highly valued items also contributed to the higher prestige accorded to the products of men's labor. Men's utilization of their hunting skills and weapons in defense of the band and for warfare further increased their prestige. Today warfare (and competitive sports) continues to convey great prestige to warriors, and women have difficulty being accepted on equal terms in those arenas of accomplishment.

In egalitarian hunting and gathering bands—whether patrilineal and patrilocal, or matrilineal and matrilocal, or some other combination of marital residence and lineage—women have significant status due to their crucial economic contributions to survival, but the division of labor by sex creates social contexts in which greater prestige is accorded to men's activities and the products of men's labor. The weapons used by men for hunting adapt readily to use in warfare and asserting dominance over women and other men. In foraging societies, as well as societies based on other types of economies, myths, rites of passage, rituals, and religious specialist roles express and reinforce gender roles and the values associated with them.

FORAGERS, GENDER, AND RELIGION IN THE PALEOLITHIC

The Paleolithic, or the "Old Stone Age," is dated from approximately 2.6 million years ago to around 10,000 B.P. and is the earliest period in which human beings existed and used stone tools that survive in archaeological records. The earliest evidence of *Homo sapiens*, which dates to about 200,000 B.P., has been found in East Africa. During the Paleolithic, Africa was hot and dry, while much of northern Europe was covered with glaciers. Paleolithic humans lived in small foraging bands.

The animals available for hunting in the Paleolithic varied according to the climate. Archaeologists have assumed that men hunted large animals such as varieties of deer, wild goat, antelope, pig, horse, mammoth, and woolly rhinoceros, and, in temperate Europe and Western Asia, aurochs cattle.[30] Studies of contemporary foraging women postulate that women living in the Paleolithic were economically productive in feeding their families by gathering honey, "insects, fruit, nuts, and plants," as well as shellfish, by fishing, and by hunting and making snares and traps to capture small animals.[31] Paleolithic women's economic contributions to survival would have been valued in the foraging bands.

According to Ehrenberg, Paleolithic women probably invented and made tools for their activities: slings made of skins to carry children, containers made of skins and woven baskets to carry gathered food-stuffs, sticks to dig out plants and roots, sharpened flints with which to cut and scrape, and special rocks to crack nuts. Ehrenberg suggests that Paleolithic women probably promoted social bonds and communication by sharing food with their children, caring for their offspring during their extended childhoods, and teaching children how to use tools and gather food.[32] Adovasio, Soffer, and their co-author, Jake Page, summarize the research of biological anthropologist Dean Falk, which demonstrates that human females' brains use both hemispheres in performing language functions, while male brains use mostly the left hemisphere. Men's brains, in general, have evolved to have greater proficiency in the "mental manipulation of spatial relationships," and males' verbal skills frequently have to catch up with those of females. Falk theorizes that early women's verbal communications with their children led to the development of human speech.[33]

Over sixty female figurines have been found that date from about 35,000 B.P. to about 10,000 B.P. in the large area from western France to Russia. Most of these Upper Paleolithic female figurines date between about 28,000 to 23,000 B.P., and range from 4 to 22 cm. in height, with the smaller sizes being more common. Most of the figurines were carved from stone or mammoth ivory, but a few were molded from clay and then baked in fire, or were carved rock reliefs. Despite the scholarly focus on the female figurines depicting nude women with large breasts and buttocks, faces with no features, and minimally shaped arms and legs, archaeologist Sarah M. Nelson points to the diversity in the female body types depicted in the figurines, which include slender figures.[34] Some of the figurines were carefully crafted, and others were very roughly made. The most famous Paleolithic female figurine, dubbed the "Venus of Willendorf," was found at Willendorf, Austria.

Whereas popular interpreters have written that the female figurines indicate there was a widespread religion dedicated to the worship of a "Great Goddess" in Paleolithic Europe, Margaret Ehrenberg cautions that we must be cognizant of the locations in which the figurines were found and that the female figurines could have served a variety of

"Venus" of Willendorf, approximately 25,000 B.P. Natural History Museum, Vienna, Austria. Adovasio, Soffer, and Page point out that she is wearing a woven hat made of coiled stitches like a basket. Courtesy of Jorge Royan, Wikimedia Commons.

functions. The female figurines have usually been located within home bases or shelters made of earth, sticks, and brush. Typically, they are discovered in the rubbish of the living site, or alternatively in piles of flint tools. Some are found near hearths of the earliest houses constructed in the Paleolithic. The female figurines often appear singly in the archaeological record, but sometimes there are multiple figures. Rough clay female figurines, along with other baked clay figures of animals, are often discovered on sites with a hearth.[35]

Anthropologist Catherine Hodge McCoid and art historian Leroy D. McDermott argue that the Paleolithic figurines that depict the female body in ample proportions were created by women modeled on their own pregnant bodies viewed as they looked down at themselves, and that this accounts for why the head is frequently turned down, the face is not delineated, and the legs narrow to barely discernible feet. McCoid and McDermott speculate that the figurines were created for teaching purposes concerning women's physiological functioning.[36] Other scholars have speculated that some of the figurines may represent goddesses. Some may have been used in sympathetic magic to promote fertility; after the desired result—pregnancy or the birth of a healthy child—was achieved, the figurine may have been thrown away.[37]

Anthropologist Barbara Tedlock suggests that the figurines may have belonged to women shamans who were midwives. A *shaman* is an individual in an indigenous religion who mediates between the forces and beings in the spirit world and human beings in the physical world. In such traditions it is often believed that harmony with the spiritual forces and beings is necessary for well-being. Tedlock points out that the figurine called the "Venus of Lespugue," a six-inch ivory sculpture found in France, has long parallel serrations carved below the buttocks, which Tedlock suggests depicts a string apron. Adovasio and Soffer confirm that the "back skirt" of this sculpture consists of eleven cords attached to a cord serving as a belt and is depicted in realistic and detailed carving. Tedlock reports that clay figurines found in the grave of a woman shaman at Dolní Vestonice (in what is now the Czech Republic) bear similar impressions made by twined rope made from plant fiber. The woman in question had been buried under a pitched roof made of mammoth shoulder blades. Traces of red on her bones indicate she had been covered with red ochre.[38] A flint spearhead was next to her head, and one hand held the body of a fox, which is frequently viewed as a spirit guide in Europe, Asia, and the Americas. Near the woman's grave was an earthen lodge containing bone flutes and a large oven filled with almost three thousand small pieces of baked clay, some in the shape of human feet, hands, and heads, and others in animal shapes.[39] Tedlock writes, "In other words, not only do the oldest known skeletal remains of a shaman belong to a woman, but she is also the earliest known artisan who worked in clay and then hardened it with fire. She wasn't making early household utensils; she seems to have been making talismans or figurines of some sort, perhaps for use in her rituals and spiritual healing."[40]

EGALITARIAN FORAGERS: CHIRICAHUA AND MESCALERO APACHES

Collected oral histories reveal the religion and gender roles of the Chiricahua and Mescalero Apache, who lived a nomadic foraging way of life within historic times.[41] Their range included what is now northern Mexico and the southwestern United States. Their memories and oral histories illustrate that when women make direct economic contributions to the survival of their families and bands, the roles of women and men are generally balanced in the society and its religion. In the foraging days of the matrilineal and matrilocal Chiricahua and Mescalero Apache, women built temporary residences (*wickiups*) made of wood and brush, gathered plants and processed them into edible and storable foods, nursed the sick and injured with plant substances possessing medicinal properties, and cared for children. The men hunted; raided ranches, farms, and wagon trains to bring back valued items; and waged war to protect their families and bands on a "metaethnic frontier" on which there were competing peoples—different groupings of Native Americans, beginning in the sixteenth century Spanish colonists, and from the nineteenth century Mexican and American soldiers and settlers. [42]

Despite traditional activities based on division of labor by sex, Apache girls and boys and women and men were all trained in the knowledge and skills to survive, and if necessary, fight enemies on a rugged desert terrain. There was considerable overlap in the types of economic and religious work performed by Apache men and women. Medicine women and medicine men were equally respected. Daughters were valued equally with sons, and the girl's puberty ritual was an important occasion that brought together members of multiple families. The puberty ritual for boys involved their accompanying the men on four raids; it was discontinued after the Apache were forced by colonial powers to live in one place and stop raiding.

Today at the Mescalero Apache Reservation in New Mexico, the girl's puberty ritual continues to be important for many Chiricahua, Mescalero, and Lipan Apache.[43] During the ritual the girl is imbued with the power of White Painted Woman (also called Changing Woman), and she, in turn, conveys healing blessing to people attending the ceremony. White Painted Woman is the model for the strong, generous, and resourceful Apache woman.

Anthropologist Claire Farrer listened to medicine man Bernard Second (d. 1988) tell his niece Delores (his sister's daughter) about White Painted Woman and her relation to the Apache girl's puberty ceremony. Farrer's report demonstrates that adults tell stories about White Painted Woman to teach girls about their roles in Apache society and instill self-esteem in the girls.

"They say [White Painted Woman] first came to us from the East. Oh! She was beautiful, a beautiful young woman. She lived with us. She showed us many things. She grew to full adulthood and lived down there. [He gestured with his lips to the south.] She had children there. Then she became old, very old. Soon she would begin her westward journey. But first she became even older with thinned skin and white, white hair, hair like the snow in the north country where our people used to live.

[Delores turned her head and glanced at me and my gray-white hair, a gesture not lost on her uncle.]

She was much older than your auntie, much older. She walked on three; she walked with gish/cane. Then one day, she died. The People were so sad; we were sad, for we loved her dearly. But, we were surprised, too. All of us were surprised, for the next morning, the next sunrise, she appeared to us in the east again, a young woman again.

That's who those girls [in the puberty ceremony] are: [White Painted Woman]. They go around that basket four times, just like she lived four stages in her life on this earth. Just like all of us live four stages: first we are babies, infants, like Nancy; then we are children, like you [and he patted Delores's shoulder]; then we are adults, like me and auntie; and, if we are lucky and live good lives, we become the elderlies, like Grandma Apache. That is a good life.

That's what my grandparents told me."

After the story, Delores whispered to her uncle, inquiring if she, too, would be White Painted Woman during the girls' puberty ceremonial.

"Of course you will be [White Painted Woman]. But I won't sing for you. Oh, no! I want to dance at your feast!" And Delores skipped out of the tipi giggling at the imagined sight of her very proper uncle dancing.[44]

Nonegalitarian Foragers: Transition to Male-Dominant Farming Societies

Summarizing anthropological literature, archaeologist Robert L. Kelly points out that in addition to relatively egalitarian foragers, there are also *nonegalitarian foragers*. Theirs is a social pattern that indicates socioeconomic factors tending toward hierarchy and patriarchy. This pattern is found among foragers who live in sedentary communities for significant periods during the year, and therefore accumulate possessions. Nonegalitarian foragers have complex societies in which there is specialization in occupations, high densities of population, storage of food, defense of ownership of resources, and status-seeking by various means. According to Kelly, "Complex hunter-gatherers are nonegalitarian societies, whose elites possess slaves, fight wars, and overtly seek prestige." These societies are frequently patrilineal and patrilocal, but they may be matrilineal. They possess characteristics leading to the development of class-stratified patriarchal cultures. The value placed on sharing and personal humility in egalitarian foraging societies shifts in nonegalitarian foraging societies to "emphasis on hoarding and boastfulness; from values that do not sanction violence to those that do."[45]

Nonegalitarian foraging societies represent social movement toward sedentary farming communities that are patriarchal, hierarchical, and class-stratified, with elite men reinforcing their status by warfare, trade, and accumulation of possessions, which include human beings. Examples of nonegalitarian foraging societies given by Kelly are Native American groups on the northwest coast of North America ranging from northern California through the Alaskan panhandle.

It is possible for formerly nomadic foragers to settle in one place to pursue horticulture in environments where they are not in conflict with inhabitants of other settlements. In that case, the transition to male dominance may occur slowly over centuries. Classical patriarchy will not develop as long as women have direct access to the production of the primary products necessary for survival.

Horticulture

In a society that relies on horticulture, or farming with a stick or hoe, men typically cut the trees and brush to clear the land for cultivation. After the land is cleared, women and men may cultivate the land together, or either only women or only men plant and tend the crops. Of these three labor patterns, Friedl suggests that since horticulture is an obvious extension of women's gathering activities, the only one requiring explanation is when men do all the cultivation and women participate "only in the harvests or as incidental assistants." Friedl asserts that a major factor contributing to the exclusion of women from cultivation is warfare. Women working in the fields risk capture by other groups to be made into slaves/wives. On the other hand, if men are absent due to warfare or the need to pursue economic tasks elsewhere, women take over horticulture.[46]

Friedl's point that warfare or raiding is the likely cause of the shift of horticultural work from women to men is supported by the explanation by Adovasio, Soffer, and Page that among Native American horticulturalists, women in most instances were the farmers while men continued to hunt. Forensic archaeology has determined this by examining the femurs of women and men, the different characteristics of which indicating the different types of work performed. The exception was the Pueblo people: "Evidently, by about 1500 AD, the Pueblo peoples' fields were so frequently raided—for both food and women—by neighboring non-agricultural people that the men had taken to doing the work in the fields."[47]

Contemporary horticultural societies may be matrilineal or patrilineal, matrilocal or patrilocal, or various other arrangements in terms of the residence of spouses. The most advantageous pattern for women is when the important economic resource for survival—the land—is tilled by women, and inheritance of the land is passed through the female line. But even in matrilineal and matrilocal societies men have political prominence and exercise leadership because they have important resources they can distribute—meat from hunting, items obtained by raiding or trade—and because they are the ones who make alliances with other peoples in their wide-ranging travels. When residence is matrilocal, husbands leave their mothers' homes to go and reside with their wives. Where enemy attack is a constant threat, men most often clear the land and perform the tasks of horticulture, and this sexual division of labor frequently corresponds to patrilineal inheritance of land and patrilocal residence of spouses. In such a case, women will not be completely disempowered if they have direct access to valued economic resources they can distribute to family members and to others beyond the family. For instance, in West African horticultural societies where men do the cultivation and pass the land to their sons, women are active and often prosperous traders, who may travel considerable distances to reach markets.[48]

Friedl points out that in horticultural societies, regardless of who does the cultivation, preparation of food is typically done by women once agricultural products are brought into the household. This is a continuation of the work of foraging women who prepare food for consumption and storage. In foraging societies and horticultural societies women also do the work involved with cleaning the domestic space. This work does not convey status to women. Women lose social status if they become separated from production of primary economic resources.[49]

GENDER CHANGES IN THE NEOLITHIC

The invention of agriculture in the form of horticulture set into motion a number of dynamics that led eventually to the decline of women's social position. In many parts of the world this occurred during the Neolithic, which itself covered different time spans, depending on location. Thus, the Neolithic in the Fertile Crescent, ranging from the Persian Gulf to the Tigris and Euphrates River areas to the east of the Mediterranean Sea, began about 10,000 B.C.E. in various locations. The Neolithic in China began about 10,000 B.C.E, and the Indus and Sarasvatī Rivers region in the Indian subcontinent entered the Neolithic about 9000 B.C.E. In the Anatolian Plateau in Western Asia, the Neolithic began about 8000 B.C.E. The Nile River region in northeastern Africa entered the Neolithic about 6000 B.C.E. Agricultural peoples from Anatolia moved their families, tools, seeds, and animals in boats to the eastern Mediterranean islands and Greece to initiate the European Neolithic approximately 7000 B.C.E. Archaeologists use the term *Formative Stage* for a similar period in Mesoamerica and South America and the Southwest in North America that began about 2500

B.C.E. and continued through 300 C.E. In various areas, the Neolithic began with increased settled agriculture and ended with the invention and use of metallurgy to make tools—first copper, followed by bronze, and then iron. Whereas women's status was generally equal to that of men at the beginning of the Neolithic, by its end a number of societies had developed intensive agriculture and were becoming patriarchal.

The Neolithic was characterized by increased sedentary farming and the development of villages and towns. The shift to farming has been termed the *Great Transition* to indicate its importance for humanity. This period was crucial for changes in the status of women. Archaeological records suggest that women had generally equal status at the beginning of the Neolithic. Yet, by the end of the Neolithic, the written records of literate peoples in some parts of the world indicate that their societies were patriarchal, even though women of elite classes did wield some power, priestesses did have significance, and goddesses were worshipped. Therefore, it is important to understand the social processes that occurred during the Neolithic. The Neolithic saw a technological revolution in the form of the development of agriculture, which further structured the division of labor between women and men and hence cultural understandings of gender, which were reinforced by religious traditions and their concepts of deity, their myths, and their law codes.

Since foraging women had extensive knowledge of plants, archaeologists assume that women in various parts of the world played the leading role in the domestication of plants. Plants that are domesticated are dependent on humans to plant, tend, and harvest them. The grains that were domesticated in the Fertile Crescent and Anatolia were barley and varieties of wheat. In North Africa the primary grains were barley and emmer wheat. The Indus-Sarasvatī civilization cultivated barley, varieties of wheat, millet, and rice. In China millet, wheat, and rice were cultivated. In Mexico and Central America corn was domesticated. Domestication of plants is necessary for the domestication of animals. Because of the large size of wild cattle, goats, sheep, and hogs, archaeologists assume that men played the primary role in domesticating large animals.[50]

During the Neolithic a number of technologies related to the sedentary agricultural way of life were invented. It is reasonable to assume that women as well as men were creative in developing tools and artwork during these periods. Techniques were developed to mold containers from clay and fire them in a hearth or kiln. Heavy containers could be utilized because people were no longer nomadic, and by farming they accumulated more food than could be eaten in a few days. Animals such as goats, sheep, cattle, and pigs were domesticated and kept near the home base for other purposes besides providing meat. Wool was plucked from sheep, spun into thread, and woven into garments and household coverings. Thus, instead of being raised solely for their meat, sheep took on significance for the secondary products that could be processed from one of their primary products—wool. The first domesticated cattle probably were kept for their meat, but during the Neolithic techniques of milking were developed. People then learned how to process the primary product of milk into the secondary products of cheese and yogurt. During the early Neolithic men probably continued to hunt and supplement the community's diet with the meat of large animals, but the keeping of domestic animals gradually reduced the need for men to hunt.[51]

Once plows began to be utilized to till the ground in some areas, bullocks (castrated bulls) were used to pull plows. When a region made the shift from horticulture to *intensive agriculture*, men usually took over the primary agricultural tasks if they had not already done so. Women then devoted themselves to the very time-consuming tasks of processing primary agricultural products into the secondary products of food and cloth. In some areas, the size of herds increased. The combination of reliance on intensive agriculture and herding frequently removed women from the direct production of primary food products. Use of the plow to till the ground and the keeping of herds usually means that men perform the tasks that produce agricultural products.

With sedentary agriculture there is increased occupational specialization with accompanying economic divisions. Full-time specialization of labor includes warfare, which contributes to the emergence of armies. Warfare is related to the subordination and commodification of women. Archaeological artifacts, ancient literature, and oral histories reveal societies in which women were warriors, but, ultimately, increase in warfare leads to the building of kingdoms and the establishment of empires. These are hierarchical, class-stratified societies, in which elite men control their wives and offspring, as well as other human beings, including slaves. Elite women may have power and influence but they are subordinated to fathers and husbands. A woman will become the ruler only if there is no male heir of the age to rule.

In horticultural societies, religious traditions reflect and reinforce gender roles shaped by the environment, available technology, and resulting economy. In the next section we will examine what can be known about gender roles and religion from the artifacts discovered at the largest Neolithic archaeological site being excavated, Çatalhöyük.

GENDER IN ÇATALHÖYÜK, A NEOLITHIC TOWN

Çatalhöyük is located on the Konya Plain in the Central Anatolia region of present-day Turkey in Western Asia. Its rich archaeological record provides information about the relatively equal status of women and men at the beginning of the Neolithic and the factors in a settled agricultural community that slowly led to male dominance and female subordination in society and religion. From the 1960s through the 1980s, based on the excavation directed by archaeologist James Mellaart in the early 1960s and his interpretations of the findings, it was thought that Çatalhöyük was a matrilineal and matrilocal culture in which a Great Goddess was worshipped and in which women were respected because of their economic productivity in horticulture.[52] The interpretations of the current team of archaeologists led by Ian Hodder complicate the picture of Çatalhöyük by pointing to the predominance of evidence that indicates that male prestige was gained from hunting large wild animals and sharing the meat in community feasts. The current archaeological project at Çatalhöyük demonstrates that this Neolithic town was the site of gradual changes relating to economy, way of life, gender roles, and religion.[53]

Çatalhöyük was a town that stretched over 33.5 acres next to the Çarsamba Çay River, which flows from the Taurus Mountains. It was inhabited for 1,400 years, from about 7400 B.C.E. to about 6000 B.C.E. The town's population ranged from about 3,000 to 8,000 people. They lived in closely packed brick houses plastered with mud, with refuse areas (middens) outside the houses, and virtually no streets. A house was entered through a hatch on the flat roof, which also served as an outlet for smoke. No fortifications were built around the town and there is no evidence of massacres or raids.

The archaeological remains of this town, called by local people Çatalhöyük ("fork mound"), are located on what is known as East Mound, the largest of two mounds on each side of the river. When Çatalhöyük was finally abandoned, people had moved to a town known by contemporary locals as Küçük Höyük ("small mound") across the river. Küçük Höyük was a Copper Age town existing on the West Mound through the sixth millennium B.C.E. It has not been excavated to the same extent as Çatalhöyük, where excavations are ongoing.

Çatalhöyük is an especially well-preserved archaeological site. When inhabitants of a house decided it was time to build a new residence, after removing their belongings and the faces and hands and feet (or paws) on figures sculpted in bas relief on the mud plastered walls, they demolished the upper walls of the house and filled in areas bounded by the lower walls with soil. Then the new house was built directly on top of the old one.

The inhabitants of Çatalhöyük buried some of their dead family members underneath the clay floors of their houses. Deceased babies and children, young people and mature adults were literally present in the house, under the floors,[54] with their biological or spiritual relatives sleeping over them on slightly raised mud platforms covered with woven mats.

Not all the houses contained burials, and some houses contain only five or six. The average number of burials in a house is eight. Houses with more than twelve burials in their various levels had the greatest number of decorations in the form of wall paintings, bucrania (the skull and horns of a wild aurochs bull) with mud plastered on it in the shape of the bull's head, and bas-relief sculptures. The number of burials in these houses range from twenty to thirty. The largest number of burials has been found in House 1, with sixty-two bodies and portions of bodies that had been exhumed and reburied by the inhabitants. Anthropologist Peter Pels has termed the houses with numerous burials "history houses," because they apparently served to commemorate ancestors and their accomplishments. All of the houses were residences, thus making Çatalhöyük a house-centered society, but the larger history houses had reduced areas for storage bins, ovens, and work, which suggests that people living in nearby houses provided food for the elders or priests/priestesses living in them to tend to the ancestors.[55]

The average house consisted of a living and sleeping room of about six by four meters and a storeroom with grain bins. A house was large enough for a family consisting of five to eight people. Most of the houses were built on a north-south axis but some were on a west-east axis. Each house had its own domed oven, usually placed on the south wall inside the main room, with an open hearth also in the south area of the room.

Çatalhöyük was discovered by archaeologist James Mellaart in 1958, and he excavated there from 1961 to 1965. Mellaart's archaeological technique was to excavate quickly.[56] In his published works, Mellaart interpreted Çatalhöyük as being a matrilineal and matrilocal society, because he incorrectly believed that women and children were buried under the large slightly raised floor platform in the main room and that males were buried under other floor platforms.

Çatalhöyük's economy was based on horticulture, herding, and trade, although men continued to hunt.[57] The domesticated plants cultivated were emmer and einkorn (early varieties of wheat), barley, lentils, peas, pistachios, acorns, almonds, apples, juniper, and hackberry. Obsidian, a black volcanic stone, was used to make blades, arrow and spear points, and polished mirrors. Thread and woven cloth were made from sheep's wool and goat hair. Men had bows and arrows, lances, spears, and sling-shots, but there is no evidence that they engaged in warfare or conquest.[58]

Mellaart concluded that the gods worshipped at Çatalhöyük included a birth-giving goddess and a bull deity. A figure with outstretched arms and legs was depicted in bas-relief sculpture made of clay modeled over reeds on the wall of the main room in some of the houses. Mellaart thought that this figure depicted a goddess giving birth. Numerous houses had bull's heads mounted on the walls; they were sculpted in mud over the skulls of aurochs (wild cattle) with their horns protruding. To Mellaart's imagination it appeared that the bas-relief goddess had given birth to the bull's head below her outstretched legs.

Mellaart's team found inside a grain bin a large headless clay figurine (16.5 cm.; 6.5 in.) of an amply proportioned seated woman flanked by two leopards. Crudely modeled clay female figurines with beaked faces or pointed heads were found, as well as roughly made clay figurines of animals, and male and female figurines of a higher quality made of stone or clay.

Feminists inclined to goddess worship in their search for alternatives to the patriarchal male God of western religions have been attracted to Mellaart's intepretations of Çatalhöyük, thinking of it as a matrilineal and matrilocal society, in which women did the horticultural work, with men assisting by doing heavy work and also engaging in hunting and traveling for trade. As a 1986 article by feminist historian Anne L. Barstow indicates, a number of feminist women were thrilled to find what they believed to be a Great Goddess worshipped at Çatalhöyük.[59]

Excavation at Çatalhöyük resumed in 1993 by an international team of archaeologists who have brought a variety of scientific expertise to what is now a slow and painstaking excavation directed by Ian Hodder. In his book *The Leopard's Tail*, Hodder discusses the disappointment of feminists who visit Çatalhöyük and find that his team is not confirming their expectations that it was a matrifocal society. Anthropologist Kathryn Rountree discusses how Goddess feminists dispute the interpretations of Hodder's team, which has not concluded that Çatalhöyük was matrilineal and matrilocal.[60]

Hodder's team finds that in the majority of the houses, adults (women and men) were buried under the large platform on the northern wall of the main room. Wall paintings at Çatalhöyük indicate that corpses may have been exposed to vultures before burial of the bones. Recent studies indicate that vultures are able to deflesh a carcass while leaving intact the tendons and ligaments that hold the skeletal remains together. Marin A. Pilloud, Scott D. Haddow, Christopher J. Knüsel, and Clark Spencer Larsen argue that after a body had been exposed to vultures for the removal of flesh, the intact skeleton was bound in a tightly flexed position to be buried in a shallow grave under a mud platform in a house. This greatly cut down on the smell of the body in the living space.[61]

Studies of the skeletons reveal similar types of wear and tear on the bones of women and men, although women may have been more involved in grinding grain and men may have been more involved in throwing, perhaps of spears. Soot found inside the ribcages of skeletons indicates that women and men spent a similar amount of time indoors next to the fire. There was no difference in the diet eaten by women and men. Study of teeth indicates that more women married into Çatalhöyük than men, presenting a picture of a patrilocal society. A full picture of the marriage patterns at Çatalhöyük has yet to emerge. Examination of skeletons indicates that there was not a high degree of biological related-ness among the inhabitants of many houses. People frequently lived and worked together on a basis of "practical" kinship rather than biologi-cal kinship.[62] Other social ties held individuals in the houses together, and these may have involved religious belief and practice. Initiation into worship societies often results in "houses" under the headship of a spiri-tual mother or father.

Hodder's team has found few grave goods in the burials of adults. Young people, most often buried under the main room's northwest platform, were more likely to be buried with grave goods. The wall above the platform was decorated with geometric patterns. Sometimes newborn babies or small children were buried in the southern part of the main room next to the domed oven, although their bodies were also sometimes buried at the threshold of the main room or placed inside the house walls. Infants and children were buried with numer-ous beads.

Wall paintings were made on the northern wall at the time of a burial, or perhaps also on the occasion of other rites of passage, and then later plastered over with white clay. Sometimes the men in the paintings wear what appear to be leopard skins around their waists. The paintings often depict groups of people teasing large wild animals—aurochs bulls, stags, boars, and a bear. In one such painting, men with beards are depicted surrounding and harassing a stag. Some of the paintings on the north and east walls depict vultures attacking decapi-tated bodies.

Wall installations of bucrania, the sculpted figure with arms and legs "splayed," to use Hodder's term, and other sculptures and installations are usually found on the east and west walls. Hodder suggests that the splayed figure was not a woman or goddess, but a bear that would have been included among the animals venerated at Çatalhöyük. A pair of leopards facing each other is often found in sculpted bas-relief on the mud-plastered walls. Archaeologist Ali Umut Türkcan argues that a clay seal in the shape of a bear, found in 2005, mirrors the posture of the bas-relief figure with hind legs stretched out and hind feet turned upwards, and front legs also stretched out with front paws upturned (before they were broken off). He argues that at Çatalhöyük the bear, leopard, and aurochs bull were regarded as sacred animals. In short, contemporary archaeologists are not confirming that the seemingly anthropomorphic bas-relief figures represent a mother goddess.[63]

Hodder points out that a dichotomy is found in the main rooms: the south side of the room was where the "dirty" and practical work of cooking and making tools from a cache of obsidian buried next to the oven occurred, versus the north side of the room, which was "clean" and appears to have been devoted to ancestor veneration and perhaps veneration of the spirits or gods of particular animals.[64] The careful orientation of the main room and its functions suggests that the four directions were regarded as sacred, each having different qualities.

Hodder reports that the contents of the houses indicate long-distance travel and trade on the part of some individuals. Obsidian was obtained from the southern Cappadocia region in central Anatolia, oak and juniper timber from the Taurus Mountains to the south, shells were brought from the Mediterranean, and some baskets were imported from the Red Sea area. There is no evidence of a ruler or chief, but there is a lot of evidence of coordinated work in farming, herding cattle, goats, and sheep, and hunting.[65]

While Hodder refrains from much speculation about work performed by women and men, it can be inferred that women and men cooperated with each other to carry out various aspects of farming and herding, with some men traveling distances to hunt and kill wild bulls, which were important to community feasts and were commemorated by installation of bucrania in relevant houses. Men also probably traveled distances to obtain obsidian and timber and to engage in trade. Women were likely to have done most of the cooking. In the early centuries of the settlement, heated clay balls were put into skin containers to cook food and liquids. Later cooking was done in clay pots. Perhaps women wove cloth, although men may have done weaving also. Probably both women and men performed work next to the oven, including cooking, knapping obsidian points and blades, and making items such as small clay figurines.

The archaeological data provide no evidence that Çatalhöyük's women were subordinated, but men had more opportunities to gain prestige through hunting large and dangerous animals and to travel long distances to trade and acquire highly valued goods to distribute within the community. This is seen in what Hodder terms "a prowess-animal spirit-hunting-feasting nexus" of activities and meaning at Çatalhöyük. The town's archaeological record indicates that wild bulls were consumed at large feasts. It is probable that killing an aurochs conferred prestige and also spiritual power to the hunters. The meat was brought into the town for a large outdoor feast, and the skull with horns was subsequently displayed in a house.[66] Lynn Meskell and Hodder point to the phallocentric imagery of the teasing of dangerous wild male animals with erect penises in the paintings and the bucrania and horns of wild goats and wild sheep installed inside the houses or in the walls.[67] Although there were domesticated sheep and goats at Çatalhöyük, there continued to be emphasis on the periodic hunting of large animals, especially aurochs bulls, which probably brought prestige to the men and which may have had religious connotations. The meat was distributed to houses in the town, and the bull's skull displayed in a house, or the horns were divided to be stacked in displays in houses.[68]

Hodder's team found that the skulls of a few adults buried under the floors had been removed. These may have been notable ancestors, and their skulls appear to have been used in ritualistic and protective magical ways. Foundations of houses sometimes contained a burial of an elder, perhaps holding the skull of another ancestor that had been plastered with mud to represent the skin. Building 42's foundation was found to contain the burial of a man holding a woman's plastered skull.[69] At the foundation of Building 1 the team discovered the skeleton of a woman who had been buried in the characteristic flexed position, holding a skull against her chest. Clay had been modeled on the skull and painted red. The woman was probably an important individual, as was the original owner of the male skull. A leopard claw, perforated for wear as a pendant, was found near the lower right arm of the woman's skeleton. It appears that the woman was a significant ancestor and perhaps a religious specialist. Hodder speculates that both male and female ancestors were important at Çatalhöyük, and lineage might have been traced through both parents.[70]

Meskell discusses the numerous anthropomorphic and animal figurines found at Çatalhöyük. The figurines made of clay were probably baked in household ovens. A few anthropomorphic figurines were carved in marble. The zoomorphic figurines depict cattle and other domesticated animals. A number of anthropomorphic figurines resemble phallic shapes. Of the 1,800 figurines discovered as of 2007 only forty are female. Many of these depict headless females with ample figures. Meskell speculates that they were portable sacred images, which perhaps were decorated and worn, carried, or kept in cloth pouches, perhaps along with other sacred items. She points out that the figurines were "(almost without exception) found in building fills and midden areas."[71] The removal of the head in the case of anthropomorphic figurines and stabbing and maiming in the case of zoomorphic figurines suggest that the object was "killed" before disposal. Hodder speculates that when a house was being demolished and filled in, the protective figurines located next to the hearth, in the walls, and in bins might have had their heads broken off before being left behind.[72]

Some figurines of women appear to be wearing leopard-skin bodices. There are male and female figurines that appear to be either sitting on or standing next to leopards.[73] If leopard skins were worn by religious specialists, then it appears that women as well as men held such roles.

Hodder sees the figurines, wall paintings, bucrania, and bas-relief sculptures within the houses as "art as practical science." They were objects believed to have magical power to effect material changes and provide protection. The many sharp animal and bird beaks, tusks, and teeth embedded in the walls may have had protective functions.[74]

Hodder argues that as life continued through the centuries at Çatalhöyük and eventually transferred to Küçük Höyük on the West Mound across the river, "gender changes were brought about by infinitesimal changes in the way people cooked, made stone tools, made pottery, used houses and so on." He emphasizes "the slow movement of the mass" of activities in effecting social change, the "long-term process of change in small daily practices."[75]

No wall paintings, bucrania, or bas-reliefs have been found in the houses excavated on the West Mound. Ancestors probably continued to be venerated, but the dead were no longer buried under house floors.[76] By the time of the Copper Age town of Küçük Höyük, life probably focused more on farming and much less on prestige and spiritual power acquired by hunting wild animals.

According to Hodder, "This changing relationship with things is the slow process that lies behind the shifts we call the emergence of village life, agriculture and social inequality."[77] If women were not subordinated at the beginning of the Neolithic period at Çatalhöyük, the social development toward subordination of women probably proceeded by the end of the Neolithic and continued in the life of Küçük Höyük. The prestige accorded to men's hunting, which is so strongly evident at Çatalhöyük, would have transferred to men as owners of the land once intensive agriculture based on tilling the ground with plows began. This process was repeated in all parts of the world as agricultural societies developed class stratification and occupational specialization.

PATRILINEAL AND PATRILOCAL HORTICULTURALISTS: THE YORÙBÁ OF SOUTHWEST NIGERIA

The Yorùbá of southwest Nigeria provide a living example of a horticultural society in which men do the farming, own the land, and pass it to their sons and in which marriage is patrilocal and polygynous (when a man has multiple wives). Despite the strong trend toward male dominance, Yorùbá society is not a classical patriarchy since Yorùbá women maintain independent economic productivity through their activities as traders as well as close connections with their natal families after they marry.

Corresponding to women's direct economic contributions to their families, in Yorùbá religion women as well as men play significant roles as initiated priests worshipping within societies dedicated to particular òrìṣà (Yoruba deities).[78] In a patrilineal and patrilocal extended family (the ilé), wives perform important priestly roles in worshipping the family's ancestors and òrìṣà by singing their oríkì ("praise poems"). Men may sing oríkì, but women are considered masters of oríkì.[79]

Women and men who are initiated priestesses and priests in worship societies are "mounts" for the òrìṣà, both female and male. Thus, women who are priestesses serve their òrìṣà, and in rituals they dance while possessed by male or female deities. In Yorùbá religious ritual, which involves drumming, singing, and dancing, the priest or priestess is dressed in clothing representative of the deity possessing him or her. If it is a male òrìṣà, the priest or priestess is dressed appropriately, carries weapons or royal staffs, and dances in an aggressive male style. When women priests are possessed by male òrìṣà, they express characteristics Yorùbá assign to men. During possession performances, "male" dancing is characterized by forceful movements including rapid spinning and high kicking, which indicate that Yorùbá consider men to be hot, violent, forceful, and aggressive. If women are priestesses of female òrìṣà, they affirm the dignity and significance of female characteristics and roles in Yorùbá society. "Female" dancing is highly controlled and dignified, indicating that women are considered to be cool, patient, gentle, and enduring. Male priests who are mounts for the "hot" warrior òrìṣà Ṣàngó, wear their hair plaited in women's hairstyles and wear women's earrings and, on occasions, women's clothing, because they are the "brides" of Ṣàngó. These men are usually polygynously married, and their wives plait their hair for them. Ethnographer Margaret Thompson Drewal writes of observing in 1975 a female priest called Ìyá Ṣàngó possessed by Ṣàngó dancing in a forceful, expansive and angular manner. Drewal points out that priestesses such as Ìyá Ṣàngó bring the qualities of their òrìṣà into their personal identities even when not possessed. Ìyá Ṣàngó "partakes of her deity's masculine character even in her daily life. She is never merely not not herself, not not Ṣango. . . . It is the nature of her 'inner head.'" Drewal notes that although Yoruba society has distinct masculine and feminine gender roles, initiation as a possession priest or priestess permits both women and men "institutionalized opportunities within ritual contexts to cross gender boundaries and to express the traits assigned to the opposite gender. Just as Yoruba construct gender, they also deconstruct it."[80]

Women, who have attained old age, wealth through their trading activities, political status, and/or religious status as initiated priestesses in worship societies are regarded as possessing àṣe, "vital force," the "power to bring things into existence, to make things happen." Women of power, especially older women, are known as àjẹ́, which has been translated into English as "witch." There are àjẹ́ who convey blessings and fertility, those who convey suffering, and those who convey death. These senior and powerful women, "our mothers," "the powerful mothers," are regarded with respect and affection.[81]

Men of a town put on a daytime Gèlèdé festival and a nighttime Èfè performance to appease the àjẹ́. In the Gèlèdé festival men masquerade as women, expressing various aspects of the female òrìṣà Gèlèdé in specially made costumes and painted masks made of wood and dancing to honor "our mothers" and Ìyá Nlá (the Great Mother), so they will not utilize their àṣe to harm. The Gèlèdé worship society contains women and men, with a woman as the Ìyálásé, the high priestess of Ìyá

Iya Odua, head priestess of the goddess Odua. Courtesy of Henry J. Drewal.

Nlá, the Mother of All. Membership in the Gẹ̀lẹ̀dẹ́ society is believed to improve the fertility of women, and masquerading in the festival is believed to enhance men's sexual potency. Art historian Babatunde Lawal observes that the festival fosters unity and cooperation between women and men and between Yorùbá who are priests of various òrìṣà and Yorùbá who are Muslims and Christians but who nevertheless belong to the Gẹ̀lẹ̀dẹ́ society, as the men masquerade and participate in this complex festival.[82]

The legacy of colonialism, the oil industry in Nigeria, and the globalized economy are pushing Yorùbá gender relations today toward increasing male dominance while simultaneously providing women with more educational and professional opportunities. The perpetuation and contestation of Yorùbá gender roles continues in Christian churches and Islamic mosques and within Yorùbá families,[83] but women continue to have significant religious roles in their Christian and Muslim communities as well as in the Yorùbá religion.[84]

Nomadic Pastoralism

Some peoples have preferred to live a nomadic way of life to herd their domesticated animals. Each nomadic pastoral society needs to be examined to determine the gender roles and their relation to religion. Archaeologist and ethnographer Jeannine Davis-Kimball reported that nomadic pastoralists on the vast Eurasian Steppe (grassland plain) had and continue to have significant roles for women. She believed that archaeological evidence found in *kurgans* (burial mounds) indicates that some steppe cultures were matrilineal in the past and that gender roles were not strongly distinct. Although the warrior role was important on this frontier so was the role of the woman at the heart of the family, "the hearth person," as termed by Davis-Kimball. Her experiences living with Kazakh nomads revealed that although they are patrilineal, women play significant roles in nomadic pastoral subsistence and that the gender roles of these contemporary nomads are not strongly distinct.

The Eurasian Steppe stretches 5,000 miles from eastern Hungary in the west to China in the east. The steppe is broken by the Altai and Tien Shan mountain ranges and then stretches across China and Mongolia into Manchuria. The steppe also reaches north into southern Siberia and south into the Tibetan plateau. Davis-Kimball studied mainly the Saka, who lived on the Tien Shan and Altai mountains and on the Eastern Steppe from the eighth through third centuries B.C.E.; Sauromatians, who in the sixth and fifth centuries B.C.E. lived in Russia's southern Ural Mountains and along the Volga and Don Rivers on the Western Steppe; and the Sarmatians, in the same region from the fourth century B.C.E. to fourth century C.E. These nomadic herders rode horses and lived in yurts, as do nomadic herders in these regions today.

The primary archaeological record left by prehistoric steppe nomads consists of burial mounds called *kurgans*, some dating to the Bronze Age, in which numerous bodies were buried around a central ancestor. Chieftan *kurgans*, called *czar kurgans* by Russians, can be as large as one hundred feet high and 350 feet in diameter. Average *kurgans* are nine feet high and 65 feet in diameter. The bodies of men and women were interred inside *kurgans* along with considerable wealth in grave goods. The largest *kurgans* containing gold objects were subsequently widely looted.

In a 1997 *Archaeology* article, Davis-Kimball argued that an unlooted fifth-century B.C.E. Saka *kurgan* burial near Issyk, Kazakhstan, of a petite individual wearing trousers and a caftan and boots covered with 2,400 arrow-shaped gold plaques, who was buried with a whip, an iron sword and dagger, as well as numerous gold ornaments, was a warrior-priestess. Davis-Kimball based her argument in part on the fact that the grave included earrings and beads of semiprecious stones and a gilded bronze mirror (used by female shamans) and on the fact that the individual was wearing a tall, richly decorated hat similar to those found in other burials of warrior-priestesses, and similar to hats worn by Kazakh women today at their weddings. Because of the richness of the burial, archaeologists had previously assumed that this individual was a chieftan and the figure was dubbed the "Issyk Gold Man."

In the 1990s Davis-Kimball collaborated with Russian archaeologist Leonid Yablonsky to excavate Sauromatian and Sarmatian *kurgans* dating from sixth century B.C.E. through the third century C.E. near Pokrovka, Kazakhstan. The grave goods indicated three statuses of people: hearth person, priest or priestess, and warrior. Ninety-four percent of the men had warrior status as indicated by bronze and iron arrowheads, swords, and daggers buried with them. Fifteen percent of the women were buried with weapons, indicating warrior status. Seven percent of the women were buried with bronze mirrors, seashells, and carved stone altars, indicating they were priestesses. About 3 percent of the women were buried with both warrior and priestess artifacts. Seventy-five percent of the women were buried with clay spindle whorls, bronze and gold earrings, and stone and glass beads, which indicate they were hearth women. Hearth women of wealth were buried in clothing richly decorated with beads and semiprecious stones from distant lands, which were probably acquired from trade or raiding along the Silk Road. Seventy-two percent of the persons in the first and central burial in the *kurgans* were women, suggestive of a matrilineal culture, and certainly of a society that valued women.[85]

While living with contemporary Kazakh nomads, Davis-Kimball noted that although their society is patrilineal and patrilocal, women and men share tasks and perform similar types of work, often side by side. Everyone pitches in to set up or take down yurts. Women do the cooking inside the yurt, while men cook horsemeat outside in sawed-off oil drums used as cauldrons. Mothers care for babies, and fathers look after toddlers while their mothers are occupied with other work. Both women and men make wool felt that is used in clothing, blankets, rugs, and on the outside of yurts. They both herd horses, sheep, goats, and yaks. Women take care of the work within the *aul*, the yurt village, when men travel to trade and buy supplies. Boys help their mothers with domestic tasks and milking livestock, and girls are taught to ride and shoot bows and arrows equally with boys. The society is generally egalitarian. In Kazakh nomad society, the youngest son inherits the father's property when he dies, because the youngest son remains with the parents to care for them in their old age. Other sons and daughters receive their inheritances when they marry. Women own the clothes and jewelry they are given by their parents when they marry. *Auls* are governed by consensus and women have input into decisions. The chieftan of the *aul* is selected based on ability; occasionally the person selected is a woman. Davis-Kimball found that nomadic women are shamans.

Although the Kazakh indigenous religious traditions were suppressed during the years of Soviet Union control (1931–1991), shamanism continued to be practiced in the yurts of nomadic Kazakhs,[86] and shamanism has reemerged in the post-Soviet Republic of Kazakhstan's villages and cities. Shamans's consultation of the spirits and their rituals to heal clients of illnesses and bad luck are blended with Sunni Islam, especially Sufism, in which saints are venerated for their closeness to Allah. Kazakhs believe a person is called to be a shaman through illness that does not respond to medical treatment. The person consults a shaman and is told that the ancestors are calling her to become a shaman, and if she does not go through the training to learn how to contact the spirits and serve them, she will not get well. In Kazakhstan, shamans are "highly esteemed," and

After covering ritual participants in the blood of a sacrificial sheep, Bifatima Dualetova punches a man to release trapped energy. Courtesy of Denis Vejas.

people go to them to be healed of illnesses that they believe are caused by the "evil eye" or magic spells. "They search for a renowned shaman only in the case of serious and persistent troubles, especially if they are believed to be a result of the interference of evil spirits . . . or particularly harmful black magic . . . which is widely feared."[87]

One such highly esteemed woman shaman is Bifatima Dualetova (b. 1940), who lives at the foot of a sacred hill outside the village of Ungurtas, Kazakhstan. She frequently performs a healing ritual in which a sheep or goat is sacrificed and its blood is poured over the participant. Then the person must wash away the blood and, along with it, their sins in the cold water of a creek. Dualetova compares the ritual to being born: "going through a birth canal, covered in blood, and cleansed with water afterward."[88]

Intensive Agriculture, Classical Patriarchy, and Complex Societies

The agricultural revolution promoted more highly specialized division of labor between men as well as between men and women and the greater accumulation of property by some people with valued occupational specializations. Anthropologists report that peoples who are intensive agriculturalists (also called *agro-pastoralists* because they have cattle) are rarely matrilocal in marriage residence and matrilineal in family and inheritance. Intensive agriculture most often corresponds with patrilineal inheritance, in which men pass ownership of the land to their sons and to patrilocal residence of spouses in extended families. In cultures where intensive agriculture is practiced, domesticated cattle are kept and some bulls are castrated to make them into bullocks, which are used as draft animals to pull plows. The work of plowing with draft animals is usually done by men. There is male dominance over economic resources, other people including family members, religious symbols and worship, and political institutions. *Intensive agriculture—pervasive in many parts of the world by the end of the Neolithic—is associated with classical patriarchy.*

Thus the ultimate result of innovations in agriculture was the removal of women in many areas from direct economic productivity and women's eventual subordination in family, society, and religion. In a settled agricultural society, it is possible for some people to accumulate more land and wealth than others, and class stratification develops. As some people accumulate more possessions than others, they also begin to think of other people as possessions. The male head of the family owns his wives, children, and slaves and exercises life-or-death authority over them. Not unusually, this type of society corresponds with the development of writing, keeping records, and formulating law codes. In other words, it is historical "civilization." This accounts for why classically patriarchal religions and their cultures are known to us through their written texts. "History" has been about patriarchal societies and their religions.

What is termed *classical patriarchy* in this book is seen in societies with economies based on intensive agriculture. When farming is done by men using large draft animals to pull plows, men generally own the land and pass it to their sons, daughters are married out of the family to become members of other families, and there is a strong parental preference for sons. A bride price may be paid to the father for the right to take his daughter as a wife, and in such cases the difference between purchasing a wife and purchasing a slave woman is only a matter of degree. The primary role of a wife is to care for her husband and his parents and to bear sons for the patrilineage. A woman gains status within her husband's family if she gives birth to sons.

In classical patriarchy, women of higher-class households—who may not have much wealth although they have social standing—are economically dependent on the men of their families. Their sexuality is closely guarded to make sure they do not give birth to illegitimate children who may become their husbands' heirs. Because his property will pass to his male heirs, a man wants to ensure that the sons of his wife or wives are his biological offspring. Women stay within the home to process agricultural products brought by the men of the family into secondary products that can be consumed or used. The religious tradition of the culture reflects and reinforces classical patriarchy, while perhaps also including some countercultural religious elements. The classical patriarchal social pattern and its values continue after urbanization, occupational specialization that does not rely on farming, and even industrialization.

In classical patriarchy, there is a double standard concerning sexual activity. Men have options for sexual intercourse with multiple types of women—wives, slaves and servants, mistresses, and prostitutes. Protected women are supposed to be virgins upon marriage, and they should have sex only with their husbands. There is emphasis on the early marriage of girls to ensure their virginity and also to train them to be obedient wives in the husband's household. The movement of women outside the home is restricted, and they are guarded by male relatives to uphold the family's honor, which is identified with the sexual "purity" of the family's women. A woman who has had sexual intercourse with a man who is not her husband—by her choice or through rape—loses her social value and may be discarded in various ways including murder.

The processing of primary products into secondary products useful for subsistence is highly time-consuming and tends to be part of women's work, particularly if this work corresponds with men's use of the plow pulled by draft animals in farming. Whereas men in horticultural societies often continue to hunt, men focus more on farming when ground is tilled using a plow. Men's strength is usually needed to guide the bullocks pulling the plow and to drive bullocks, oxen, or other draft animals pulling carts. Women spend their time producing secondary products by processing primary products. When greater numbers of domesticated animals are kept, men take over their care and herding, effectively controlling another source of primary production. Men no longer have as much time or the need to hunt.

Patrilineal inheritance and patrilocal residence of spouses in extended families are associated with intensive agriculture. Removing the bride from her natal family to go and live with her husband's family effectively isolates the married woman from her relatives who may prevent her husband and his relatives from abusing her. The young wife coming into her husband's family typically has very low status until she produces sons for the patrilineage. If she has no children or produces only daughters, her status remains low, and her husband either divorces her or takes additional wives. Women's labor is crucial to subsistence, but it is removed from primary production so it is devalued within the family and society. Women are dependent on their husbands for the primary resources for survival. In the event of divorce, a woman has no economic support unless her natal family agrees to take her back. Her children belong to her husband's family, but the family is less likely to want daughters.

Whereas foraging women space their children by three or four years,[89] women in sedentary agricultural communities have more children. Agriculture requires more laborers, and increased numbers of children are necessary to offset high infant mortality. The need for increased offspring as agricultural laborers encourages men to regard their children as economic assets and their wives as the means to produce children. This contributes to the commodification of women. Women are increasingly viewed as assets to be purchased as wives or slaves, or captured in warfare, enslaved, and used to produce more male children to enhance the master's economic wealth. In anthropologist Ernestine Friedl's words, women become "movable property,"[90] owned, sold and purchased, and stolen by men. Having too many daughters is an economic liability, and a man has full authority to kill his infant daughter or to sell his young daughter into slavery, including for prostitution. At this point in classical patriarchy, females are regarded as objects to be owned and utilized for the pleasure and aggrandizement of men. Females are viewed as property to be accumulated by men, and if they lose their value (by being raped or engaging in illicit sexual activity) or are superfluous (by having too many daughters), they are destroyed, cast aside, or perhaps sold for a profit.

In contrast to traditionally matrilineal and matrilocal societies, such as the nomadic, foraging Apache society, in which men were treated respectfully by the families into which they married, classical patriarchy imposes many disabilities on women, which are reinforced by religious law codes and customs. The worship of goddesses in classically patriarchal cultures does not mean that women are equal in families and society.[91]

Women in classical patriarchy have their own household religious rituals; exceptional women may serve as religious specialists and sometimes as rulers; goddesses from the earlier social patterns may continue to be worshipped and new goddesses may be created by the human imagination; but in general women are subordinated. They are often abused in their husbands' families, and their work is not valued as much as the work of men. These gender roles and values continue after intensive agriculture gives rise to cities, kingdoms and empires, and, ultimately, industrialized and information-age societies.

INTENSIVE AGRICULTURE, CLASSICAL PATRIARCHY, AND RELIGION IN NORTH INDIA

Life in the North Indian village of Karimpur, Uttar Pradesh, India, with a traditional economy based on intensive agriculture, was studied from 1925 to 2000 by anthropologist and Presbyterian missionaries William H. Wiser (1890–1961) and Charlotte Vial Wiser (1892–1981) and anthropologist Susan S. Wadley.[92] Their publications illustrate gender roles, class stratification, and expressions of Hinduism and Islam in Karimpur. Karimpur is as an example of classical patriarchy, based for millennia on farming using the plow, in which sons are valued over daughters due to economic and social factors, the work of Hindu high-caste (Brāhmaṇa) women is confined to their homes, men own and farm the land and pass it to their sons, girls from other villages leave their natal families at a young age to be married into their husbands' extended families in Karimpur, while Karimpur's daughters are married into families living in other villages. High-caste wives gain status in their families by producing sons. Low-caste women and their husbands engage in the work assigned to their hereditary castes to earn a meager living by serving high-caste patron families.

Hindu women in North India perform religious rituals called *vratas* (vows) in the hope of securing long life and prosperity for their male relatives—brothers, husbands, and sons—on whom their own well-being depends. Performing *vratas* is viewed as part of women's religious-social duty as wives and mothers. One of the *vratas* performed by women in Karimpur is the worship of Siyao Mata (Lampblack Mother) to secure the welfare of their sons and to acquire more sons. Stories told during the ritual of the origin and benefits of the *vrata* are about child-less women who bear sons after worshipping Siyao Mata. Women of a household mold a figure of a cow (Siyao Mata) from fresh cow dung and immerse a silver coin in the oil of a burning lamp. They collect soot by holding a spoon over the flame and apply it around children's eyes to protect them from evil spirits. The women next engage in several actions of imitative magic. They take turns sweeping behind themselves with a bundle of sacred grass while saying, "Give me wealth. That which is bad run away." Then they take turns holding a *puri*, a puffed and hollow fried bread, under their clothing next to their wombs, saying, "Siyao, don't give daughters, give sons. Keep all well in the next year." If a woman already has sons, she will say, "Keep my sons alive and give them many children." The women then sing devotional songs to conclude the *vrata*. According to Wadley, "To the Karimpur women having many sons is extremely important. Equally important is their belief that the goddess will give them sons and will help them keep their sons healthy."[93]

Wadley's ethnographic work in Karimpur from 1967 through 1998 demonstrates that with technological and economic changes and in-creased education for some girls and women as well as for some boys and men, women's roles are starting to become less restrictive. The age at marriage for young women has increased according to the number of years they spend in school, with half of Karimpur's twenty-two castes sending girls to high school (grades 9 and 10), and five castes sending girls to intercollege (grades 11 and 12). Young women from Brāhmaṇa families, who have the greatest access to education, may be twenty or twenty-five when they marry, especially if they attend college. Educated women have increased mobility outside the home in being able to travel unchaperoned to the nearby city. However, economic and social factors continue to perpetuate classical patriarchy. Motherhood remains the im-portant role for women, sons remain valued over daughters because sons look after their parents in their old age, and the number of daughters is reduced in Karimpur due to parental neglect (for instance, by not providing daughters with the same healthcare as sons) and perhaps more active measures.[94] In the villages of northern India today, the economy is impacted by modern and information technology, and people's lives are changing due to exposure to western values, but in general the gender roles of classical patriarchy remain strong.

The *vrata* involving the worship of a relatively new goddess who was popularized in a 1975 Bollywood film, Santoṣī Mā, who fulfills wishes and protects husbands who are away from the village working, has become popular among the women. The Hindu women in Karimpur continue worshipping the goddess housed in the shrine next to the bus stop and every Thursday visit the tomb of a Sufi saint located on top of a nearby hill to pray for his assistance with family concerns.[95]

COMPLEX SOCIETIES

Some of today's major world religions—and a number of religions that have died out—have origins in complex societies—states or kingdoms based on agriculture, with towns, class hierarchy, and work and craft specialization—characterized by classical patriarchy. Complex societies correspond with the invention of writing. When the script can be translated, historians can study these ancient literatures to trace out the processes involved in the expansion and institutionalization of classical patriarchy.[96]

The agricultural revolution unleashed economic and social forces that in many regions led to the subordination and oppression of classes of people. As people accumulated more wealth, land, children, and domesticated animals, some men began to use their hunting skills in armed raids to steal other people's property. Eventually this became full-scale warfare in which victors killed defeated men and seized women and children along with other booty.[97] An enslaved woman's body is owned by her master; she has no protection from rape. Once she gives birth to the children of her master, a woman may be less likely to try to escape and return to her own people. She has been domesticated. Such a woman can only seek to make the best of her situation, and if she bears sons, she may find favor with her master.

Daughters and wives in classical patriarchal families are also controlled and owned by their fathers and husbands. The selling of a daughter in marriage is structurally not very different from selling a slave to another man, or the selling of a daughter into prostitution. The difference in the statuses of women of different classes is a matter of degree. Women's sexuality and reproductive capacities are reified and commodified. The "double standard" is taken for granted.

In class-stratified societies, a man's class status is influenced by the amount of property, including women, which he owns or does not own. Perhaps another man owns him. The amount of property a man owns is related to his military prowess, or his skillful manipulation of political allies, or his business acumen, or inheritance, or all of these factors. But a woman's class status is defined by her sexual status and her relationship to men. Female relatives are exchanged in marriage to seal men's alliances and business agreements. A virgin daughter can have high status as a priestess in the organized religion. If a woman is possessed by one man, either her father or her husband, and is protected by him so other men do not have sexual access to her, her status is higher than that of female slaves to whom virtually any man can have sexual access. The concubine, being a slave whose sexual service is reserved solely for her master, is in a middle position between a wife and a slave. Even more demeaned than the slave is the prostitute, who actually is a slave whose master (the pimp) rents out her sexual services. According to feminist historian Gerda Lerner, the sexual exploitation of girls and women is the means of exploiting women as a class.[98]

The post-Neolithic economic and sociological processes that initiated the development of archaic states in complex societies operated gradually—archaeologist Ian Hodder's "slow movement of the mass"[99]—and not all women were subordinated to equal degrees. It took a long time for theology to adjust fully to support male domination. Particularly in the earliest stages of the shift to classical patriarchy in complex societies, individual women of high class could exercise a great deal of political and religious power. But eventually high-class women came to exercise their power only by virtue of being related or married to powerful men. Lerner points out that these women gained their wealth, power, and privilege by serving as "stand-ins" for the male ruler. Daughters or other female relatives may command considerable respect and exercise authority as priestesses in a system of worship that supports royal rule. Powerful goddesses from the earlier more egalitarian period continue to be worshipped for centuries, but classical patriarchal gender roles frequently require that goddesses either be repudiated and eliminated, which occurred, for example, as Jewish monotheism developed through the centuries B.C.E., or demoted to being consorts of the gods, which is frequently, but not always, the case in Hinduism. In Hinduism, powerful independent goddesses believed to exercise the power of life and death are usually not regarded as models for the behavior of Hindu women.[100] In many places in the world, the centralization of the nation-state corresponds with setting one god, who is masculine and epitomizes kingly qualities, above other gods. In places such as India and Japan, where goddesses continue to be strong presences, particular goddesses were utilized to support the power of kings and emperors, and occasionally, the stand-in queen or empress.

Religious law codes, such as Manusmṛti (Laws of Manu) in India and the Confucian Five Relationships in China, which gave sanction to the roles and duties of different categories of men and women, are developed and enforced by custom in complex societies. These law codes spell out distinct, and dichotomized, gender roles, with women being subordinate to and controlled by men. Male priests and their written scriptures teach that gender roles are divinely sanctioned to correspond with the different natures of men and women, and not unusually, women's nature is described as being subhuman and evil, unlike the complete and god-like human nature of men.

Typically in religions shaped within classical patriarchal complex societies, the origin of evil and of the suffering and mortality involved in human existence—the "fallenness" of the human condition—is blamed on women. The story of Adam, Eve, and the Serpent in Genesis 2–3 is the best-known example of this, but the phenomenon of blaming women collectively for human affliction and finitude can be discerned in many patriarchal religious traditions. Women are often regarded as being impure due to the blood of their menstrual cycles and childbirth. Women's bodies are regarded as making them antithetical to holiness.

Classically patriarchal complex societies are sex-segregated cultures in which the public and religious spheres belong to men, and women are restricted to the domestic sphere. Women in classically patriarchal cultures are frequently excluded from education that would make them cognizant of their rights within their religious traditions.

Industrialized Societies

The Industrial Revolution, initiated in the west, began a process of economic development that, while damaging to the environment and to people exploited as workers, began processes in which women gradually gained access to education and economic earning power. Increasing prosperity enjoyed in some areas creates contexts in which daughters are provided with nutrition and healthcare equal to that of their brothers, and women can take advantage of educational opportunities, which, interestingly, may be justified by appeals to religion.

For example, in the nineteenth-century United States, the gender ideology termed by historians the "cult of true womanhood" asserted that women's purity and Christian spirituality must be preserved by restricting women's activities to the domestic sphere, but since in cities men left the household to work during the day, it was argued that women needed to be educated so that they could raise their children in Christian piety and exercise a subtle reforming influence on their husbands. The cult of true womanhood and the Protestant revivalism associated with the Second Great Awakening (ca. 1790–1840s) and the Third Great Awakening (ca. 1850–1900) justified women's joining "voluntary associations" to be active outside their homes to reform society. They believed that their personal experience of being saved by Jesus Christ required them to testify publicly about their experience in order to extend salvation to others and that their sanctification meant they had an obligation to work to reform social ills.[101]

Adding to the complexity of interacting economic forces, the technology of the information age—computers, internet, cell phones, smart phones, and tablets—is increasing the rate of change based on women's access to education, information, and ability to earn a living. One result of industrial and postindustrial development and accessible education is the breakdown of strictly distinguished gender roles and division of labor by sex. In industrial and postindustrial societies, women often work outside the home, and women have access to education that enables them to do so. Increasingly, wives as well as husbands are breadwinners. Single women may have economic earning capacity. More women have education that enables them to challenge inequality, and they have the skills and technological tools to work together with other women and men for women's rights. As wives working outside the home have less time to do housework, more husbands are sharing the household chores. Increasingly more fathers are nurturing their children equally with mothers.

The contemporary steady, but uneven, breakdown of distinct gender roles in heterosexual marriages and increase in the social expectation of gender equality moves societies toward acceptance of equality for LGBTQ persons. Same-sex marriage and families with two moms or two dads are being accepted more, depending to a great extent on the nature of the religious culture. The decision by the United States Supreme Court in 2015 to legalize same-sex marriage nationwide ended the patchwork situation in which same-sex marriage was legal in some states and not in others. The popular vote in Ireland in 2015 in favor of legalizing same-sex marriage indicated that Ireland had moved beyond being a strict Catholic state in which the ethics taught by the Roman Catholic Church strongly influenced laws.

Instead of dividing the human race into two types of people, one with "masculine" qualities and the other with "feminine" qualities, *very gradually* more individuals are finding scope within their respective religions and societies to be human beings who express themselves in holistic ways. Additionally, as industrial and postindustrial technology and economy provides scope for change in gender roles, educated women and men, including gender nonconforming persons, are reimagining and recreating their respective theologies and religious traditions to make them more egalitarian.[102] They are demanding that their religious institutions change to accommodate social expectations of equality, and if they do not, many women move on to more accommodating religions or give up religious affiliation.

Women's subordination continues in industrialized and information societies, but since these societies grant increasing access to education to girls and women, more women become educationally and economically empowered to benefit themselves and their children and to work for social change. The shift to greater equality for girls and women is slow, and uneven, in part because of the conservative features of religion based on claimed revelation of truth.

Lessons from Anthropology and Archaeology concerning Women and Gender for the History of Religions

The interdisciplinary study of women in religions and cultures reveals that *religious worldviews and gender roles interact with each other in complex ways.* A society's economy, based on the available technology and resources, has a direct influence on family structures and political organizations, beginning with the division of labor by sex, and these affect the content of myths and theology. As patriarchy develops, myths, theology, and religious law codes are utilized to reinforce unequal gender arrangements, as well as divisions of labor and class hierarchy. The content of patriarchal myths, scriptures, and religious law codes establish the subordination of some groups, including women, to groups of dominant men.

However, religious traditions and scriptures shaped within patriarchal societies are internally diverse. They contain resources that can be used to support women's equality as well as those that can be used to support the subordination of women.[103] These resources include passages in scriptures, myths, significant foremothers, and conceptions of the divine. Which religious resources are utilized and become predominant are influenced by the economic structures of that culture, which promote either a social expectation of equality or a social expectation of the subordination of women.

When technological and economic changes in society lead to the breakdown of the patriarchal division of labor by sex in ways that are supportive of women's equality, women begin to press for equality in their religious traditions, including equal access to positions of religious leadership. Women reinterpret or reject patriarchal interpretations of myths that have been used to justify women's subordination. Women work to change patriarchal theologies and religious organizations. If women seeking meaningful equality encounter too much opposition to their full participation in their religious traditions, and if they live in free societies, they may opt to leave and form or join new religious movements.

The prehistoric division of labor according to sex based on the available technology and means of subsistence precipitated a long series of interacting changes, which through the millennia ultimately restricted women to subordinate positions in religious societies. The economic theory of the emergence of patriarchy asserts that a complex process of interacting economic and sociological factors led to the development and continuation of patriarchy.

Different societies in the world today can be seen as representing configurations of forces that have interacted to create unequal class societies as well as relatively egalitarian societies. The situations involving women in religions are even more complex today, since societies in various stages of technological and economic development interact and impinge on each other, even within the same nation.

3

Psychological Theories of Gender Roles and Women's Self-Esteem

The social factors traced out in the economic theory of the emergence and transformation of patriarchy are compatible with feminist psychological theories about attitudes that create and perpetuate patriarchy, as well as other attitudes that lead to increased equality in society. These different types of psychologies impact gender roles, and also views of God and other concepts of the sacred manifested in religious cultures. While these psychological theories were formulated by second-wave feminist scholars in the United States, members of younger generations and persons in other countries can consider and discuss these theories to determine whether or not they find them relevant to their family and social contexts today.

Patriarchy Perpetuated by Men's Lack of Involvement in Childrearing

One feminist theory of the origins of patriarchy places importance on the psychological consequences of strongly distinct gender roles. Feminist sociologist, psychoanalyst, and object-relations theorist Nancy Chodorow sees her psychological theory as complementing analysis of socioeconomic factors.[1] Chodorow theorizes that the different gender identities of men and women are due to their being parented primarily by women in patriarchal societies and that the resulting different psychological make-up of women and men perpetuates (in her words, "reproduces") male dominance and female subordination.

According to Chodorow, girls develop a less differentiated sense of self-identity because they identify with their mothers, who are their primary parents. Therefore, according to Chodorow, adult women possess a self-identity that has a sense of interconnection and relationship with others. Chodorow describes girls' acquisition of gender identity as being relatively unproblematic, because their primary caretaker models feminine behavior and nurturing on a daily basis. Therefore, most girls grow up prepared to become the primary parents of their own children. Only later, in a patriarchal society, when a girl realizes that her mother's role and contributions are devalued, does the female gender role become problematic for her.

Chodorow theorizes that boys also have a sense of identity with their mothers, who are their primary nurturers, and thus boys' first experience of human nature is that of a female human being with whom they identify. But in order to develop a masculine identity within a patriarchal culture that requires different ways of doing gender for women and men, the boy must learn to distinguish himself from his mother and gain a sense of being not-female. According to Chodorow, in a patriarchal society, a boy's development of gender identity is more problematic; he remains fearful of his retained inner sense of being female. If the father is absent (physically and/or emotionally) most or all of the time, the boy can define himself as masculine only by rebelling strongly against his mother and any perceived feminine characteristics in himself. Thus, according to Chodorow, men raised in a patriarchal culture have a psychological need to define women as being other than themselves, as being weaker, less desirable human types, and they feel a need to control women.

Chodorow acknowledges the complex economic and sociological factors that create and perpetuate patriarchy, but she believes that her psychological theory of the reproduction of patriarchy accounts for the intensity of men's dread of powerful, or even mildly assertive, women.[2] While acknowledging that psychoanalytic theories cannot be proven, Chodorow believes that her theory accounts for the persistence of the fear many men feel of being controlled by women.

Dorothy Dinnerstein, another psychoanalytic theorist, attributes the irrational unease that both men and women feel about women in positions of authority to the rebellion that *both* sons and daughters, growing up and living in patriarchal societies, direct against their primary caretakers—their mothers—in order to achieve independent identities. According to Dinnerstein, both daughters and sons fear being reabsorbed into the overwhelming presence of the mother. Both sons and daughters—long after they are grown—do not want to hear a woman's voice telling them what they should do.[3]

The fear of women in leadership positions can be seen in the resistance to women in ordained positions of religious leadership—in other words, religious leadership that is not solely based on charisma (belief that a person has access to an unseen source of authority).[4] Sociological surveys of women in ministry show that women rabbis and ministers are called mainly to serve small congregations, which are often congregations that male rabbis and ministers do not want. A large wealthy congregation will usually have a male rabbi or minister at its head, while women might be hired as assistant rabbis or ministers. Members of large, wealthy congregations appear to be more comfortable with a male leader than a female one, while ministering to a small congregation can be seen as congruent with a woman's nurturing role as mother. This reluctance to have ordained women in significant positions of leadership of congregations or national denominations is why it is so significant whenever clergywomen break through this barrier—one that church historian Susie C. Stanley calls "the stained glass ceiling."[5]

A similar phenomenon is observed in politics. More women are being elected heads of state, but many in the American public do not appear to be ready for a woman as president of the United States. The number of women elected to Congress remains low. In 2020 women held 127 (23.7 percent) out of the 535 seats in Congress: 26 percent of the one hundred seats in the Senate (seventeen Democrat, nine Republican), and 101, or 23.2 percent, of the 435 seats in the House of Representatives (eighty-eight Democrat, thirteen Republican). Of the 127 women in Congress in 2020, twenty-two were African Americans, thirteen were Latinas, eight were Asian American/Pacific Islanders, two were Native American, one was Middle Eastern/North African, and one was multiracial. In 2020 only nine women were governors (three Republican, six Democrat) among the fifty states in the United States (18 percent).[6]

The psychological theory that locates the perpetuation of patriarchy in men's lack of involvement in childrearing does not blame mothers for patriarchy. To the contrary, in patriarchal religions and cultures, *men* blame women collectively for the limitations of human existence and for the evil, suffering, and death that finitude entails. Not unusually in patriarchy, men blame individual women for being evil and perverted mothers, or "witches." The psychological theory of the perpetuation of patriarchy associated with Dinnerstein and Chodorow points out that the division of labor by sex, which in many patriarchal cultures assigns parenting virtually to women alone, produces psychological dynamics within men and women that perpetuate sexist attitudes toward women as well as patriarchal social and family structures.

According to the theories of Chodorow and Dinnerstein, in order to break the cycle that continually reproduces patriarchy in the psychologies of men and women, men must become equally involved in childcare. If a child is nurtured equally by a man and a woman, the feelings of youthful rebellion are no longer directed solely toward the mother figure—the father figure gets a share. An infant's earliest sense of unity with its caretaker is diffused between its male and female parents. The child will have to differentiate itself from both a woman and a man, so it will not be necessary or possible to subjugate and control members of one sex in order to achieve individuation.

When the strict division of labor by sex is broken down, and women and men perform similar and/or identical tasks in family and society, a boy or girl raised by both a man and a woman or by a same-sex couple who share the tasks of childcare, homemaking, and breadwinning, can select from both or either of the parents the traits and characteristics that he or she wishes to emulate. A daughter or a son can take a parent of either sex as a model of adult behavior and roles.

Men's equal involvement in parenting is seen by many feminists as one key to breaking the cycle that perpetuates psychological attitudes that undergird patriarchy. But it will take a long time for equal parenting to become widespread. Even men with good intentions may find it difficult to remain consistently involved in the nurture of their children if they were not parented by their fathers and society does not reinforce men's parenting. In general, there remains a strong social expectation that children will be nurtured primarily by their mothers.

A 2010 U.S. Census report on statistics collected in 2005–2006 found that only 32 percent of fathers with wives in the workforce were providing regular care for their children under age fifteen, which was up from 25 percent in 2002. However, the Census Bureau survey defined the mother in a two-heterosexual-parent household as the "designated parent," stating, "If the mother is not available for an interview, the father of the child can give proxy responses for her." A single parent of either sex was the designated parent in the survey. The survey did not investigate childcare arrangements for children of same-sex couples. Jonathan Liu, an author and stay-at-home father, notes that the Census Bureau survey considered only care provided by persons or groups other than the mother as "childcare" and that only those hours were recorded. The work of stay-at-home mothers as "designated parents" was not recorded since it was considered the social norm. If the mother worked or attended school, her childcare hours were counted in the survey. Liu concludes that the survey "does a disservice to both dads and moms, perpetuating stereotypes and writing off anything that doesn't fit conventional gender roles."[7]

As men become involved in raising their children, it will take some time for society to move away from the assumption that the mother is the primary, or "designated," parent. According to the theories articulated by Dinnerstein and Chodorow, until women and men in various societies parent more equally, men and women will have their unconscious fears of "controlling women" activated when they encounter a woman in a position of authority. Women will continue to appear less threatening and more reassuring to both women and men when they are engaged in activities of homemaking and caring of others.

The Problem of Dichotomous Thinking

Psychology professor Linda E. Olds has provided analysis that locates the basis of patriarchy in dichotomous thinking that is commonly found in religions and cultures.[8] Olds points out that dichotomous thinking promotes a simplistic view of complex reality in conceptualizing what is or is not permissible behavior. Furthermore, dualistic conceptions of gender roles do damage to individuals insofar as they require them to disown or bury deep within themselves significant qualities of their personalities: Men are discouraged from revealing their emotions or becoming involved in the intimate life of their families; women are discouraged from being goal-oriented in pursuing success and achievement outside the domestic sphere, or openly articulating their deepest concerns. Dichotomous thinking does not adequately represent complex realities, particularly the complex realities of human personalities.

According to Olds, worldviews that permit only dichotomous gender roles create unhealthy psychological contexts in which individuals project their own repressed and most devalued and feared qualities onto the opposite sex (or any other despised class of people).

After conducting interviews with women and men in the United States, Olds concluded that in today's society there are *feminine-identified women*, who see and comport themselves according to patriarchal female gender roles; *masculine-identified men*, who see and comport themselves according to patriarchal male gender roles; and *androgynous women and men*, who strive to be whole human beings with a variety of qualities and roles. During their youth in a patriarchal society, androgynous women and men are likely to feel social discomfort because they do not fit into traditional and "popular" gender roles, but maturity can bring self-confidence. According to Olds, feminine-identified women and masculine-identified men can reevaluate their gender roles. Raising daughters may prompt feminine-identified women, in particular, to reconsider the gender roles they learned as children.

Olds advocates adopting the metaphor of *androgyny*—a balance of both "feminine" and "masculine" elements in one whole—as an ideal, *until* a cultural revolution is accomplished that eliminates distinct gender roles and permits every human being to develop her or his talents and capacities in a holistic manner most fitting for the individual. "Androgyny" for Olds does not mean "unisex," or abandoning or disguising the differences between men and women. As explicated by Olds, androgyny as a personal goal refers to the cultivation of balance within oneself of the qualities that in patriarchal societies have been identified as being "masculine" and "feminine," so both women and men can be nurturing and self-assertive, and both can care for their children and engage in meaningful work beyond the family. Olds argues that androgyny as a personal and cultural goal results in flexibility of roles and permits individuals to make choices and manifest a range of behaviors that adjust to different contexts, life stages, and personal needs and capacities. Olds suggests that when greater balance of the constructed "feminine" and "masculine" qualities is achieved in society, the metaphor of "androgyny" can be dropped. *Wholeness*—being *fully human*—is a *process* that is pursued throughout one's lifetime in changing ways.

Olds points out that there are two possible pitfalls for women attempting to achieve balance in personal development and gender roles. First, there is the possibility that women who become active in the public arena may put too much emphasis on the "masculine" values of work, competition, intellect, achievement, and thus perpetuate in their own lives the patriarchal devaluation of the "feminine" qualities of personal relatedness, communication, nurture, and homemaking. The second possible pitfall is that women wishing to rectify the previously dominant patriarchal values by affirming embodied femaleness, motherhood, intuition, and closeness to nature may come to see these "feminine" qualities as ends in themselves, thereby inhibiting the development of a balance of socially constructed "masculine" and "feminine" qualities. Balancing one's personal assertive and achievement-oriented qualities with one's nurturing and reproductive qualities is an on-going process.

By applying Olds's analysis to the economic theory of gender roles in family and society, we can see that wholeness as a goal of personal development within families and societies addresses the problems caused by distinct gender roles, childrearing by women to the virtual exclusion of men, and the devaluing of "feminine" qualities and women's work. When children are nurtured by both parents and both are involved in breadwinning, the division of labor by sex breaks down in a relationship of heterosexual parents as well as in a relationship of same-sex parents. A single parent performs all of these roles for the benefit of the children, and the outcome for the children and the parent will be optimum when society is supportive of a single parent performing both child-nurturing and breadwinning roles.

The increase in same-sex parenting challenges the traditional division of labor by sex in raising children and providing for families. It was reported in 2001 that a study by two University of Southern California professors found that children raised by lesbian mothers were less likely to adopt feminine-identified and masculine-identified gender roles. Sons of lesbian moms are more likely to express nurturing characteristics and daughters are more likely to aspire to professional careers than children raised by heterosexual parents. Typically, both moms are involved in child-nurturing as well as breadwinning.[9] In 2013, the American Sociological Association filed an amicus brief with the U.S. Supreme Court, which reported, as summarized by ASA President Cecilia Ridgeway, "There is no evidence that children with parents in stable same-sex or opposite-sex relationships differ in terms of well-being. Indeed, the greater stability offered by marriage for same-sex as well as opposite-sex parents may be an asset for child well-being."[10]

As distinct gender roles break down in families and society, parents will be perceived by the child as having personal qualities and work valued by society that may be emulated.

Self-Esteem: The Revolution from Within

Gloria Steinem, one of the foremost activists in the second-wave feminist movement in the United States and founder of *Ms.* magazine, concluded after many years of activism that the external revolution in society toward equality must be matched with an internal personal revolution toward self-esteem.[11]

Steinem asserts that hierarchical class systems characteristic of patriarchy inculcate in many children a sense of their personal lack of worth. Steinem argues that equality is not possible for any formerly subordinated class of people until they develop a positive self-image and value themselves as human beings. In a patriarchal society, even members of the ruling class and sex are dominated during childhood by the older members of their family and class, so later as adults they often bolster their damaged self-esteem by dominating other people who are physically and socially weaker. Lack of healthy self-esteem is perpetuated through the generations in a patriarchal society, because fathers and mothers who lack self-esteem are unable to convey self-esteem to their children. The vicious cycle continues, because older family members may physically, sexually, or psychologically abuse their children to bolster their own weak sense of self-worth. These children may grow up to convey their own lack of self-worth to their children, by failing to model healthy self-esteem and/or by abusing their children.

The harm caused by patriarchal attitudes to the self-esteem of girls and women can be imagined from the following accounts of how the birth of infant daughters is regarded in some Asian classical patriarchal cultures in which sons are valued over daughters.

A mother and father in Pakistan named their infant daughter Joya because of their happiness at her birth. The mother reported that while she was in the hospital strangers came to peer in at the new mother and baby. When she asked the nurse what they were doing the reply was: "They want to see what is so special about this baby girl at whose birth the family is distributing sweets." Another visitor was more direct asking, "Why are you so happy at the birth of a girl?"[12]

An Indian woman had a similar experience when she and her husband distributed sweets to honor the birth of their baby girl. A few months after the birth, a female relative visiting the young mother remarked, "Nani, could I ever imagine that one day, I too would have children? When, the first two times, I gave birth to stones, I wept day and night, wishing that I had been fortunate enough to have a child." When the young mother expressed her sympathy at such a strange problem, the relative replied angrily, "I had stones just as you had a stone." She was referring to daughters as "stone."[13]

If the mother values herself only as a producer of sons, and both the mother and father regard the daughter as an economic and social burden, how can a daughter develop self-esteem? In a classical patriarchal culture, from the beginning of her life, a daughter's humanity and worth may not be acknowledged by her parents. How then can such a woman value her own daughters and convey self-esteem to them?

Gloria Steinem argues that self-esteem can be developed in many ways at any point in one's life. If society does not acknowledge one's value, then one can look within to develop self-esteem utilizing techniques of meditation, visualization, keeping a journal, and talking with friends.

Steinem believes that self-esteem is essential to motivating women and men to work for social change to correct injustice. The revolution within is necessary to fuel the social revolution without. This is Steinem's personal manner of balancing the culturally defined "masculine" activities of speaking, writing, thinking, and political lobbying with the culturally defined "feminine" values of introspection and caring for others and oneself. In classical patriarchal cultures, women are socialized to care for others while their own personal worth is devalued, so it often does not occur to women that they can and should nurture themselves. Steinem advocates the formation of small "full-circle groups," in which people can share their experiences, pain, and wisdom as they strive to achieve interior emotional and mental health and balance these with exterior work and activism.

Religion, Psychology, and Women's Self-Esteem and Equality

In the study of women in religions, the teachings, beliefs, law codes, social structures, myths, scriptures, and theologies are examined to see if they promote the valuing of women, and hence if they are resources for individual women's self-esteem and social equality. Since most of the historical religious traditions are patriarchal, much is found that is detrimental to the personal self-esteem of women. However, each patriarchal religious tradition contains within it revolutionary messages about social equality and the full humanity of all persons. In its scriptures and traditions, each patriarchal religion remembers strong women who may be taken as models. However, in searching for models among significant foremothers, today's women need to evaluate the extent to which the lives of particular foremothers express liberating values.

Women make creative efforts to promote women's self-esteem while living in patriarchal cultures. When they are supported by technology, the economy, education, and increasing social expectations of equality, women work to make their traditional religious institutions more inclusive, or women go outside patriarchal religions to create their own religious traditions, or they leave religions altogether.

When studying religious traditions and their cultures to ascertain the status of women and gain understanding of their religious lives, particular issues affecting girls and women should be examined. These will be discussed in the following chapter.

4

Issues for Women in Religions

Eleven issues in particular contribute to whether women are relatively equal or whether they are subordinated in a religious culture. The issues are: (1) gender roles; (2) marriage and divorce; (3) property rights for women; (4) myths and doctrines about the cause of the limitations of the human condition; (5) views of women's bodies; (6) violence against women; (7) women as religious specialists, (a) as shamans or other leaders with charisma, or (b) as credentialed religious leaders; (8) goddesses and other concepts of the divine; (9) rituals—whether women are included in rituals, if there are women's rituals, and rituals that affirm women; (10) whether a religion and believers extend equality to LGBTQ persons; and (11) whether or not there is movement beyond patriarchy. Examination of these issues reveals a great deal about the status of women in a religious tradition, how gender roles are reinforced by religion, and how women utilize resources within the religious tradition to challenge patriarchal gender roles and support new roles for themselves. These eleven issues do not preclude other pertinent issues from influencing women's status in religious cultures.

Gender Roles

Religions and cultures define what are considered to be proper roles and behaviors for females and males, and for persons who do not fit neatly into those binary categories. Some societies do not have strongly distinct gender roles, which means there is considerable overlap in the activities of women and men. This is true of a number of traditional Native American societies, which also have religious and cultural roles for men and women who do not conform to male and female gender roles.[1] In contrast, patriarchal religions and cultures have *distinct gender roles*, which define what are "feminine" and "masculine" characteristics, and girls and boys are socialized into those ways of behaving.

Human beings often think in simplistic either/or terms: either black or white, good or bad, hot or cold, high or low, soft or hard, easy or difficult, conservative or liberal, and so on. The most basic of the "pairs of opposites," as they are termed in Hinduism,[2] is male and female. In numerous philosophical/religious worldviews, these polarities are seen as being the qualities that make up physical existence. In the best conceptualization, one polarity is not seen as being better than the other—the interaction of both polarities produces existence. For example in the Chinese Daoist text, the Daodejing (ca. 200 B.C.E.) attributed to the sage Laozi, the qualities of *yin* (femaleness, darkness, wetness, softness, humility, lowliness, the earth) and *yang* (maleness, brightness, dryness, hardness, assertiveness, heaven) exist in a nondichotomous way within the ever-moving and ever-changing Dao, the dynamic and creative ultimate reality. The Daodejing advises men governing the Chinese empire to "work against their traditional gender conditioning" by adopting the qualities that patriarchal society attributes to women: humbleness, softness, and pliability. Although the nature of the Dao is ineffable and cannot be captured in binary gender stereotypes, the Daodejing "exalts the female" by utilizing metaphors associated with motherhood and the valley as feminine symbols to point to the nature of the Dao.[3] According to scholar of Chinese philosophy and religions Judith Chuan Xu, the Daodejing's vision of "masculinity" and "femininity" dissolves the gender binary by articulating that one becomes "truly human" by cultivating human qualities, not qualities that in patriarchal society are socially constructed as being "male" or "female."[4] Thus the Daodejing opens the possibility for women to go beyond the female gender role in patriarchy and cultivate independence and self-determination. The changing forces of yin and yang within the Dao are also within each human person. According to Xu,

> Perhaps, like the Dao, an individual cannot be defined. The Dao is constantly in the process of change and creation; it is forever creating, transforming, and transcending. Likewise, individuals must create their own identities and not limit themselves to culturally constructed stereotypical gender roles.[5]

In contrast, in patriarchal religions and societies, the masculine is seen as better, more perfect, and valuable than the feminine, which is seen as inferior, imperfect, and even demonic. Even worse, patriarchal world-views assert that men, individually and collectively, possess the positive "masculine" characteristics, and women, individually and collectively, have the evil "feminine" qualities.

Study of history indicates that the problem with the dualistic per-spective is the ease with which it dichotomizes groups into "us versus them." Evil or subhuman characteristics are attributed to members of the sex, race, ethnic group, class, sexual orientation, gender identity, nation, political party, and religious group who are classified as "other." Demonizing the "other" makes it socially acceptable to commit acts of violence against them, fight wars against them, attempt to eradicate them, enslave them, exclude them from education and economic earn-ing power, and politically disenfranchise them. Dualistic thinking gives rise to prejudice, which sanctions violence against the despised group and blames the victims for their suffering. The dualistic view of human-ity is how men in a classically patriarchal society justify their control over and oppression of women: Women deserve no better, and great harm will result if women are not controlled and subordinated.

Although various religious cultures identify different characteris-tics as being "masculine" or "feminine," a classically patriarchal society values the "masculine" qualities and attributes them to men as a class, and devalues the "feminine" qualities and attribute them to women as a class. Gender conceptualizations that construct personal qualities as ei-ther "masculine" or "feminine" dictate different roles for women and men. Children are socialized to adhere to their respective gender roles, and they are punished if they do not conform. All persons possess both socially constructed "masculine" and "feminine" characteristics. How-ever, in a patriarchal society, individuals are pressured to repress or hide the qualities that are assigned to the opposite sex in order to manifest only those qualities that are defined as being appropriate to their gender. If no gender role is permitted for nonconforming persons, individuals who persist in manifesting qualities assigned to the opposite sex will be ridiculed or despised, and they are at risk of being killed. Dualistic thinking demands conformity to specified gender roles, and does not tolerate diversity or independent thinking and expression.

In classical patriarchal societies, girls are taught that they should be under the protection of their fathers and that they should be virgins when they marry. After marriage the woman is under the protection and control of her husband, and her role is to be a good wife serving her husband and his parents, especially by bearing sons. A widow is supposed to be under the care of her grown-up sons or other male relatives. Women's roles are defined by their sexual status and the men to whom they are related by birth or marriage. Boys and men also have restricted gender options in classical patriarchal societies. Although their activities can be determined by their sexual status, as in the case of religious celibacy, they are not necessarily so determined. Some religious codes of conduct enforce gender roles. For example, in the Confucian Five Relationships, family harmony is preserved when the wife is subordinate to the husband. The *Manusmṛti* (Laws of Manu), which is influential in the Hindu tradition, states:

> By a girl, by a young woman, or even an aged one, nothing must be done independently, even in her own house.
>
> In childhood a female must be subject to her father, in youth to her husband, when her lord is dead to her sons; a woman must never be independent.
>
> She must not seek to separate herself from her father, husband, or sons; by leaving them she would make both (her own and her husband's) families contemptible.
>
> She must always be cheerful, clever in (the management of her) household affairs, careful in cleaning her utensils, and economical in expenditure.[6]

Girls and boys, and women and men experience stress when their personal qualities and talents make an uncomfortable fit with their assigned gender roles in patriarchal societies, unless a way to circumvent the restrictive roles is possible. In some religious traditions, such possibilities for persons to shape their lives in meaningful ways are available—for example, by becoming a shaman within some religions, such as the Korean indigenous religious tradition. Jainism, Buddhism, and Christianity offer women celibate religious roles as nuns as significant alternatives to the roles of wife and mother.

Many religious and cultural traditions assert that women and men are different from each other but equal: Women and men are regarded as having different personality and physical characteristics and hence they have different jobs to perform in family and society, but they are conceived as being complementary to each other. Yet in a patriarchal religion and society in which women have limited or no access to independent economic earning power as well as positions of religious and political authority, this concept of *complementarity* slips quickly in practice into male dominance. In such a cultural situation, the ideology of gender complementarity is utilized by men to rationalize and mask male dominance.

Religious individuals and institutions wishing to maintain patriarchal gender roles in today's society promote theologies and gender ideologies stressing complementarity by claiming that women and men are different but equal, with different talents and roles. Gender complementarity is the view that in marriage a man and a woman complete each other, and complementarity of married heterosexual couples is stressed: Man is the head, woman is the heart; man is intellectual, strong, and in charge, woman is emotional, empathetic, caregiving; man works outside the home, woman works inside the home cleaning, cooking, and rearing children.

Complementarity as a gender ideology is challenged by increasing changes in women's gender roles and by the legalization of same-sex marriage. In response, in 2014 the Vatican's Congregation for the Doctrine of the Faith sponsored "Humanum: An International Colloquium on the Complementarity of Man and Woman" in Rome to discuss "the fundamental good of the complementary union of man and woman."[7] The speakers in the symposium presented their perspectives on complementarity in Catholic, Jewish, Anabaptist, Muslim, philosophical, Buddhist, Anglican, Evangelical Christian, Hindu, Pentecostal, Daoist, Mormon, and Baptist traditions. In his preface to the published collection of the colloquium's papers, Cardinal Gerhard Ludwig Müller (b. 1947), prefect of the Congregation of the Doctrine of the Faith, wrote that complementarity "encompasses the equality of women and men while neither obscuring nor diminishing their differences." He immediately followed this assertion with a statement using Vatican-style language to assert that married couples should not use artificial birth control: "[complementarity] benefits spouses directly while also being open, receptive, and life-giving."[8] Pope Francis (papacy 2013 to present) asserted in the title of his address that complementarity is "Not Just Good, but Beautiful." According to Pope Francis, complementarity is a gift from God and the basis of marriage and family. He characterized the "decline of the marriage culture" with increased poverty, social problems, and the "crisis in the family" as being causes of the environmental crisis.[9]

Feminists advocate *mutuality* in committed heterosexual and same-sex relationships. Mutuality describes a relationship of equal partners, each seen as possessing a complete human nature, who within their committed love for each other make decisions about sharing the tasks of breadwinning, homemaking, and child-rearing in ways that are not dictated by patriarchal gender norms. Catholic scholar of ethics Margaret A. Farley, who is a member of the Sisters of Mercy of the Americas, describes the "principle of mutuality" as being based on "a view of human persons as embodied subjects, essentially relational as well as autonomous and free."[10]

The examination of gender roles in a religious culture raises a number of questions about the status of women. Are women and men supposed to perform certain jobs that are different from one another? In the religious tradition, are women taught to be nurturing and passive, while men are taught to be intellectual and active? Does the religion teach that women's roles and responsibilities are primarily inside the home, while men are supposed to be active in the world outside the home? What are the respective economic contributions of women and men? Are women believed to be more religious than men and more in touch with what is sacred? Or, are women believed to be too deficient, impure, and/or morally degraded to have direct contact with the divine, and is the religious realm believed to be available only to men? Do men lead and women follow, or is it the other way around? Do women and men share leadership roles equally?

Gender roles and religious beliefs interact with each other and mutually influence each other in complex ways. The comparative study of women in religions and cultures, combined with social analysis provided by anthropologists and archaeologists, leads to the conclusion that gender roles are influenced first by the available technology to achieve economic survival and then by the division of labor between women and men. In societies where gender roles are not strongly distinct, both women and men play significant roles in religious activities. In classical patriarchal religious cultures with distinct gender roles, myths, theologies, and religious laws are used to reinforce subordination of women to men. But if the patriarchal division of labor by sex becomes less rigid because of technological and economic developments and increased availability of education, women and supportive men begin to assert the necessity of changing or abandoning patriarchal theologies and religious law codes. Women who aspire to or already occupy positions of religious authority look to the lives of significant women in the past as role models as well as to conceptions of a female deity (or deities) to validate themselves in positions of authority, just as men in patriarchal religious cultures have utilized significant men of the tradition's past as role models and conceptions of a male deity (or deities) to validate their authority.

Marriage and Divorce

The rules governing marriage and divorce are very important to understanding women's status in a culture and its religious tradition. Relevant questions to explore include: Are very young girls married to older men (as in classical patriarchies)? Do girls and women have any say about whom they marry? Is same-sex marriage sanctioned? If married heterosexually, does the wife go to live with her husband's family, or does the husband go to live with the wife's family? Does the newly married couple set up a separate household or live in an extended family? How do these different family structures affect the status of women? Is there any exchange of wealth between the two families at marriage, and if so, who receives the wealth and how does it affect the bride? Upon the death of a spouse, is a widow as free to remarry as a widower is?

In the classical patriarchies within which a significant number of the world's religions emerged and which continue to exist, only heterosexual marriage is approved and married women have no right of divorce; only the husband can choose to divorce his wife and often that is done very easily. If women do have the right to divorce in a patriarchal religion, frequently girls and women are not educated about the circumstances in which they can divorce their husbands. In classical patriarchal societies, due to religious tradition and the wife's financial dependence on her husband, a wife in an abusive marriage has little choice but to remain married.

In Judaism marriage is viewed as a sanctification of the conjugal love between a man and woman. The husband and wife are to be loving companions to each other, and their marriage evokes the covenant relationship between God and the people of Israel. The rabbis of the Talmudic period (from the destruction of the Second Temple in Jerusalem in 70 C.E. to approximately 500 C.E.) instituted the marriage contract, the *ketubah*, stating how the husband will support the wife, what her rights are to the property she brings into the marriage, and the amount of support that will be given to the wife if the husband divorces her. The *ketubah* was necessary, because since biblical times Jewish men have had complete control over divorce (see Deuteronomy 24:1-4; Isaiah 50:1; Jeremiah 3:8). Divorce is effected only when the husband gives his wife a *get*, a certificate of divorce. Before the *ketubah* was implemented to provide economic protection to the wife, a Jewish man could easily act on his prerogative to divorce his wife without providing economic support for the woman's post-divorce life. The *ketubah* and *get* remain a feature of Jewish marriage and divorce lived according to *halakha* (Jewish religious law). Reform Jews are not concerned with adhering to everything in *halakha*; since the *get* is irrelevant to their religious lives, a couple is free, if they wish, to draw up a personalized *ketubah* expressing their love and commitment to each other and how they will live out their mutual obligations in their marriages.[11]

Although Israel was founded in 1948 by primarily secular Jews, in order to stress the Jewish nature of the state of Israel, Orthodox rabbis were given authority to govern personal family law concerning marriage and divorce according to *halakha*. In Israel in divorce cases, some husbands have withheld the *get*, frequently to pressure the wife to agree to a division of property that is favorable to him. A woman whose husband refuses to give her a *get* is an *agunah*, a wife "anchored" to her husband, even if she is separated from him. A woman also becomes an *agunah* if her husband disappears, or if he is presumed to be dead but there is no verifying evidence. A woman who is an *agunah* is still married and she cannot remarry according to *halakha* in Israel. Any children whom she bears while separated from her husband but still married to him are considered *mamzerim*, illegitimate, and according to *halakha* they cannot marry legitimate Jews. The offspring of *mamzerim* are also considered to be *mamzerim* so the religious and social ostracism is passed on to subsequent generations. The same predicament does not apply to a husband who has children with another woman while he is still married to his wife, because *halakha* permits the taking of a second wife. Feminist activists are working to assist *agunot* in securing their divorces in Israel's religious courts, and they are also pressing the government to remove marriage and divorce in Israel from being governed by the ancient rules in *halakha*.[12]

The Roman Catholic hierarchy made marriage a sacrament, a sign and means of conferring divine grace, in 1274 at the Council of Lyons. In Catholicism, a marriage is considered to be valid if the wedding was sacramental and if subsequently the marriage was consummated. Church authorities have interpreted passages in Mark 10:2–12 and Matthew 19 as indicating that Jesus Christ condemned divorce, and if either the man or the woman remarried they were committing adultery. Mark 10:2–12 in the New American Bible reads:

[2]The Pharisees approached and asked, "Is it lawful for a husband to divorce his wife?" They were testing him.

[3]He said to them in reply, "What did Moses command you?"

[4]They replied, "Moses permitted him to write a bill of divorce and dismiss her."

[5]But Jesus told them, "Because of the hardness of your hearts he wrote you this commandment.

[6]But from the beginning of creation, 'God made them male and female.

[7]For this reason a man shall leave his father and mother [and be joined to his wife],

[8]and the two shall become one flesh.' So they are no longer two but one flesh.

[9]Therefore what God has joined together, no human being must separate."

[10]In the house the disciples again questioned him about this.

¹¹He said to them, "Whoever divorces his wife and marries another commits adultery against her;

¹²and if she divorces her husband and marries another, she commits adultery."

Based on these scriptures, the Roman Catholic Church automatically excommunicates any divorced person who remarries without receiving an annulment, which declares that in the eyes of the church the first marriage was invalid. Excommunication means that the civilly remarried Catholic may not partake of the Eucharist. This is problematic for individual Catholics' continued participation in their church, especially given that Catholics divorce at the same rate as other persons in their respective countries. A significant reason that Catholics and their children move away from participation in the Roman Catholic Church is that one or both of the parents has civilly remarried after divorce.

While arguing against the excommunication of remarried Catholics, theologian Michael G. Lawler points out that Jesus's statement against divorce in Mark 10:9 and Matthew 19:6 is a moral demand, a "you should not," and not an ontological reality, a "you cannot not." In 1994 the Vatican's Congregation for the Doctrine of the Faith reaffirmed that such persons may not receive the Eucharist because they are in a state of sin. Pope John Paul II (papacy, 1978–2005) reiterated this position in 1997. Contrary to John Paul II's statement that scandal would result if civilly remarried Catholics were allowed to receive the Eucharist, causing "error and confusion" on the part of the faithful "regarding the Church's teaching about the indissolubility of marriage," Lawler concludes that scandal resides instead in the policy of the Roman Catholic Church toward divorced and remarried Catholics.[13]

In Islam there are diverse schools of *shari'a* (Islamic law) shaped according to the opinions of jurists about the meanings of passages in the Qur'an and the collections of *hadith* (accounts of the things that Muhammad said and did). Therefore, there are no fixed understandings of the rules of marriage and divorce in Islam. Some Muslim-majority countries enforce *shari'a* through Islamic courts or through the formulation of civil laws, while many other Muslims living in western societies that enforce only civil laws make choices about the extent to which they will voluntarily adhere to *shari'a*.

Islamic marriage involves a contract, which stipulates the value of the *mahr*—property or money the groom will give to the bride—and when it will be given. The *mahr* can be minimal or substantial, it can be given upon the marriage or in the event the husband divorces his wife, or the woman can waive the *mahr*. Islam scholar Kecia Ali points out that Islamic jurists have generally agreed that the *mahr* "constitutes compensation paid by the husband for exclusive legitimate sexual access to his wife." Some Islamic jurists have referred to the *mahr* as "the vulva's price." The *mahr*, therefore, appears to be what Qur'an 4:24 refers to as "the *ajr* (reward, compensation) paid by a man for 'what he enjoys from her.'"[14] According to Ali, "In the development logic of the jurists . . . dower [*mahr*] came to be understood as compensation in exchange for *milk al-nikah*, the husband's exclusive dominion over the wife's sexual and reproductive capacity, which also conveys his sole right to dissolve the marriage tie by unilateral divorce."[15] Ali explains that the classical Islamic jurists' understanding of *mahr* paralleled their understanding of paying a price to purchase a slave, and that the husband's right to divorce his wife unilaterally at will paralleled the right of an owner to choose to free a slave. Currently the *mahr* is understood by many Muslims as an expression of a Muslim woman's right to own property and is a means to provide the wife with financial security in the event she is divorced by her husband.[16]

Qur'an 4:3 permits a man to have up to four wives if they are all provided for equally. Although the majority of Muslims are in monogamous marriages, polygyny (having multiple wives) continues to be practiced by Muslims in Muslim-majority countries. Where it occurs in the west, marriages subsequent to the first are necessarily unregistered. Regarding the practice of polygyny among African American Muslims affiliated with the American Society of Muslims, religious historian Debra Majeed writes that "the positive examples of multiple-wife marriages are outweighed by those led by men who are financially, spiritually, and/or mentally ill-equipped for such responsibilities and involve women who feel they have no other options."[17] A survey of 1,224 Malaysians in polygynous families undertaken by the advocacy group Sisters in Islam with three Malaysian universities found the same thing. It was common that the first wife was not told by her husband that he had taken another wife, with 69 percent of first wives saying they were treated unfairly by their husbands, 61 percent were unhappy with their situation as a co-wife, and 87 percent of children were negatively affected by polygny. Sisters in Islam executive director Rozana Isa points out that the Qur'an states that it is impossible for a man to treat all his wives equally (Sura 4:129) and argues that therefore a Muslim man should have only one wife:

> The Prophet was monogamous for a very long time when he was married to Siti Khadijah and his subsequent marriages were done with other interests.
> And the fact is, he is a Prophet. People tend to forget that they are not.[18]

Although Muhammad is quoted as saying, "God did not make lawful anything more repugnant to Him than divorce,"[19] divorce in Islam is traditionally permitted to a man by stating *talaq* ("release," or "I divorce you") three times, preferably over the course of three of the wife's menstrual cycles. It is possible for a husband to pronounce *talaq* three times at once. Upon the third pronouncement of *talaq* the husband's obligation to support his wife ends. In the case of *talaq* divorce, the wife does not have to return any of the *mahr*, and if the husband had not yet paid all or a portion of the *mahr*, he is supposed to do so when he divorces her. The husband's right to divorce his wife unilaterally has been limited in various ways in many Muslim-majority countries. In 2017, the Supreme Court of India, where Muslims constitute a sizable minority, ruled that triple *talaq*, or instant divorce, was unconstitutional because it violated the equal rights of Muslim women.

According to Islamic law, if a wife wishes to divorce her husband, she may be able to exercise the option of a *khul'* divorce, in which she returns the portion of the *mahr* that she has received, waives the portion that she deferred, and perhaps pays an additional sum to her husband. Ali explains that requiring a wife to purchase her freedom from her husband in *khul'* divorce parallels the circumstances of a slave purchasing her freedom from the master. A Muslim woman may also be able to seek a religious judicial divorce on the grounds that her husband has failed to fulfill his obligations to her—for instance, if he is not providing her with economic support, has abandoned her, or injured her. Judicial divorce does not require the woman to pay her husband compensation as does *khul'*. The marriage contract may stipulate terms by which the woman is entitled to a judicial divorce—for instance, if the man takes another wife.[20] Ali suggests that it is reasonable for Muslims living in western countries who desire egalitarian marriages to exercise the option of a civil prenuptial agreement and resort to civil law for marriage and divorce.[21]

Property Rights

Related to marriage and divorce is the question of whether or not a woman has rights to inherit and/or own wealth and other property. Women have greater equality in societies where women have earning power and they own and control their wealth and pass it to their children as they see fit. In matrilineal horticultural societies, daughters inherit property, notably land, from their mothers. In classical patriarchy, women are economically dependent on, first their fathers, then husbands, and later grown-up sons.

In classical patriarchal societies, since land and property pass from the father to sons, daughters may be given gifts as their inheritance when they marry and go to live with their husbands' families. Problems arose in India because most of the marriage gifts were appropriated by the groom and/or his parents. Some in-laws may essentially hold their daughter-in-law hostage to possible mistreatment if her parents do not respond to their demands for more dowry. Payment of dowry to the groom's family has been illegal in India since 1961, but it is still considered necessary by many Indians to secure a good husband for a daughter.[22] Indian feminists have argued that dowry is an economic, not a religious arrangement, and can be eliminated without adversely affecting the practice of Hinduism. Sociologist Madhu Kishwar points out that dowry as practiced in India functions as a bribe to a man and his family to accept a daughter in marriage. She argues that a return to including daughters in inheritance will eliminate dowry and associated evils and thereby contribute to women's equality. Kishwar advocates reviving the traditional practice of parents giving the daughter who marries *strīdhan* ("gifts to the wife"). The items received as *strīdhan* would belong to the woman and be utilized as she sees fit. Kishwar advocates that inheritance for daughters should equal the inheritance of their brothers. She encourages parents with financial means to give a daughter income-generating property and/or a house of her own upon her marriage.[23]

In Islam, *shari'a* provides women the right to own and inherit wealth based on statements in the Qur'an. A daughter inherits one-half the amount that her brothers receive, because men are expected to use their wealth to support their wives and children, while a woman owns and manages her inheritance herself. According to *shari'a*, a man should pay a *mahr*, or dower, in the form of money and/or property to his bride when they marry. The woman is supposed to own the *mahr* and utilize it as she sees fit.[24] However, there is a great deal of variation in whether an adequate *mahr* is paid to a bride. According to agreement stipulated in the marriage contract, there is also variation in whether she receives the *mahr* upon her marriage or at a later date, perhaps when her husband divorces her. Hence, the economic protection provided by the *mahr* has been limited. In patriarchal societies, instead of the *mahr*, a financial gift may be paid to the wife's legal guardian, usually her father.

Societies vary on whether a woman, particularly a wife, may keep and utilize income she has earned, and whether or not a woman may own property in her own right. Women living in predominantly Christian countries struggled to obtain these rights in the nineteenth and twentieth centuries. Whether or not women have rights to own wealth and property and inherit contributes to women's equality or subordination.

Myths and Doctrines about the Cause of the Limitations of the Human Condition

In the religions of classical patriarchal societies, women are frequently regarded as the source of evil. For instance, in the Jewish and Christian traditions, patriarchal interpretations of the myth of Adam and Eve (Genesis 2–3) blame Eve (and thus all women) for "the Fall"—that is, the limitations of the human condition, in other words, mortality. In patriarchal interpretations within Hinduism, women are identified with the philosophical concept of *māyā*, the delusion of the senses and the mind and their desires, which binds souls to the suffering of constant rebirth.[25] Thus women may be seen as temptresses who distract men with the promise of physical delights and cause them to fall away from the spiritual life. In patriarchal religions, women are often blamed collectively for the finitude and suffering of the human condition. Women's presumed guilt in this matter is the justification used to keep women subordinated and under men's control.

On the other hand, religions in matrilineal and matrilocal cultures, in which women make direct economic contributions to their families' survival, and in which women make equal or greater contributions to telling the stories in which wisdom is passed to younger generations, appear not to describe women as the source of evil. For example, Chiricahua and Mescalero Apache stories do not blame women for suffering and evil. Instead they blame Coyote or other mythic animals. Coyote is depicted as a male figure possessing the possible foibles of human men. Stories about Coyote explain how evil behaviors such as incest, stealing, and duplicity became part of the human repertoire of actions.[26] In Apache culture, both women and men tell stories that teach lessons, and remember and interpret events. Women as well as men therefore create Apache oral literature. In a society where women are creating sacred literature, it is unlikely that they will perpetuate myths that blame women for the limitations of the human condition.

The popularity of the "invasion theory" of the origin of patriarchy, discussed earlier, in some contemporary feminist spirituality circles prompts the following questions: Do women sometimes construct worldviews that blame men as the source of evil? If so, under what conditions?

Views of Women's Bodies

Views of women's bodies differ within egalitarian and classical patriarchal societies, and they are frequently related to whether or not impurity is attributed to women's bodies. In Native American cultures that are matrilineal and matrilocal, the view appears to be that women's blood is powerful and potentially harmful to men and animals, and therefore it is subject to taboos, but it is not seen as being impure. For example, Chiricahua and Mescalero Apache believed that women's menstrual blood caused men's joints to ache or become deformed, so sexual intercourse was avoided during that time. Menstrual blood was believed to harm male horses also. The blood of childbirth was believed to have the same effect on men, so the father would not be present at the birth.[27] Although menstrual blood was seen as harmful to males, Mescalero and Chiricahua Apache menstrual taboos did not convey the idea found in highly patriarchal religions that menstruating women are impure.

In classical patriarchal cultures, women are usually seen as being impure because of their periodic bleeding and the blood of childbirth. Women's state of impurity is often regarded as perpetual, so women are prohibited from contact with sacred things and performing sacred functions. Women's blood, therefore, is regarded as disqualifying them from performing religious and/or priestly functions. The most extreme beliefs about women's impurity correspond with the most extreme forms of patriarchy.

Religious cultures have different perspectives on whether or not women's bodies contain or may be imbued with divine forces. If women's bodies are believed to contain divine forces, people in egalitarian and patriarchal cultures draw different conclusions about what to do with that power. In Hinduism women's bodies are believed to contain *śakti*, the power that creates and sustains the universe, but in patriarchal manifestations of Hindu culture it is important that women's power and sexuality be controlled through subordination to men.[28] In the Tantra tradition within Hinduism, girls and women may be worshipped as embodying Śaktī (the Goddess). Women and men may even engage in ritual sexual yoga that transgresses caste and menstrual taboos, but in patriarchal societies this may turn out to be men using women's bodies to achieve enlightenment.[29] Viewing women as the embodiment of divine energies may not empower women to equality when a general social expectation of equality is absent.

In patriarchal cultures, female bodies may be mutilated to fit females into the gender role assigned to them. One form of this violence is female genital mutilation (FGM) or female genital cutting (FGC), which are indigenous practices among some African and Middle Eastern cultures. Female genital cutting is a pre-Islamic and a pre-Christian practice found in a number of populations that are now Muslim or Christian. There is nothing in the Qur'an or the Christian Bible that requires female genital mutilation, although practitioners may believe it is required by their religion.

Islam scholar Kecia Ali points out that although proponents of the elimination of female genital cutting argue that it is non-Islamic, the classical jurists who formulated the schools of Sunni and Shi'i *shari'a* all concluded that it was either recommended or required.[30] In Islam, there is a *hadith* that states:

> A woman used to perform circumcision in Medina. The Prophet (peace be upon him) said to her: "Do not cut severely as that is better for a woman and more desirable for a husband."[31]

Ali points out that "do not cut severely" may be better translated as "do not ruin" or "do not uproot" and also that this *hadith* was considered by Islamic scholars as being an unreliable account. Another *hadith* considered to be weak states that circumcision is *sunnah* ("tradition," referring to a custom of the Prophet, thereby to be emulated by other Muslims) for men, and a noble act for women.[32] Nevertheless, there are many populations of Muslims who do *not* practice female genital cutting.

Although frequently called "female circumcision," female genital cutting is in no way analogous to male circumcision, which leaves the penis intact. Female genital cutting is performed on girls usually between the ages of four and fourteen, but it may also be performed on infants. FGC takes many forms but they are all aimed at controlling women's sexuality, as well as surgically making sure that a female has no signs of "maleness" in the form of a clitoris (often considered analogous to a penis), or any sort of external genitalia. Female genital cutting ranges from pricking the clitoris or its prepuce (hood) without removal of tissue, to partial or complete excision of the clitoris and surrounding tissues in the labia minora (medically called a clitoridectomy, known as *sunnah* circumcision among Muslims), to infibulation, termed "pharaonic circumcision" in Sudan.[33] According to anthropologist Ellen Gruenbaum, pharaonic circumcision consists of slicing off a girl's "prepuce, clitoris, labia minora, and all or part of the labia majora—and infibulation, or stitching together, of the vulva." Gruenbaum writes of infibulation:

> Once healed, this most extreme form leaves a perfectly smooth vulva of skin and scar tissue with only a single tiny opening, preserved during healing by the insertion of a small object such as a piece of straw, for

urination and menstrual flow. The extremely small size of the opening makes first sexual intercourse very difficult or impossible, necessitating rupture or cutting of the scar tissue around the opening. In a variation of infibulation that is slightly less severe, the trimmed labia minora are sewn shut but the labia majora are left alone. Reinfubulation is done after childbirth.[34]

Female genital cutting, especially infibulation, is very life-threatening due to loss of blood at the time of the cutting and the subsequent high possibility of infection.

Nahid Toubia, a Sudanese surgeon and women's health rights activist, reports that Christian missionaries in Africa took varying stances toward female genital cutting. Protestant missionaries opposed it and worked to have laws passed forbidding it, while Roman Catholic priests did not speak out against it. She reports that Protestant Africans therefore tend to eschew female genital cutting, while it is found more often among Catholic Africans. African Indigenous Churches blend traditional customs with African Christianity, so female genital cutting is more likely to be practiced. Coptic Christians in Egypt and Sudan practice both clitoridectomy and infibulation. In the Ethiopian Orthodox Church "a woman is considered unclean if she is not circumcised, and many priests refuse to let such women enter their church."[35] Toubia says that the only Jews known to practice female genital cutting are Ethiopian Jews (Beta Israel) who now live in the state of Israel. When Jewish women from Ethiopia were interviewed after being relocated to Israel in 1991, they reported that they intended to discontinue the practice with their daughters.[36] In 2013 United Nations Women partnered with the Ethiopian Orthodox Church to hold workshops to educate religious leaders about gender-based violence, including female genital mutilation, so they could take steps to work against it with their congregations' members. In 2017 the Coptic Orthodox Church launched an awareness campaign against female genital mutilation.

Infibulation is practiced primarily in Sudan and Somalia and is clearly the most life-threatening form of female genital cutting. Anthropologist Janice Boddy has described how in the 1970s and 1980s women in an agricultural village named Hofriyat (a pseudonym), on the Nile River in northern Sudan, performed this operation on their daughters and granddaughters to prepare them for marriage. Hofriyati women were socialized through the searing pain of infibulation into an extremely restricted female gender role, and they believed they must pass this on to their daughters for their well-being. Prepubescent infibulation ensured that a girl was a virgin when she married. The women said "circumcision" was to make girls' bodies clean (*nazif*), smooth (*na'im*), and pure (*tahir*). They called it *tahur*, cleansing, purification. A girl who had not been "purified" by circumcision could not marry. Marriage provided the opportunity to advance a woman's social position by giving birth, particularly to sons. Boddy reported that men who had traveled to work in other Muslim countries learned that "female circumcision" was not Islamic and that they did not particularly want their daughters subjected to it, but Hofriyati women were convinced that it remained a necessary ritual for their daughters to be married and socialized into the female gender role.[37]

In an update published in 2016, Boddy reports that some Hofriyati families moved to Khartoum and that more young Sudanese Arab women are attending high schools and universities. Development in Sudan is based on the oil industry, and the construction of roads and the wide availability of cars, cell phones, and satellite television have caused changes in Sudan's families and society. For instance, cell phones provide a way for parents to stay in touch with their daughters while they are attending university. Boddy reports that as of 2015 women made up approximately four-fifths of the students at universities. "Thus more twenty-something Hofriyati daughters than sons have university educations, but few of either are married or permanently employed"[38] due to economic and cultural conditions, such as young men having to go abroad to find work and the high cost of a wedding. With women and men marrying at older ages, "today single women seek companionate spouses of their choice; several have successfully eluded 'good' matches arranged by kin."[39] According to Boddy, men and women in a family who watch television together are familiar with the message disseminated by medical education programs that female genital cutting is harmful, and they "are increasingly prepared to rethink their gender aesthetics." While medical treatment is provided by the government, people purchase private health insurance to pay for expenses the public healthcare system does not cover. People are more likely to conclude that if female genital cutting causes health problems, "it now makes economic sense to stop."[40] But as female genital cutting has started to decline in Sudan, the practice of elective female genital cosmetic surgery (FGCS) is increasing in the west. Female genital cosmetic surgery in the form of labiaplasty (the surgical trimming or removal of the labia minora and/or parts of the labia majora) can make the appearance of a woman's genitalia "smooth," like a that of Barbie doll.[41] Boddy expresses concern that western pornography available on DVDs sold in Sudan in conjunction with Sudanese traditional genital aesthetics for women may prompt a return to resorting to surgery to obtain a "smooth" and "closed" appearance.[42]

Statistics provided by Sudan's Central Bureau of Statistics support Boddy's observation that female genital cutting is beginning to decline in Sudan due to changed socioeconomic conditions. A 2014 report indicates that 86.6 percent of women between fifteen and forty-nine years of age in Sudan had been subjected to female genital cutting, but the percentage of daughters age fourteen and younger who had been subjected to female genital cutting was down to 31.5 percent, as reported by their mothers. Among women between fifteen and forty-nine years old, 40.9 percent stated that female genital mutilation should be continued, leaving 59.1% of women who are ready to discontinue the practice.[43] In 2020 Sudan's government banned female genital mutilation and established a criminal penalty of a possible three-year prison sentence and a fine for anyone who performs it. However, more work remains to be done to prevent the practice from going underground.[44]

UNICEF and the World Health Organization work with a variety of local organizations to provide education to women on sexual and reproductive health so that women themselves will elect to stop carrying out genital cutting on girls. African feminists engage in educational work to eliminate female genital cutting, pointing out that change will come only through efforts that are compatible with the societies' values.[45] Islam scholar Kecia Ali agrees that work for reform must aim for incremental change. This may involve persuading people to reduce the amount that is cut off rather than eliminating the practice totally. Ali points out that shifting the practice to medical professionals has resulted only in larger amounts of tissue being surgically removed.[46]

There are religions with positive views of women's bodies. As suggested by Paleolithic and Neolithic female figurines, women's bodies may have been viewed positively as conveying power and blessings in prehistoric religions. Another example, the Apache puberty rite of passage for girls, imbues their bodies with the healing power of the Apache cultural heroine White Painted Woman.

Views of women's bodies in religious cultures inform us about socially constructed gender roles and the extent to which there is equality or subordination of women. It is also worth considering what views of women's bodies tell us about women's status in today's more secular cultures.

Violence against Women

Violence is the ultimate means of oppressing any class of people. Religiously sanctioned violence against girls and women may be committed by men or women. Expressions of violence toward women occur in numerous religious cultures.

It is unknown precisely how many women and men were tortured and killed during the "Burning Times" in European Christian lands. The major witch hunts occurred between 1560 and 1760 C.E. Historian Anne Llewellyn Barstow estimates that 200,000 people were accused of being witches and that the a death rate for them (from starvation, torture, and execution) was 50 percent. Barstow reports that 80 percent of persons accused were women or girls, and 85 percent of those killed were female. The men and boys who were accused and killed were usually related or married to the women convicted of being witches. The largest number of alleged witches killed—about 30,000—died in German-speaking lands of the Holy Roman Empire, with women constituting 82 percent of those accused and killed.[47]

A woman arrested for suspicion of witchcraft was stripped, either in prison or in public, and her body pricked and inspected for fleshy growths, believed to be the marks of the devil and teats by which to nurse demons. The search for these marks included the woman's genitals. During and subsequent to this sexual abuse, accused women were frequently raped. Various tortures were applied to get women and men to confess to being witches and name others. A woman might be tied to a table and have water poured into her mouth and nose until she confessed. The strappado was a strap or rope that was used to tie a woman's wrists behind her back and then hoist her to the ceiling, which pulled the shoulders over her head, dislocating them by the weight of her body; rocks might be tied to her feet to increase the pressure. Torture by strappado would be made even more excruciating by pulling the rope taut and then releasing it to drop her repeatedly. The accused witch might be subjected to stretching on a ladder used as a rack. The woman might be made to sit on a metal "witch's seat," which was heated to the point of burning. Hot metal pincers were used against women's bodies in terrible ways. Children were tortured to make them testify against their mothers.

After the authorities had condemned a person to be executed as a witch, torture was continued as public spectacle at the execution. Hot pincers were used to tear flesh off. A woman might have her breasts cut off and perhaps pressed into her mouth and the mouths of her adult sons, as was done to Anna Pappenheimer and her sons in 1600 outside Munich. A man might be impaled through his rectum, as was done to Anna's husband, Paulus Pappenheimer. Then the witches would be burned at the stake,[48] or hung, as in England. Some villages would have virtually all the women killed as witches. Misogyny and sadism flourished during the burning times.

Barstow argues that the persecution of women as witches during the Burning Times had the effect of silencing women, making them less likely to serve as "magic-workers" and village healers, and less likely to speak up to state their opinions and criticize or curse those who crossed or harmed them. The torture and execution of women as witches made women keenly aware of their precarious status in families and society, and diminished their self-esteem through their powerlessness and association with evil.

In contemporary evangelical Christianity, it is common for Christian pastors and counselors to encourage women to remain in abusive marriages based on the story of Adam, Eve, and the Serpent (Genesis 2–3) and on passages in the New Testament saying that the husband is the head of the wife and the wife should obediently submit to her husband (e.g. Ephesians 5:21–33; 1 Timothy 2:8–15; Colossians 3:18–4:1). These same passages say that a husband should love and treat his wife well, but when that is not the case, these passages have been used to encourage a woman to stay with an abusive husband. A woman may be told that her husband beats her because she does not submit, or a woman is counseled to leave while her husband is violent, but to return later after the husband has cooled down—bad advice for a woman whose life is threatened by an abusive husband. It is easier for a wife to leave a husband or domestic partner if she has the resources—income and family and social support—to do so. Evangelical Christianity, which overlaps with a contemporary movement to revitalize "Christian Patriarchy," creates a culture in which it is difficult for a woman to remove herself from an abusive marriage.[49]

In patriarchal Islamic societies, Surah 4:34 in the Qur'an has been understood as Allah giving permission to husbands to beat their disobedient wives. In illustration, Iranian American religious studies scholar Reza Aslan quotes the translation by scholar of Islamic philosophy Majid Fakhry:

> Men are in charge of women, because Allah has made some of them excel the others, and because they spend some of their wealth. . . . And for those [women] that you fear might rebel, admonish them and abandon them in their beds and beat them [*adribuhunna*].[50]

In 2016, national television in Saudi Arabia released a video in which Saudi family specialist Khaled Al-Saqabi instructed men on how to beat their wives lightly in an Islamic manner. In his talk, Al-Saqabi asserted that the early Islamic scholar Ibn Abbas (ca. 619–ca. 687) had indicated that, after a husband resorted to the measures listed earlier in Surah 4:34 without success, a disobedient wife should be beaten only with a twig used for cleaning teeth or a handkerchief "to make the wife feel she was wrong." Although Al-Saqabi advocated treating the disobedient wife compassionately, he still affirmed the patriarchal assumption that a wife is a ward of her husband—which she is according to Saudi law and custom—and that it is her husband's duty to discipline her.[51]

Reza Aslan points out that as in most languages, Arabic words can have various meanings, and Surah 4:34 can be understood as saying something completely different. In illustration, Aslan quotes the translation by Pakistani scholar, translator, and author Ahmed Ali:

Men are the support of women [*qawwamuna 'ala an-nisa*] as God gives some more means than others, and because they spend of their wealth (to provide for them). . . . As for women you feel are averse, talk to them suasively; then leave them alone in bed (without molesting them) and go to bed with them (when they are willing).

Aslan points out that the Ahmed Ali's translation instructs Muslim men not to press unwanted sexual intercourse on their wives. Nevertheless, the common understanding in patriarchal Islamic societies is that this verse gives Muslim men the right to beat disobedient wives.

An edited book produced under the auspices of Musawah ("Equality"), an international association that advocates for "equality and justice in the Muslim family,"[52] includes chapters that contextualize and analyze Surah 4:34. In one, American Qur'an scholar Amina Wadud argues that the male dominance in Surah 4:34 is descriptive rather than prescriptive, and that the social context for Muslim gender roles has changed such that Muslim women are frequently breadwinners who support themselves and their families. She argues for a relational ethic of egalitarianism and reciprocity based on the Islamic doctrine of *tawhid* (the oneness of Allah). According to Wadud, Muslim women are frequently fully active in their families and society, and patriarchy is "unsustainable, untenable and un-Islamic."[53]

Violence against girls and women can also be committed by women, as in female genital cutting described earlier, footbinding in China before the People's Republic of China was established in 1949, and the murder of young wives in India by mothers-in-law aiding and abetting the violent actions of their sons. Occasionally a mother will kill her daughter if she feels the daughter's independent actions have sullied the family's honor, as in the case of Pakistani mother Parveen Rafiq, who in 2016 with the help of her son tied her seventeen-year-old daughter, Zeenat, to a cot, doused her body with kerosene, and set her on fire, because Zeenat had married a man without her widowed mother's permission. In January 2017 Parveen Rafiq was sentenced to death, and her son was sentenced to life in prison for the murder of Zeenat Rafiq.

An example of religious condemnation of violence is Surah 81:8–9 in the Qur'an, which condemns female infanticide. Female infanticide remains a problem in today's world due to the preference for sons in patriarchal societies in which sons support their parents in their old age, inheritance is passed to sons, and daughters are expensive to marry off. In 1990 Nobel Prize–winning economist Amartya Sen published an essay entitled "More Than 100 Million Women Are Missing," in which he argues that women in fact do not make up half of the world's population due to discrimination, poor nutrition and healthcare, and active killing of female infants and neglect of female children. He points out that for every one hundred female babies born, about 105 or 106 male babies are born. Although more male babies are born, male infants have a higher mortality rate than females during the first year of life. By the end of the first year the sex ratio of females to males is generally balanced if nutrition and healthcare are equal. However, women have a longer life expectancy than men and, therefore, in countries where healthcare is of good quality and equal for women and men, the sex ratio can be 105 or 106 females to every one hundred males. Sen points out that in South Asia, West Asia, and China, depending on the particular state, province, or region, the sex ratio can be 94 females or lower for every 100 males, indicating active elimination and poor healthcare of females. He calculates that in China alone 50 million women are missing; adding statistics for South Asia, West Asia, and Northern Africa, he suggests that a total of more than 100 million women are missing.[54]

Female infanticide, withholding nutrition and healthcare from young daughters, and now selective abortion of female fetuses utilizing amniocentesis and later ultrasound to determine the sex of the fetus are major factors in skewing the sex ratio in highly patriarchal societies. A shortage of women in the general population is the result of sexism and does not increase the status of women. Instead, women are often harassed and/or raped by men, in addition to being sold to men wanting wives.

Even if a religion does not call for violence against girls and women, the silence of religious leaders may create conditions for its perpetuation.[55]

Women as Religious Specialists

An exploration of women as religious specialists raises the question of the type of religious tradition in which women are leaders. In *basic religions* (including many indigenous religions), in which people live close to the powers and spirits believed to exist throughout nature, women are often *shamans*, whose religious leadership is based on *charisma*, which is present when it is believed that a person has access to an unseen source of authority.[56] Credentialed knowledge for certain types of religious leadership may be obtained orally in a religious tradition that was originally preliterate. In institutionalized religions today, more women are earning credentials in seminaries to be ordained to ministerial leadership roles, but charisma may continue to be regarded as the ultimate source of the religious leader's authority.[57]

Basic Religions

The most prevalent pattern of human religiosity is what many world religions textbooks call *indigenous religion*. Since many originally indigenous religions are now practiced by people in various parts of the world, I prefer Lewis M. Hopfe's term, *basic religion*, which indicates that this is a pattern fundamental to human religiosity.[58] Basic religion is indicated by prehistoric artifacts, and it is found in Hinduism, Shinto, traditional African religions, Native American religions, and Chinese religious tradition, among others.

The cosmology of basic religion consists of *animism*. The Latin word *anima* means "soul," or "life." An animistic cosmology involves the belief that plants, animals, and human beings are animated by life forces and souls. *Animism* involves two overlapping beliefs: (1) that there is an impersonal force or forces underlying everything in nature and within humans and (2) that these forces take on personal expressions as spirits (good and bad), ancestors, and gods. Basic religion is polytheistic, with goddesses as well as gods, and there is often belief in a high god or goddess.

Because belief in impersonal forces and belief in personal gods and spirits are equally important in the animistic cosmology, there are two possible developments as religious traditions change over time. If believers are seeking the one God or Goddess, who is the creator and ruler of the universe, out of the plurality of deities, the end result will be *monotheism*, although basic religion often continues as a substratum of monotheistic traditions. If philosophers and ascetics seek the one source of the universe in the impersonal forces believed to exist in nature, the end result will be philosophical *monism*, the belief that there is one impersonal ultimate reality underlying the universe, although, again, monism is usually blended with the continuing basic religion.

The Abrahamic religions of Judaism, Christianity, and Islam stress monotheism but continue many basic religious practices and beliefs such as veneration of ancestors and saints and even spirit possession. Daoism (Taoism) in China stresses a monistic, dynamic energy, the Dao, but it is not separate from what may be called the Chinese basic religion. Hinduism, originating in the Indian subcontinent, is an internally diverse tradition that contains basic religions, monotheistic trends, and philosophical monism in an ever-changing kaleidoscope of colorful elements. Buddhism is a psychological analysis of the human condition, which seldom exists apart from basic religious expressions, of which it has been very tolerant. African and Native American religions are basic religions, with their own complexities and particularities within the overarching basic religious pattern.

Basic religions are very compatible with today's postmodern, postindustrial, information age world, as illustrated by Shinto, the indigenous religion of Japan. While basic religions are being revived in various parts of the world, others are being created today, such as the New Age movement, and Wicca and Neopaganism. Basic religions are the religions of people who live close to nature—or wish to—and sense forces and spirits throughout nature.

In a basic religion, survival and well-being are dependent on being in harmony with the impersonal forces and personal gods and spirits and the ancestors. A variety of methods are practiced to achieve this ultimate goal. *Magic* is the belief that words combined with sacred substances and ritual actions have the power to make material changes in the natural world. *Divination* is foretelling the future by various means. *Taboos* are actions or contacts that are forbidden in order to protect against harm and/or impurity. *Totems* are natural or human-made objects that are closely identified with individuals or a sacred group or nation. Totems, such as national flags, are often closely associated with the sacred dead.[59] *Sacrifices* are offerings—ranging from prayers and lighting candles or incense to giving money or gifts that can be inexpensive or costly—to placate spirits, gods, and ancestors believed to be more powerful than the worshippers. *Myths* are stories that explain why things are the way they are and/or convey values important to the people; they are told, reenacted, and read in ritualized fashion. *Rites of passage* are rituals designed to help an individual safely traverse key moments in the life cycle, including death. *Ancestor veneration* involves making offerings, and sometimes observing taboos, to prevent ancestors from harming their living relatives and to gain their blessings. *Sacred time* and *sacred places* are times and places where people may come into close, and harmonious, contact with the divine forces and beings.

Shamanism

Shamanism is a very important method in basic religions to preserve and/or regain harmony with sacred forces and beings. It is the first specialized religious role in human religious expressions. Women and men may be shamans in egalitarian foraging, nonegalitarian foraging, horticultural, nomadic pastoral, and plow agricultural societies. Shamanism has continued to manifest in industrial and postindustrial societies, despite the fact that in these societies religious leadership is more likely to be based on credentials gained through education and ordination. Shamanism is an important means by which women and those of alternative gender, as well as men of low social status, gain their voices and some degree of empowerment in patriarchal societies.

In the language of the Evenki of Siberia, *shaman* means "one who knows."[60] The term is used in religious studies to refer to a specialist who is believed to gain knowledge by contacting unseen spirits. People in different cultures variously understand these unseen beings to be gods, ancestors, spirits, angels, saints, and in Christianity, the Holy Spirit. In contemporary industrial and postindustrial societies, some shamans claim that extraterrestrials or space aliens speak through them. In some cultures the shaman's role is reserved for men; in other cultures the shamans are women; and in yet other cultures both women and men may be shamans.

Shamanism involves *charisma*.[61] The phrase *extraordinary charisma* refers to the believed capacity of the leader of a religious group to have access to direct revelation, which is not available to other members of the group. *Shared charisma* can be used to refer to experiences of what is considered sacred by multiple members of the group.[62] Charisma of all types is socially constructed. No individual has charisma unless people believe that she or he has access to an unseen source of authority. Shamanism involves complex and not fully understood phenomena, which probably fulfill a variety of functions in women's lives, including therapeutic ones. Shamanistic techniques and behaviors in many cases are learned behaviors.

There are several expressions of shamanism. In one form, which religious studies scholar Robert S. Ellwood terms *traveling shamanism*, the soul of the shaman is believed to leave the body to travel in the spirit world and consult spirits. When the shaman's soul is reported as having returned to the body, the cause of a problem and the means to cure it is announced. Another type, *possession shamanism*, involves the belief that a spirit comes into the shaman's body during trance, speaks through the shaman's mouth, and causes the shaman to behave in particular ways.[63] Frequently numerous spirits speak through a shaman. We may use the term *psychic shamanism* to refer to religious specialists who receive information from the spirit world through visions, dreams, or intuitions rather than through possession or out-of-the-body experience.

Clients consult a shaman seeking to alleviate the ills and sufferings of life. The shaman's knowledge is considered to be authoritative because it comes from beings residing in the unseen world. The shaman indicates what is needed to restore harmony with the spirit world and thus regain well-being. Healing may take place with the shaman serving as the vehicle of healing power.

Since information gained through the shaman is often about the future, shamanism frequently involves divination. The shaman's role as religious specialist overlaps with the roles of the practitioner of magic (for good or evil purposes) and the priest (ritualist). Shamanism always involves knowledge of and contact with the spirit world.

Anthropologist Erika Bourguignon observed that possession shamanism seems to be associated with early socialization to accept hierarchical authority, whereas childhood socialization geared to producing independent and self-reliant individuals within a predominantly classless society is not conducive to experiences that the society will interpret as possession trance. Bourguignon estimated that nearly 50 percent of Native American cultures in North America do not have belief in and practice of possession trance.[64] Instead psychic shamanism is often found in Native American religious expressions. Native Americans may induce altered states of consciousness by dancing, drumming, singing and chanting, gazing at a blazing fire, fasting, participating in sweat lodges, or ingesting psychotropic plant substances (entheogens), or they may report spontaneous visions. Dreams are considered important sources of knowledge in Native American religions.

In some cultures the possession shaman is a religious specialist whose ability to communicate with spirits is not widely shared among the community. This is termed *specialist possession* by anthropologist Susan Starr Sered. In other cultures, numerous people can be possessed by spirits during rituals performed especially for that purpose. Sered terms this *lay possession.*[65] I prefer a term such as *shared possession* to indicate that multiple members of the group become possessed. The indigenous Yorùbá religion provides examples of shared possession in worship groups in which there are one or more senior initiates who prepare and initiate others into the worship society. This type of possession worship is also seen in Haitian Vodou, which combines elements from the religions of the Fon, Ewe, Yorùbá and Kongo peoples with responses to the Haitian context; Santería, also known as Lucumí (a Yorùbá people and language), which developed in Cuba; and Candomblé, which preserves Yorùbá worship forms in Brazil.

Often a person is called to become a shaman through intense suffering, which scholars have termed *possession sickness*. Possession sickness can be mental and emotional torment and actual physical illness. It is not unusual for women in highly restrictive patriarchal societies to manifest symptoms of emotional, mental, and physical distress. Usually, numerous healing methods must be attempted without result before consulting a shaman, who diagnoses the person as suffering from possession sickness. Possession sickness is regarded as a call from the spirits to serve them, and the only way to get well is for the person to receive training and initiation to become a shaman. The ill person often resists becoming a shaman, because there will be significant costs in terms of finances, time, effort, and social standing. However, it is believed that the person must become a shaman in order for healing to occur and thereafter must function as a shaman in order to maintain well-being. If not, it is believed that the person will be killed by the spirit(s).

The Yorùbá goddess Yemǫnja, a significant river and mother goddess, manifests in a priestess during a religious festival in Abeokuta, Ogun State, Nigeria. In Candomblé in Brazil and Santería in Cuba, she is associated with the ocean. June 6, 2014. Courtesy of Portal Ifá Nigéria, Wikimedia Commons.

For example, anthropologist Janice Boddy found that in the village of Hofriyat in northern Sudan in the 1970s and 1980s, the women who had suffered the pain of infibulation when they were girls, and who continued to suffer from oppression in their husbands' families and the pain of sexual intercourse and repeated childbirth, often became possessed by spirits called *zayran* (singular, *zar*). In order for them to get well, their families paid for training and rituals to heal them and initiate them into *zar* worship. Initiation meant that the characteristics of the *zar* or *zayran* were incorporated into a woman's identity, giving her permission to act in ways a good Muslim woman in Hofriyat was not supposed to act. Within the context of the possession rituals, Hofriyati girls and women sang, drummed, and, once possessed, danced and articulated their grievances about their lives to other women. Since some of the *zayran* are males, in this society where gender is rigidly—and painfully—distinct, women possessed by *zayran* gain cultural permission to act in more "masculine" ways, such as speaking boldly. Many Muslims regard the *zar* cult as polytheistic and therefore heretical, but *zar* possession exists in many strict Muslim countries. It performs therapeutic functions for women, who gain voices and greater freedom of behavior that they would not otherwise have.[66] Although public *zar* possession rituals have been eliminated in the village in Sudan where Boddy did her fieldwork due to the attitude that they are not consistent with Islam, the work of anthropologist Susan M. Kenyon has shown that *zar* rituals continue elsewhere in Sudan among women.[67]

Very often a culture utilizes language with strong sexual overtones in referring to shamans as the "mounts" or "horses" of the spirits or to their marrying the deity in their initiation and becoming the deity's "bride." In some cultures, such as the Yorùbá, a man who is a possession shaman dresses like a woman. An understudied phenomenon is the extent to which LGBTQ persons gravitate to possession shamanism in a patriarchal society with rigid gender roles.[68]

Following the psychoanalytic theory of gender of Nancy Chodorow discussed earlier, Susan Starr Sered suggests that in societies in which women are primarily responsible for childcare, male identity formation involves the male needing to separate himself from his mother and all femaleness (i.e., women and their gender characteristics) to establish his distinct identity with culturally assigned masculine traits. Therefore, Sered suggests, men tend to have more well-defined ego boundaries and are more likely to have soul-traveling, out-of-the body, shamanistic experiences, than the internal, in-dwelling experiences of possession shamanism more common to women.[69] The study of world religions suggests that women are indeed typically involved in possession shamanistic experiences. However, many men are also possession shamans, as Yorùbá religions demonstrate. Accounts of soul-traveling shamanism are usually about men. One well-known example is Muhammad's Night Journey experience of traveling on the back of a steed from Arabia to Jerusalem, to touch down on the sacred rock on Mount Moriah and from there ascend through the heavenly realms to speak with Allah.

Possession shamanism functions in a variety of ways to heal and empower individual women. After being diagnosed with possession sickness, the woman who undertakes the training and initiation to become a shaman gains personal integration and healing. She may also gain social status, although in many patriarchal societies shamanism is considered a low-class occupation, as, for instance, in Korean shamanism, in which women predominate. In such cultures a woman shaman uses her role as a means to support herself and her children.[70]

In South Korea the word *mudang* refers to a shaman, and the majority of these shamans are women. Some *mudang* experience possession while performing *gut* (shamanic rituals), but other hereditary *mudang* do not experience possession. All *mudang* are priests in the sense that they mediate between humans and gods and spirits by performing rituals. The Korean women shamans prefer to call themselves *manshin* ("ten thousand spirits").

Anthropologist Youngsook Kim Harvey described Korean women called to possession shamanism as going through a lengthy *sinbyŏng* (spirit sickness) when they find themselves trapped in intolerable family situations involving emotional, and sometimes physical, abuse. They manifest numerous physical and psychological symptoms of stress, including hallucinations and unresponsiveness, in addition to behavior that is considered antisocial, such as speaking openly about their own and their neighbors' personal problems. When such women consult a *mudang* and are diagnosed with *sinbyŏng*, the only way for them to be healed is to undergo training to become *mudang*. The outcome may be the overturning of patriarchal family relationships as the new *mudang* acquires paying clients and begins to support her family. Harvey described how one *mudang*'s husband took over food preparation, childcare, and housekeeping, because his wife saw thirty to forty clients daily. The husband's mother could not bear to see her son doing women's

Manshin KɪM Keum-hwa carrying out a three-day ritual at her shrine in Ganghwado, South Korea, October 20–22, 2017, to celebrate her seventieth anniversary as a shaman. This was her last ritual before her death on February 23, 2019 at age eighty-eight. In 1985 she was designated a "Human Cultural Treasure," and two of her rituals were designated "Intangible Cultural Properties" by the South Korean government.[71] Photo from the series *On Distant Objects and Hungry Gods* by Jorge Mañes Rubio. Courtesy of Jorge Mañes Rubio.

work, so she began running the household, thereby reversing the relationship in which the daughter-in-law serves her mother-in-law in a classical patriarchal family.[72]

Possession rituals provide women with opportunities for catharsis, emotional release, and social support, and even occasions to take on male gender roles and express "masculine" behaviors when possessed by male spirits. In a society that rigidly distinguishes between male and female gender roles, possession shamanism may serve to help an individual express qualities that are culturally assigned to the opposite sex and thus help the individual achieve personal balance.

A woman shaman does not typically question patriarchal family and social structures. She may teach other women to conform to patriarchal norms, even while she helps them to be healed of physical and emotional ailments and find peace. For instance, scholar of Japanese religions Carmen Blacker writes of a healer named Mrs. Ryuun HIROSHIMA, who in the early 1940s treated a woman who had been stricken with an overwhelming headache after her husband's death. During her husband's final illness the woman had nursed him devotedly while continuing to work to support the family, but her husband criticized everything she did, and he was extremely possessive of her. When Mrs. Hiroshima arrived at the woman's residence, she found the woman prostrated at the altar to her husband's spirit. Mrs. Hiroshima recited the Mahāyāna Buddhist *Heart of the Perfection of Wisdom* scripture for two and a half hours and then she was able to speak to the ghost.

> "Who are you?" she demanded.
> "The new ghost," it replied. "I have been waiting and waiting for you to come. Indeed, it was to get you to come here that I caused my wife to have this fearful headache. Magotarō, I died with great resentment in my heart and because of this I am wandering with nowhere to go. I died hating and loathing my wife because she was continually making me doubt her. If she marries again I cannot bear it."[73]

Mrs. Hiroshima made the woman promise that she would not remarry and that she would always venerate the spirit of her deceased husband. When the woman promised, Mrs. Hiroshima

> thereupon recited with ear-splitting force the nine magic syllables.
> "Rin-byō-tō-sha-kai-jin-retsu-zai-zen."
> And at that instant the headache which had been tormenting the woman for so long vanished.[74]

Shamanism provides women with explanations for their sufferings. Possession shamanism removes the blame from a woman for not successfully fulfilling her socially assigned gender role, because her problems are interpreted as being the fault of the spirits possessing her.[75] Very importantly, in patriarchal cultures in which women are expected to be obedient and silent, possession shamanism provides women with acceptable ways to articulate their grievances to their husbands and in-laws. A woman who does not dare speak directly about her complaints in a patriarchal context is not held responsible for what a spirit says through her mouth. In classical patriarchal societies, in which women's public verbal expression is not permitted, shamanism can empower a woman to speak legitimately in public. For example, religious studies and women's studies scholar Ann Braude reports that during the 1850s in the United States, trance mediums in the Spiritualist movement were "the first sizable group of American women to speak in public."[76]

Shamanism serves the various functions it does for women only in contexts in which the spirits and the possibility of possession are believed to be real. If there is no belief in the reality of spirits and possession in a society, then a woman's symptoms will be diagnosed as having some other cause.

Sered points out that possession shamanism is the primary leadership option for women in many strongly patriarchal cultures. While possessed during rituals, women shamans may act out and articulate critiques of patriarchal gender roles, but they are not empowered by their possession to take direct action to change society. "In short, the possessed woman is not acting from a position of power." According to Sered, possession religions "provide individual women with immediate assistance, but in that they individualize and mystify the true source of women's suffering, they undermine the ability of the religion to offer collective empowerment."[77]

Sometimes women religious specialists found their own religious groups and movements, usually based on their claimed charismatic access to the divine. This has been relatively common in Japan. NA-KAYAMA Miki (1798–1887) is the founding prophet of Tenrikyō, which has its sacred temple at Tenri City in Japan, and which regards Nakayama as the mouthpiece of God the Parent, Tenri-Ō-no-Mikoto. Nakayama is believed by devotees to continue to live in her quarters adjacent to the temple over the spot where humanity was created. KITA-MURA Sayo (1900–1967) founded Tenshō-kōtai-jingū-kyō, known as the "dancing religion," on the basis of her experience of being possessed by Tenshō-kōtai-jingū, whom Kitamura identified as being the "absolute god of the universe,"[78] and being adopted by the divine couple, Tenshō-kōtai-jingū and Amaterasu-ōmikami, the Sun Goddess and ancestor of the imperial family.[79]

As a new religious movement founded on charisma becomes institutionalized in a patriarchal society and develops leadership offices, typically women are excluded from positions of ordained leadership and are relegated to serving their congregations and denominations in ways that do not require ordination. This is what African religions scholar Rosalind I. J. Hackett discovered in churches founded by women in Calabar, Nigeria.[80] The Seventh-day Adventist Church, which relies on the revelations given to the prophet Ellen G. White (1827–1915), has so far failed to gain worldwide ordination of women to ministry.[81] This pattern is repeated in new religious movements and religious organizations founded by women and men around the world. But as access to education increases, more women are going beyond relying on the charisma of shamanism to legitimate their religious authority by earning credentials and even becoming ordained.

Credentialed Religious Leadership

Since the nineteenth century, and especially since the 1970s, women's demands to be admitted to Christian and Jewish ordination as religious specialists after earning educational credentials have been very controversial. Religious institutions have responded in various ways. After much struggle on the part of women to be included equally, some religious denominations have approved women's credentialed religious leadership. However, it is one thing to ordain women as rabbis, ministers, and priests, and another to hire them in pastoral positions and pay them equally. Similarly, it is one thing to give full ordination to Buddhist nuns and quite another to give them the financial support and cultural respect commensurate with that given to monks. Some religious organizations and traditions continue to refuse to ordain women or grant them other forms of leadership based on credentials. Women who feel called to ordained religious leadership may move to another denomination that does ordain women. In the case of the Roman Catholic Women Priests movement, women have proceeded with receiving ordination in ways not approved by the pope and Vatican officials in order to model a new type of priestly ministry for the Roman Catholic Church.

One example of a religious organization's movement toward inclusiveness in its ordained leadership is the Episcopal Church in the United

States of America, which since the 1970s has progressively taken steps to ordain women priests, elect and consecrate women bishops, elect and consecrate openly gay men and lesbian bishops, and move women into denominational leadership. These changes did not come about uncontested.[82] Many political battles were fought before the Episcopal Church's General Convention, consisting of a House of Bishops and a House of Deputies (lay delegates elected by dioceses), passed resolutions approving these changes. Opening the Episcopal Church's priesthood and episcopate to women, gay men, and lesbians, and then in 2012 to transgender and transsexual persons has created considerable tension between the Episcopal Church and other national Anglican churches within the consortium known as the Anglican Communion. In 2016 two-thirds of the bishops in the Anglican Communion voted to suspend the Episcopal Church from the Anglican Communion for three years because Episcopal priests were officiating at same-sex weddings. A spokesman for the Episcopal Church said, "We can accept these actions with grace and humility but the Episcopal Church is not going back. We can't repent what is not a sin."[83]

Despite the fact that Anglican churches permit marriage for priests and bishops, the national churches in the Anglican Communion are considered to be closest in polity and liturgy to the Roman Catholic Church. However, a significant difference in polity is that in the Roman Catholic Church ultimate decision-making authority concerning faith, morals, and practice is vested in the pope, while Anglican churches have democratically elected lay representatives and bishops.

It is useful to examine the recent history of the Roman Catholic Church as an example of a religious organization refusing to update itself to ordain women. Since the 1970s the Roman Catholic Church's proclamations against the ordination of women as priests can be seen as responding to changes in the Episcopal Church, in addition to responding to feminist Catholic woman and men seeking equality for women in their church.[84]

In the early 1970s, after Episcopal women had completed their seminary training and were ordained deacons, they began to lobby the General Convention for ordination to the priesthood. After their efforts were rebuffed, four retired bishops ordained eleven women deacons as priests in 1974, in what the General Convention subsequently declared "irregular" ordinations. The irregular ordinations provoked heated discussion of the question of ordaining women in the Episcopal Church, and in 1976 the General Convention passed a resolution that women could be ordained priests.

Catholic women were watching these developments with interest and in 1975 held the first meeting of the Women's Ordination Conference. Second-wave feminism and its promotion of the social expectation of equality of women put the Vatican under pressure to explain why women could not be ordained priests. The old assumption that women were misbegotten males, and that obviously defective human beings could not be priests, was no longer culturally acceptable.

Two theological rationales against women's ordination in the Roman Catholic Church were put forward in a "Declaration on the Question of Admission of Women to the Ministerial Priesthood" (*Inter Insigniores*) issued by the Congregation for the Doctrine of the Faith on October 15, 1976.[85] The first was that because of the "nuptial analogy" of Christ's relation to the Church as bridegroom to bride, the priest stood in the place of Christ and therefore had to be male in order to act in the person of Christ (*in persona Christi*). The second is that Christ had indicated his intent to have only male priests in his Church by selecting only men to be apostles.

Feminist Catholic intellectuals critiqued these rationales by pointing out that in the first place, an analogy is not meant to be taken literally and that the Congregation for the Doctrine of the Faith was not only applying it literally, but doing so only in relation to the priest, especially in the context of the Eucharist, and not to the congregation, which contains men and women.[86] In the second, there is no evidence that Jesus of Nazareth intended to found a church, much less a male priesthood. The disciples of Jesus included women and were not restricted to the twelve men who were probably selected to represent the twelve tribes of Israel and who were commissioned to go out among the Jews and proclaim the kingdom of God was at hand, heal the sick, raise the dead, and drive out demons, as did Jesus.

In the early centuries, the Christian tradition had a broader understanding of the word *apostle* than the twelve men sent out by Jesus, and this understanding included women. *Apostle* means "one who is sent," and in Matthew 10:5–15, where the twelve men are termed "apostles," it is clear that they were sent out by Jesus with the mission to proclaim the kingdom of God. The mission is clear also in Mark 3:13–19, the earliest gospel (ca. 68–73 C.E.), where the twelve are *not* termed *apostles*. They are termed *apostles* in Luke 6:12–16, which also describes the selection of the twelve men.[87] Paul, a Pharisee (rabbi) who converted about ten years after the death of Jesus and became a Christian missionary to the gentiles, called himself an *apostle* on the basis of his reported vision of Jesus on the road to Damascus (Acts 9:3–9). Paul became accepted in Christianity as an apostle, and his letters (ca. 50s and 60s C.E.) are the earliest writings that are included in the New Testament. Statements in Paul's letters (1 Cor. 15:5–11; 1 Cor. 1:1, 9:1) indicate a broader understanding of *apostle* than the twelve men selected by Jesus. In these passages *apostle* means primarily someone who has seen the resurrected Jesus Christ and has been sent out by him to proclaim the good news of resurrection. Paul's letters and the book of Acts describe a number of traveling missionaries, including Priscilla and Aquila, which Christian tradition includes among the seventy (or seventy-two) disciples sent out by Jesus (Luke 10:1–20) to spread the news of the kingdom of God. Priscilla, also called Prisca, is mentioned before her husband, Aquila, in three of the six passages that refer to them (Rom. 16:3–4; Acts 18:18; 2 Tim. 4:19), suggesting that she was a very active Christian missionary. They are both described in an episode in which they taught theology to a man and in this instance Priscilla is mentioned first (Acts 18:26). In Paul's Letter to the Romans, 16:7 is notable because it refers to a woman, Junia, and her husband, Andronicus, as being "prominent among the apostles, and they were in Christ before I was." (To conceal that Junia could be construed as being an apostle on the basis of Romans 16:7, for centuries Junia's name was transcribed as a purported male name, Junias.) Hippolytus (d. ca. 235), bishop of Rome, called Mary Magdalene (Mary of Magdala) "apostle to the apostles," because Mark 16:9–11 and John 20:1–18 describe the resurrected Jesus appearing first to her, and she went to tell the other disciples. Also, in Matthew 28:8–10, Jesus appears to Mary Magdalene and "the other Mary." In Luke 24:1-12, Mary Magdalene is listed first among the women who found the empty tomb and saw two men in gleaming clothes who told them that Jesus had risen.

On October 7, 1979, when Pope John Paul II made his first visit to the United States, Sister Theresa Kane (b. 1936), one of the Religious Sisters of Mercy of the Americas, as president of the Leadership Conference of Women Religious, addressed the pope during a welcoming Mass in the Basilica of the National Shrine of the Immaculate Conception in Washington, D.C., and respectfully challenged him to open all the ministries of the Roman Catholic Church to women.

During the 1980s and the 1990s, Pope John Paul II and Cardinal Joseph Ratzinger (later Pope Benedict XVI in office 2005–2013), head of the Congregation for the Doctrine of the Faith, responded to progress in the Episcopal Church and the larger Anglican Communion concerning women as priests and bishops by issuing statements designed to preclude Catholic women from becoming ordained as priests. In the late 1980s there were discussions in the Episcopal Church about electing and consecrating women as bishops. An African American woman, Barbara Harris (1930–2020), was elected in 1988 and consecrated Bishop Suffragan (assistant bishop) of the Diocese of Massachusetts in 1989. In 1988 Pope John Paul II issued an apostolic letter "On the Dignity and Vocation of Women" (*Mulieris dignitatem*), explaining that women have equal human dignity, and giving a feminist interpretation of the story of Adam, Eve, and the Serpent (Genesis 2–3), but stating that women's vocations are to be modeled after the Virgin Mary and that therefore the two options open to women are to be either mother (a married woman) or virgin (a nun) and that women cannot be ordained priests.

The Episcopal Church in the United States of America continued consecrating women as bishops, and in 1992 the Anglican Church of New Zealand consecrated its first woman bishop. In 1994 Pope John Paul II published an apostolic letter "On Reserving Priestly Ordination to Men Alone" (*Ordinatio sacerdotalis*), in which he stated that "the Church has no authority whatsoever to confer priestly ordination on women" and that this view was "to be definitively held by all the church's faithful." In 1995 Cardinal Ratzinger, as head of the Congregation for the Doctrine of the Faith, responded to questions about this letter by arguing that its teaching was infallible. In published discussions, however, Catholic intellectuals pointed out that the letter did not meet the standards of infallibility set by the Roman Catholic Church. In 1998 Pope John Paul II issued another apostolic letter entitled "To Protect the Faith" (*Ad tuendam fidem*) saying that anyone "who rejects those propositions which are to be held definitively is opposed to the doctrine of the Catholic

The Right Reverend Barbara Harris in 1999. She was elected to serve as Bishop Suffragan of the Diocese of Massachusetts in 1988. Courtesy of Episcopal Diocese of Massachusetts. Photo by David Zadig.

Church," and anyone rejecting a "definitive" doctrine would "no longer be in full communion with the Catholic Church." In other words, proponents of women's ordination excommunicate themselves. This document effectively silenced feminist Catholics employed in the Roman Catholic Church and related organizations, including religious sisters, brothers, priests, and bishops.

In 2006 Katharine Jefferts Schori (b. 1954) was invested as the presiding bishop of the Episcopal Church in the Washington National Cathedral making her the first woman primate (chief bishop) elected within the Anglican Communion. She served a nine-year term of office that ended in 2015. The bishops then elected Michael Curry (b. 1953) as the Episcopal Church's first African American presiding bishop.

Catholic women in the Roman Catholic Women Priests (RCWP) movement have been receiving ordination as deacons, priests and bishops, but they are not recognized by the Roman Catholic Church. In 2002 seven Catholic women were ordained priests by a former Catholic bishop (who was no longer recognized by the Vatican) and a male bishop whom he had consecrated, while on a boat in the Danube River. Subsequently, in 2002, two bishops, one of whom had participated in the ordination of the Danube Seven, consecrated two of the Danube Seven, Gisela Forster (b. 1946) and Christine Mayr-Lumetzberger (b. 1956) of Germany, as bishops. In 2003, they were consecrated bishops again by an anonymous bishop emeritus of the Roman Catholic Church known as Bishop X. In 2005 Patricia Fresen (b. 1940) of South Africa was consecrated bishop by Bishop X. Since that time the Roman Catholic women bishops have ordained women as deacons and priests and consecrated other women as bishops. The women ordained within the Roman Catholic Women Priests movement claim valid ordination in the apostolic succession (consecration by bishops in an unbroken succession of bishops going back to Saint Peter conveying spiritual power by laying on of hands).[88]

As of 2020 the Roman Catholic Women Priests movement is represented in the United States by two organizations, Roman Catholic Womenpriests-USA, and Association of Roman Catholic Women Priests (ARCWP). Both of these organizations have ordained women who live in other countries and three men as priests. There is also Roman Catholic Women Priests Canada and Roman Catholic Women Priests Europe. The majority of women priests are in the United States. In 2020 these four organizations had a total of fourteen active women bishops, nineteen women deacons, and 193 women priests. Additionally, some women bishops and priests in the movement have retired or are deceased.[89]

The Roman Catholic women priests celebrate the Eucharist in congregations gathered in homes or in the buildings of churches belonging to sympathetic denominations such as the Unitarian Universalist Association, the Episcopal Church, the United Church of Christ, and the United Methodist Church, all of which ordain women as ministers.

The women ordained in the Roman Catholic Women Priests move-ment are primarily of the Baby Boomer generation or older, although there are younger women who are ordained and women ranging in age from their thirties to their fifties who are preparing for ordination.[90] They hope that their presence as ordained women will promote the inclusion of women priests in the Roman Catholic Church.[91] At the present time the Roman Catholic hierarchy has excommunicated them and rejects their claim to having received valid ordination within the apostolic succession.

Concerned about keeping the younger generations of Catholic women in the Roman Catholic Church, a coalition of thirty Catholic so-cial justice organizations, including the Association of Roman Catholic Women Priests and the Women's Ordination Conference, submitted a petition in 2016 to the American Catholic bishops asking for structural and theological changes that will create "A Church for Our Daughters." The petition asked the bishops to "work with us to build a Church that strikes down every oppressive practice, teaching, and law that assigns women and girls to a subordinate status. We call on our leaders to cre-ate a Church that is truly inclusive and alive with the gifts, spirit, and potential of all its members."[92]

Goddesses and Other Concepts of the Divine

In the 1960s and 1970s many western feminists were inspired by the discovery of goddesses in religions such as the "ancient Mediterranean, pre-Christian European, Native American, Meso-American, Hindu, African, and other traditions,"[93] and the realization that God did not have to be imagined only as male. There are important goddesses in many religious traditions. To understand them thoroughly one must investigate the various ways goddesses are viewed within their own cultural contexts, and what that indicates about how real women are viewed in society. It cannot be assumed that the presence of goddesses in a religious culture is evidence that actual women have high status. In fact, many societies with goddesses are classical patriarchies, which sub-ordinate and devalue real women. Nevertheless, in cultures where the social expectation of equality is increasing, goddesses may be utilized as resources for the empowerment of women.

In India, for example, the Hindu goddesses and Devī, the Great Goddess, are related to real women in complex ways. Śrī, also known as Lakṣmī, wife of Viṣṇu and goddess of wealth and fertility, is the epitome of the beautiful, young Hindu wife whose fertility and dowry bring good fortune to her husband's extended family. Lakṣmī is auspicious because she obediently subordinates herself to her husband.[94] In a number of Hindu kingdoms in the past, Śrī-Lakṣmī was considered to be the source of the king's sovereignty and auspiciousness. During his coronation ritual, he was considered an embodiment of Viṣṇu and was married to Śrī-Lakṣmī. If he failed to rule righteously, it was believed that she would depart from him and the kingdom would experience decline.[95] Among Śrī Vaishnavas (worshippers of Śrī and Viṣṇu) in South India, Lakṣmī is regarded as the supreme being who creates, protects, and will ultimately destroy the universe.[96] Sītā is an avatar ("descent," incarnation) of Lakṣmī, born on Earth to be with her husband Rāma, an avatar of Viṣṇu. Gender messages conveyed in the Rāmāyaṇa of Vālmīki (ca. 200 B.C.E. to 200 C.E.) are that Hindu wives should strive to be like Sītā, always devoted to her husband no matter how badly he treats her and that Hindu men should be like Rāma, strong, resisting evil, and upholding social order and righteousness (*dharma*) even when it is personally painful.

The Hindu goddess Durgā is a beautiful warrior goddess who bears multiple weapons in her many hands to slay a demon in the form of a water buffalo. She was worshipped by some Hindu kings who performed annual buffalo sacrifices during the Navarātrī (Nine Nights) festival to obtain her protection of their rulership.[97] She is celebrated in the influential scripture *Devī Māhātmya* (fifth or sixth century C.E.) as Goddess, the Supreme Deity. Kālī, the naked black goddess wearing a garland of severed heads, and an apron of severed arms and legs, with fangs bared and bloody tongue protruding from her mouth, her unbound hair flying wildly, is usually not seen as a model for women to emulate in patriarchal society in India. While Durgā and Kālī are considered to be versions of the wife of Śiva, they are depicted in Hindu myths and iconography as independent, powerful, and dangerous goddesses.[98]

Particular goddesses, and traditions containing goddesses, thus need to be examined in depth to determine how they relate to the roles and experiences of women, and whether the goddesses are empowering to

Goddess Adhiparashakthi in the Devi Parashakthi Matha (Eternal Mother) Temple in Pontiac, Michigan, December 28, 2012. Courtesy of Rashkesh, Wikimedia Commons.

living women, or if they function to empower men and subordinate women. As we can see in the discussion of Hindu goddesses above, Hinduism is an example of a religious tradition that is shaped within various classical patriarchies in India and that subordinates women, even though it has numerous important goddesses. There are countercultural aspects to the Hindu tradition, notably in Tantra, but in each case, close examination is required to determine if the goddesses empower real women.

Whether or not there is a social expectation of equality of women and men determines the extent to which goddesses may serve to empower women. As increased expectations of women's equality are found in India and Hindu societies around the world, the Hindu goddesses and belief in *śakti* (the power that creates the universe and is associated with goddesses and all women) become resources to support women's religious and secular authority, as well as their self-esteem, and improve how women are regarded by men. Hindu women are reinterpreting goddesses such as Sītā and Kālī to create strong female models mean-ingful to them. A number of women in the west have found the Hindu goddesses to be valuable lenses through which they can view themselves as empowered.[99]

The Adhiparasakthi (Ādi Parāśakti, Primordial Supreme Śaktī) movement originated in Tamil Nadu state in southern India with a man named Bangaru Adigalar (b. 1941), who is regarded by his devotees as being an incarnation of the great goddess Adhiparasakthi. Both the Goddess and Adigalar are called Amma (Mother) by devotees. Adigalar created a movement in which women and men perform *pūjā* (worship) in temples themselves, without the mediation of (male) Brahmin priests, and women are not required to refrain from entering a temple and wor-shipping while menstruating. Menstruation is not regarded as making a woman impure. During *vilakku pūjā* (lamp *pūjā*) on full-moon days and special holidays, each worshipper performs the same ritual offerings in the temple while seated before the flames of lit oil lamps.[100] For temple worship, women, men, and children like to wear red, the color of Śaktī and women.

Religion scholar Nanette R. Spina's ethnographic work at the Adhi Parasakthi Temple Society of Canada in Toronto, where the worshippers are Tamils from Sri Lanka, illustrates that due to women's ritual prac-tice in the temple, women's leadership of the temple society is strong. A woman is the president of the temple society, and there are other active women leaders. Men also find meaning in their egalitarian ritual wor-ship and temple society participation. Spina reports that women find their worship of the Goddess and leadership in the temple, as well as friendships with other women active in the temple, empowering, es-pecially due to the greater expectations of social equality in Canada. In Canada, older women feel freer to leave behind the restrictions they grew up with in Tamil society in Sri Lanka. Many of the women who are members in the Adhi Parasakthi Temple Society of Canada work outside the home. The women venerate Tamil women saints, such as Karaikkal Ammaiyar (ca. 500 C.E.),[101] but especially they look up to the women leaders in the temple society as models they can emulate.[102]

Comparative history of religions research indicates that when there is a social expectation of equality, viewing the divine as female, as hav-ing both female and male characteristics, or as being impersonal can be supportive of women's religious leadership, whether it is credentialed through education and ordination, or based on charisma.[103] As the social expectation of women's equality continues to increase, these understandings of the divine are being created or revived in alternative religious movements, and they are being incorporated in some mainstream religious denominations.

Women and Religious Ritual

The ways that women participate in the rituals of their religious tradition indicate much about their status in their tradition and whether or not they are considered equal. Are women found in leadership roles in worship, or are they primarily worshippers and members of congregations? Are women included equally or sidelined from ritualized worship?

Women living in patriarchal societies carry out personally meaningful religious rituals of their own, such as *vratas* (vows, Hindi *vrat*), which are similar to those performed in Karimpur discussed earlier. Throughout India women perform rituals as part of *vratas* to obtain divine favors from deities to protect the health of their husbands, brothers, and sons—the men a Hindu woman is tasked to care for as a *pativratā* (woman who devotes herself to serving her "lord," *pati*, husband) to fulfill her *strīdharma* (sacred social duty as a wife). Men observe *vrats*, but women specialize in observing *vrats* for various purposes on sacred holidays throughout the year. Women observe *vrats* to obtain boons from a deity, categorized as *sakāma vratas*, vows performed to fulfill wishes for material blessing. Women also perform *niṣkāma vratas*, vows performed without desires for boons, but to express devotion (*bhakti*) to the deity and to cultivate self-discipline.[104]

Women's *vrats* are often performed in a gathering of household or neighborhood women. The *vrat* begins with taking a ritual bath, making a declaration of resolve to complete the vow, and following the rules and actions required by the *vrat*. For the duration of the vow, whether it is hours, a day, or weeks, a woman fasts or eats only pure foods permitted in relation to the *vrat* as a sacrifice that purifies the woman and her intentions. Alone, or with other women, she prepares simple images, perhaps made of cow dung (considered pure), a pot decorated with colored powders and flowers, or drawings on the mud walls of the house or rice powder drawings on the floor of the courtyard, which represent the deity to be worshipped in *pūjā* (worship directed toward the deity in an image). Songs are sung, offerings are made, and a story (*kathā*) is told or read about how the woman who first performed the *vrat* gained benefit.

Vrats are performed by girls to obtain a good husband; by sisters to protect their brothers; by wives to obtain sons; by mothers to protect husbands and sons; by women to benefit the family. Women interviewed by religious studies scholar Anne MacKenzie Pearson said that performing *vrats* brings them peace of mind. The mental peace can come from a sense that women have the power (*śakti*) to affect their environments to benefit their families and the men on whom their well-being depends or it can come from using the *vrat* as a meditative ritual and ascetic experience. In the latter case, women also feel that their *śakti* is strengthened by the renunciation (giving up desired things, such as the foods that are avoided) and devotion of the *vrat*.[105] As the social expectation of equality continues to grow among Hindus, there is scope for women to continue the practice of *vrats*. The greatest challenge for their continuity will be the fast-paced lives and distractions of young, urban, and westernized generations.

Religious cultures that are generally egalitarian have rituals that affirm the value of girls and women. An important example preserved in Apache tradition is the girl's puberty ceremony, which may be performed for a single girl, or for a group of girls, such as the one on the Mescalero Apache Reservation in New Mexico around July Fourth of each year. The entire rite of passage takes twelve days—four days of preparation, four days of rituals and feasting, and four days of instruction for the new woman afterward. The ceremony is believed to convey to the girl the blessings of long life, strength, good health extending into old age, prosperity in food, and the moral qualities to be an Apache woman—strength, pride, generosity, and kindness, which are qualities that all Apache should cultivate.

The Apache girl's family feeds everyone who attends their daughter's feast for four days. Men and women contribute to the ceremony in various ways—men doing heavy labor, men and women butchering cattle, women cooking and serving food with men helping, male and female members of the girl's family and the family of her sponsor (godmother) engaging in spiritual preparations, and women and men playing roles in the ceremony itself. At the July Fourth ceremony on the Mescalero Apache Reservation, everyone attends the daytime entertainment—a parade, rodeos, Apache war dances, guest appearances of Native American celebrities, and dancing. Both sexes are present for religious aspects of the ceremony.

Different groups of Apache have different approaches to performing the girl's ceremony. In the Mescalero Apache ceremony, the medicine man, or singer, sings the story of creation in archaic Apache language. The godmother, or sponsor, guides the girl through the complex rituals, as well as instructs her in gathering foods and medicinal plants, how to prepare plants and meat for consumption, and how to comport herself as an Apache woman.

During the Apache girl's puberty ritual the most important religious specialist is the girl herself, who is imbued with the power of White Painted Woman (also called Changing Woman) by prayers, pollen blessings, and her own fortitude during strenuous controlled dancing for up to four days and three nights. The sponsor and a medicine man bless the girl by placing her at the center of the four sacred directions and marking her face, shoulders, hands, feet and head with pollen. The girl in turn blesses adults and children who queue up with pollen to bless the girl and to receive the healing power of White Painted Woman. The many rituals involved in the puberty ceremony include Apache women dancing at night around a blazing fire, where the Mountain God dancers come out to dance and bless the girl.[106]

As the expectation of equality is increasing in societies that have been patriarchal, women religious specialists are adding female-affirming rituals and rites of passage to their traditions, and some rituals are created for women-only groups. In recent decades, women rabbis have created naming ceremonies, frequently called *simhat bat* ("rejoicing in a daughter"), to welcome Jewish baby girls into the covenant with God as a member of the people of Israel. For thousands of years, the rite of passage for infant boys has been the *brit milah* ("covenant of circumcision"), in which an eight-day-old baby boy is circumcised, thereby including him in the people of Israel's covenant with God. From the 1970s, in Reform, Reconstructionist, and Conservative Judaism the ritual for the twelve- or thirteen-year-old *bat mitzvah* ("daughter of the commandment") has been made comparable to the

Sonia Epstein pictured with the Torah on the occasion of her becoming a bat mitzvah. Photo used with permission from Melissa Hammer and Sonia Epstein.

ritual for the *bar mitzvah* ("son of the commandment"). A Conservative, Reconstructionist or Reform *bat mitzvah*, who has been educated in Hebrew and Torah, reads from the Torah scroll in a ceremony in a synagogue or temple. The ceremony for most Orthodox *bat mitzvah*s, however, differs from that of an Orthodox *bar mitzvah*, since an Orthodox synagogue tends to be a sex-segregated space for worship where women should not be seen or heard by the men. To preserve modesty, an Orthodox *bat mitzvah* may read a passage from Torah and give a talk on it at a ritual held in her home or during a women-only worship service. Rarely will the rite of passage for a *bat mitzvah* take place during congregational worship of both sexes in an Orthodox synagogue.[107] Since the 1970s and second-wave feminism, Jewish women have been creating new rituals for women, including returning to the observance of Rosh Chodesh (new moon) as a special time for Jewish women, their gatherings and rituals.

Women and men outside mainstream religions are also devising women-affirming religious rituals. During the second wave of feminism, women began looking outside mainstream religions to find spiritual resources, and by the late 1960s, a number of women were part of the feminist Wicca movement, identifying with the indigenous basic religions of Europe, honoring the Earth and women, and worshiping a Great Goddess as well as goddesses and gods they believed were repressed during the Burning Times. Feminist Wiccans reclaimed the word "witch" as referring to the wise women to whom people went for healing and knowledge about procreative functions, who were demonized by the Inquisition as aligned with Satan and consorting with devils. The Wicca movement has spread and is now considered part of a diverse Pagan movement. Feminist witches and Pagans have been prolific in publishing books of rituals. *The Spiral Dance: A Rebirth of the Ancient Religion of the Goddess* (1979) by Starhawk is a noteworthy example.[108] The Wicca movement consists of covens of women and men, women-only groups such as Dianic covens, and numerous solitary practitioners. Since the first Pagan Census conducted by sociologist Helen A. Berger in 1993–1995, the number of solitary practitioners has increased from 51 percent of contemporary Pagans to 78 percent of contemporary Pagans, as revealed in Berger's census of 2009–2010.[109]

For their part, feminist Christian women also began devising their own rituals, affirming women's bodies and life cycles, reinterpreting the story of Eve, and sharing religious specialist roles, in what Catholic theologian Rosemary Radford Ruether has termed Women-Church. This movement provides ritual spaces set aside from mainstream Christian worship that participants find meaningful.[110]

Inside mainstream religions, religious specialists are increasingly using gender inclusive language for human beings and God in liturgies.

Often these changes are inserted by the minister or rabbi into the liturgy without comment to avoid alienating conservative members of the congregation. These changes may be made explicitly by congregations and denominations out of a commitment to equality. Sometimes inclusive language is resisted and androcentric language is retained to avoid encouraging change, as occurred, for instance, with the 1994 English translation of the *Catechism of the Catholic Church* in which the gender-inclusive language of an earlier translation was changed to sexist language using "man" or "men" to describe all human beings.[111]

Religious Traditions and LGBTQ Persons

Religious traditions and religious organizations, as well as the individuals that take part in them, take different positions on whether LGBTQ persons have rights and freedoms equal to those of heterosexual persons. The issue of LGBTQ rights is an important part of the story of women in religions.

LBGT studies, according to religious studies scholar Melissa M. Wilcox, "refers to scholarly works that attempt to add the experiences of lesbians, gay men, bisexuals, and/or transgender people to existing disciplines or schools of thought." "Queer theory" refers "to analytical approaches that radically challenge societal norms and assumptions regarding gender and sexuality."[112] Therefore, the scope of LGBTQ studies overlaps with women and gender studies, and queer theory overlaps and parallels the goals and outlooks of feminist scholarship.

In the United States in the late 1960s, about the time of the Civil Rights movement and second-wave feminism, lesbian, gay, bisexual, and transsexual persons began to speak up and advocate for their equal rights in society and also in their religions. LGBTQ persons in all countries seek equality in civil rights, respect for their personhood, their right to express their love for those they choose, and freedom from violence. Where religious or secular cultures begin to permit it, LGBTQ persons seek equality in marriage, inheritance, the right to be with hospitalized partners, spousal health insurance, and respect for their children. LGBTQ persons may seek to become religious leaders in their religious traditions. In some religions they are welcome, but in many they are not.

Melissa M. Wilcox points out that heterosexuals' obsession with sexual activities of LGBTQ persons

> erases our identities as whole persons and reduces us to sexual bodies. It also has a second effect that is particularly destructive in the context of religion: in changing "LGB people" to "homosexuality" it narrows our sexual orientations from identities to acts. Thus religious organizations can more easily suggest that "homosexuality" is simply a behavior, something that one learned in the past and that one can unlearn in the future.[113]

Since the 1970s a number of conservative Christian organizations have been created to administer "conversion therapy," also called "reparative therapy," to "change" a person's "sexual orientation or gender identity or expression." Some persons, especially minors, may be subjected to reparative therapy against their will. Reparative therapy is not supported by the American Psychological Association as being beneficial to the patient. Instead the APA has issued a statement concluding "that homosexuality per se is not a mental disorder" and stating that the APA "encourages mental health professionals to avoid misrepresenting the efficacy of sexual orientation change efforts."[114] By 2020, conversion therapy for minors was banned by twenty states in the United States.[115]

When society permits it, LGBTQ persons may form their own religious organizations. For instance, the Metropolitan Community Churches were initiated in 1968 in Southern California to welcome LGBTQ persons in Christian worship. From there it has grown to become an international movement with 160 affiliated churches, 45 emerging congregations, and 7 oasis congregations in 33 countries.[116] The majority of the ministers are LGBTQ persons. MCC congregations welcome everyone, including heterosexual persons.

Some religious denominations have taken steps to include LGBTQ persons in worship and leadership. For instance, in the Episcopal Church in 2004, Gene Robinson (b. 1947), an openly gay man, was consecrated Bishop of New Hampshire, causing great dissension and threatened schism within the Anglican Communion. In 2010, Mary Glasspool (b. 1954), who is openly lesbian, was consecrated Bishop Suffragan of Los Angeles, again causing disruption in the Anglican Communion; she was the seventeenth woman bishop consecrated in the Episcopal Church. In 2012, the Episcopal Church's General Convention approved the admission of transsexual and transgender persons to its clergy and lay leadership roles. The General Convention also approved a blessing ceremony for same-sex couples.

In the United States, the Reform, Reconstructionist, and Conservative denominations of Judaism ordain gay and lesbian rabbis and perform same-sex marriage ceremonies. The Unitarian Universalist Association and the United Church of Christ ordain gay and lesbian ministers and perform same-sex marriages. The Religious Society of Friends (Quakers) performs same-sex marriages.[117]

In 2009, the Evangelical Lutheran Church in America (ELCA) passed a resolution to ordain qualified persons who were in committed same-sex relationships and immediately experienced a drop in membership and donations, especially in the southern states. In 2013, the ELCA consecrated its first openly gay bishop when Guy Erwin (b. 1598) became bishop of the ELCA's Southwest California Synod. The Presbyterian Church U.S.A. ordains openly gay, lesbian, and bisexual persons as ministers. In 2012 Katie Ricks became the first open lesbian to be ordained a Presbyterian minister.

Same-sex marriage is a topic of heated dispute in religious communities in many nations. SHIH Chao-hwei (b. 1957), a Mahāyāna Buddhist nun, social activist, and educator in Taiwan, became the first person to officiate at a same-sex marriage in Asia, when she married two lesbians and stood in as parent of one of the brides in 2012.[118] In May 2017 Taiwan's Constitutional Court ruled that prohibition of same-sex marriage contradicted the Taiwan Constitution's guarantee of equality. The court gave Taiwan's legislature two years to amend marriage laws to bring them into conformity with the Constitution. On May 24, 2019, Taiwan became the first Asian nation to legalize marriage equality when the new law went into effect.

In May 2015, Ireland became the first country in the world to make same-sex marriage legal as the result of a nationwide referendum, thereby demonstrating that the majority of Ireland's citizens had moved beyond the Roman Catholic Church's influence on matters of marriage and sexual ethics.[119] By 2015 in the United States, same-sex marriages were recognized as legal in thirty-seven states and the District of

SHIH Chao-hwei (seated, bottom row, middle) with the two brides, YU Ya-ting and HUANG Mei-yu, after officiating at the first same-sex marriage in Taiwan in 2012. Same-sex marriage was legalized in Taiwan in 2019. Courtesy of the Hongshi Buddhist Theological School.

Columbia. On June 26, 2015, the United States Supreme Court declared that it was unconstitutional for states not to recognize same-sex marriages as legal. There was great rejoicing at this legalization of same-sex marriages by many in all states even while it caused consternation among many religious conservatives.

Native Americans living on reservations in the United States and First Nations people living on reserves in Canada constitute separate nations that pass and administer their own tribal laws while also being subject to federal laws and law enforcement. First Nations and Native American peoples have diverse cultural traditions, with a number of them having honored spiritual and life-roles for persons who do not conform to binary gender roles and work as determined by sex. All First Nations and Native American cultures have been disrupted by the colonialism of European Christians, which caused loss of the majority of their ancestral lands, a diminishing of traditional religious identities, and changes in gender roles. Many First Nations and Native Americans people have adopted a homophobia based on Christian scripture and teachings. In 1990 lesbian and gay Native Americans coined the term *two-spirit* or *two-spirited* to express identity as a woman-man or man-woman. "Using the term 'two-spirit' emphasizes the spiritual aspect of one's life and downplays the homosexual persona."[120] By 2015 some Native American tribes on reservations had legalized same-sex marriage, but many continue to prohibit it. Because of tribal sovereignty on reservations, the United States Supreme Court decision in favor of legalization of same-sex marriage did not enforce a change of laws prohibiting same-sex marriages on reservations.

LGBTQ children growing up in conservative religions can receive pushback and rejection if they make their sexual or gender orientation known publicly. On May 7, 2017, twelve-year-old Savannah stood before her Mormon congregation in Utah County, Utah, to give her testimony about her conviction that her Heavenly Parents "did not mess up when they gave me freckles, or when they made me gay. God loves me just this way because I believe that he loves all of his creations." Savannah went on to describe her aspirations to date, go to college, find a partner, get a good job, get married, and have a family. She said, "I want to love myself and not feel ashamed for being me," but before she could go on, her microphone was cut off, and a church leader asked her to sit down.[121] Her mother led Savannah, sobbing, outside to reassure her that she is perfect the way she is. Some members of the congregation came out to comfort Savannah, and they asked her to read her statement in full to them as they sat on the grass.

Savannah and her mother were interviewed by psychologist John Dehlin on June 19, 2017, for his *Mormon Stories* podcast. Savannah explained that she wanted to make her testimony "because I would say my religion wasn't treating the LGBTs the way they should be treated, and they deserve respect and support for who they are, and they just want to be loved for that, and a lot of people aren't doing that." Her mother explained why she and Savannah's father decided to let her come out to the congregation, although they knew there could be a backlash: "We . . . talked it over and decided that showing our support to her in being authentic was more important than what other people might think." Savannah flashed a big smile in response to her mom's statement.

Savannah reported that of her congregation's members she received the most affirmation from the young women. At the time of the interview with Dehlin, she was not inclined to go back to church.[122]

In June 2019, during Pride Month, the Vatican issued a statement concerning transgender persons. Cardinal Giuseppe Versaldi, prefect, and Archbishop Angelo Vincenzo Zani, secretary, of the Vatican's Congregation for Catholic Education, released "some reflections" in a document titled "'Male and Female He Created Them': Towards a Path of Dialogue on the Question of Gender Theory in Education." In it, the authors express concern about what they term "transgenderism," which they view as arising from incorrect education in schools about "gender theory" instead of correct education on gender complementarity as taught by popes. Although the authors articulate a desire to promote respectful dialogue and inclusive listening, their document cites only other published statements from Vatican departments and popes. "'Male and Female He Created Them'" reflects no effort to listen to transgender people. It cites no publications by scholars and scientists who study sex and gender. The authors encourage Catholic educators to engage sensitively and patiently in the formation of young people to adopt complementary gender roles in "an environment of trust, calmness and openness," which does not promote "unjust discrimination," while conveying to students the knowledge that they are loved.[123] It remains to be seen if, and how, this statement will affect transgender students attending Catholic schools and universities. Reverend James Martin, S.J., author of *Building a Bridge: How the Catholic Church and the LGBT Community Can Enter into a Relationship of Respect, Compassion, and Sensitivity* (2018), has reflected that "sadly, [the document] will be used as a cudgel against transgender people, and an excuse to argue that they shouldn't even exist."[124]

The rights of LGBTQ persons to live, thrive, marry, raise their children, participate in their religions, and serve as religious leaders will continue to be contested throughout the world for some time. Scholar Melissa Wilcox concludes that the contemporary decline in membership of organized religious denominations with the concomitant increase in religious individualism in many parts of the world is conducive to LGBTQ persons having the social space "to create their own religious identities rather than accepting the identities shaped for them by family, friends, society, religious leaders, and the like."[125] LGBTQ persons wish to be seen as fully human with the same range of talents and capacities as heterosexual persons, and they assert that LGBTQ persons should have the freedom to develop and use their talents and live as they deem best without being oppressed and/or harmed by religious persons and religious organizations. If they have allegiance to religious traditions, they wish to be acknowledged as full-fledged members in their faiths.

The Extent to Which a Religion Is Moving beyond Patriarchy

The eleventh issue to be examined in order to understand the status of women in a religious tradition is the extent to which the religion is changing and moving beyond patriarchy. Some religious traditions and denominations are moving beyond patriarchy at different paces, whereas other religious cultures and denominations have been refusing to make changes. Not infrequently there is backlash on the part of conservatives against feminism and changing roles for girls and women in society and religion.[126] In many patriarchal religions and cultures, the present is often quite bleak for women who are subjected to numerous forms of subordination, oppression, coercion, and violence.[127]

In literate religious traditions, women have been articulate about the changes they desire and for which they are working, and these aspirations have been preserved in durable media. In oral religious cultures, women are articulate about their lives and circumstances, but until a literate researcher records their voices, their views are not widely accessible. It is important to hear and learn from women's aspirations for equality in their societies and religious traditions and their work to accomplish their goals. Women's new gender roles as they have been conceptualized in the west have flaws and are often not appealing to women working for equality in their respective religious societies.

One example of religious backlash against changing gender roles in the United States, which has spread its influence abroad, is the Christian Patriarchy movement among conservative Protestants. Christian Patriarchy stresses male headship in evangelical Christian marriages based on a literalist reading of Bible passages. Related to this is the Quiverfull movement in which Christian couples do not use contraception and have as many children as they believe the Lord intends for the wife to bear. These parents homeschool their children to socialize them into conservative Christian values and gender roles. Articulate women in the Christian Patriarchy and Quiverfull movements have created careers for themselves by holding workshops and retreats and writing blogs and books instructing other women about how to be full-time homemakers who subordinate themselves to their husbands. Women and men in these movements see feminism and contraception as the tools of Satan. They are adamantly opposed to marriage equality for LGBTQ persons.[128]

Women in Religions Today

In the twenty-first century, we are seeing the gradual—and uneven— decline of patriarchy in societies and their religions due to changes in technology and economy and the erosion of a strict division of labor between women and men. As economic, social, and educational factors change, religious cultures are starting to move beyond patriarchy at different rates. There is also plenty of regression in relation to women's status and welfare in society. When analyzing the status of women in specific religious cultures, it is informative to examine the eleven issues that affect the status of girls and women highlighted in this chapter.

Conclusion

This book has argued for an economic theory of women in religions in conjunction with several psychological theories. Its thesis has centered on the development of patriarchy, how patriarchy may be transformed, and issues that need to be understood by persons wishing to promote equality of women in societies and their religions. Drawing on the work of anthropologists and archaeologists, it has argued that the available technology shapes economy and the ways that women and men divide labor; this, in turn, leads to the social construction of gender roles, which are then reinforced as the norm by religious myths, scriptures, rituals, and law codes. A culture's gender customs and values impact the psychology of girls and boys, women and men, who may draw on religious elements to appropriate gender roles as constructed in society or to attempt to broaden or escape those gender expectations. When the available technology changes, the economy changes, as do the ways that women and men divide labor and the ways that gender is socially constructed. If the cumulative changes are in the direction toward women's increasing equality in families and society, women will begin to demand equality in their religious traditions, or they will relocate to religions more supportive of equality, or they will leave religions altogether. In the archaeological, ethnographic, and historical records, no straight line can be traced from egalitarianism to subordination of women, and in contemporary times there is no straight line moving from subordination to equality. However, factors and dynamics supportive of subordination of women and those supportive of women's equality with men can be discerned.

Gender roles are the products of complex processes, and religious worldviews and conceptions of gender interact with each other in complex ways. Religious traditions that have been shaped within patriarchal cultures are internally diverse; therefore, they contain resources that can be used to support women's equality as well as other resources that can be used to support the subordination of women.

Which types of resources are emphasized is influenced by the economic structures of the society and related gender roles, and whether there is a social expectation of equality or not.

We have learned that the division of labor by sex is influenced by available technology and the resulting economy. Decisions about division of labor by sex influence gender roles and whether or not roles for women and men are strongly distinct. A society's views of gender are reflected in its concepts of a deity or deities, stories and myths, heroes and heroines, religious customs, rituals, including rites of passage, scriptures, and religious law codes. Division of labor by sex led to a long series of economic consequences, which from the beginning allocated to men the most prestigious social roles, including proficiency in weapons, and thus, to military and political power. As long as women are involved in the production of the primary resources for subsistence, the roles of women and men are relatively balanced in families and societies. Generally, when women have access to economic productivity, a religious culture will express respect for women and be more likely to have female religious leaders.

When women do not have access to economic productivity, the culture and its religions are patriarchal. When men control the land and farming in horticultural and intensive agricultural societies, and men are less involved in childrearing (even though the children belong to the father and his patrilineage), social customs such as patrilineal inheritance and patrilocal residence of spouses, along with religious law codes, create conditions in which men—and frequently older women—restrict, subordinate, and oppress girls and women.

Patriarchy is produced by complex combinations of technological, economic, and psychological factors that shape gender roles in family and social structures. Patriarchy, which took millennia to develop into its classical forms, is based on division of labor by sex, which in prehistory was shaped by climate and the technology available for subsistence. This division of labor led to cultures attributing different characteristics to females and males. Societies have variously divided the labor between women and men, but in many societies women have primary responsibility for the care of infants and small children.

In classical patriarchy, sex segregation allocates economic, political, and religious empowerment in public arenas to men, and restricts many of the activities of mid- to upper-class women to the domestic sphere. Classical patriarchy frequently involves the enslavement of classes of women and men. Constructions of gender in classical patriarchy are reflected in the society's gods and goddesses, myths, religious leadership roles, rituals, and worship customs.

Women in classical patriarchy frequently collude with men to perpetuate women's subordination for a variety of reasons, including women's own gender socialization, lack of self-esteem, internalized misogyny, and gaining privileges in return for voluntary subordination. It is not unusual for women to punish other women who refuse to conform to the subordinate female role. Religious scriptures, law codes, and customs are frequently invoked to make members of society conform to patriarchal gender roles. Witch hunts are a means to get rid of women who are deemed not properly subservient to the authority of men.

While anthropologists have traced the emergence of patriarchy to the division of labor by sex, according to feminist scholarly analysis, the end of patriarchy will be accomplished when division of labor by sex is broken down, fathers are involved in childrearing, there is no stigma against same-sex couples raising children, and women have access to the ability to gain economic resources that they can distribute to family members. Anthropologist Ernestine Friedl asserts,

> Only as controllers of valued resources can women achieve prestige, power, and equality.
>
> Within the household, women who bring in income from jobs are able to function on a more nearly equal basis with their husbands. Women who contribute services to their husbands and children without pay . . . are especially vulnerable to dominance.[1]

As women directly acquire valued resources to support themselves and distribute to others in their families, they gain greater equality in their marriages, families, and societies. Such women have a basis on which to work for equality in their religious traditions.

When division of labor by sex is diminished, then qualities of intellect, talent, temperament, and physical ability are much more likely to be regarded as being present in various ways among individuals, and are no longer attributed solely to one sex. Friedl points out, "In many countries where women no longer devote most of their productive years to childbearing, they are beginning to demand a change in the social relationship of the sexes."[2]

As women are acquiring equality in society, they are expecting equality in their religious traditions. As part of the movement beyond patriarchy, women seek to educate themselves in their religions, so they know the rights accorded to them and can then struggle to have their rights recognized. Women in many religious traditions are doing the research to recover the stories of foremothers to serve as inspiring models as they build up their self-esteem and engage in work to achieve equal rights in religions and societies. Women in mainstream religions and in alternative religions are developing feminist theologies, rituals, and liturgies that include and affirm women. Women are working to make religious leadership, theology, and symbols inclusive of women. If the majority of the members of their religious tradition are resistant to incorporating changes that affirm women's equality, women desiring equality may leave the religion for other meaningful options.

Religious leadership is opening up to women in various ways. Women in religious traditions with written scriptures and law codes assert that they should have access to institutionally credentialed roles of religious leadership. Women in organized religions are no longer relying solely on charisma—believed access to unseen sources of authority—which has empowered exceptional women to become religious specialists in the past and present.[3]

Many women are working to change patriarchal religions, while others are helping to shape new religious movements.[4] Within internally diverse religious traditions, women are mining the resources they can use to promote women's equality. They are utilizing those resources to increase social expectations of equality and to counteract religious resources that are used to subordinate women to men. Women's support by and partnership with informed, egalitarian men is crucial in facilitating movement beyond patriarchy.

Although women's struggle for human rights and equality will continue to be a long one, information technology is being utilized to promote change more rapidly in many countries and moving agricultural and/or industrialized countries into the global information age. This continues the process of breaking down the division of labor by sex that was begun by industrialization. Economies in which women and men perform similar and overlapping tasks in the workplace and in the home produce societies in which women are valued equally with men. Increasingly in the future, each person will be able to strive to be fully human rather than remaining confined to patriarchal gender roles.

Information technology and international travel enable women in different countries to learn of each other's challenges and strategies for empowerment. More and more women are finding that by working with each other and with feminist men, practical solutions can be found to alleviate the suffering of girls and women and to achieve equality.

With globalization, which involves among other things interdependent national economies and rapid communications and travel, perhaps the movement out of patriarchy will not take the thousands of years it took for classical patriarchy, the most extreme form of patriarchy, to develop. The myths, theologies, and law codes of religious traditions are under pressure to change to validate women's equality. Growing numbers of women are gaining education in their religious traditions, thereby becoming empowered to critique and work to reform their religious cultures.

Given certain economic and social circumstances, women who feel restricted in their patriarchal religions increasingly have the option of adopting a different religious affiliation. Women will continue the trend of abandoning their birth religions to create their own egalitarian religions or of leaving religion altogether.[5]

Feminist women who remain in their religious traditions and those who leave to create or join alternative religions have many outlooks and concerns in common. They influence each other in their shared tasks of creating feminist theologies, ethics, liturgies, music and art, styles of leadership, and institutions.[6] Persons committed to patriarchy in religions and societies find this development highly threatening.

An insightful student who took my "Women in World Religions" course in 2016 concluded after reading material I had drafted for this book:

> It's kind of like a slow religious revolution. Women have been gaining more power and assuming some of the "traditional male roles." They're reshaping laws, reimagining and reinterpreting scripture and stories.

Even the nuns mentioned in the beginning of [this] book who were seen as radical by the Vatican are a part of this new way of rethinking and reimagining females and their role in religion. Women are making changes in the way they practice religion. It makes me wonder about what will be accomplished in this process.

She then went on to ask a number of questions about the continued developments in the future for women in religions:

Will we see more texts from females that are considered religious texts? Will women start creating new religions or sub-religions of their current one . . . ? Will we see more women pastors, even women priests and other female religious leaders? Will we start to see people who are openly a part of the LGBTQ+ community start to assume more religious positions and roles . . . as time goes on?

We are living in a transitional period in which patriarchy is slowly being transformed and some persons are responding by embracing and promoting equality for girls and women, while others in patriarchal religions are clinging to the old theologies, religious polities, and views of gender. Updating Friedl's statement about future prospects for women, we may say: "As women gain access to positions that control the exchange of resources, male dominance may become archaic, and industrial [and information-age] societies may one day become . . . egalitarian."[7]

This will be a long process, because there is considerable resistance to women's equality in patriarchal religious cultures. Some male leaders resist women's attempts to become religious specialists, some men block the education of girls and women, many men exercise control over women's bodies and their reproductive power, and some male religious leaders seek to control women who are vowed celibate religious. At the same time, particular religious traditions are opening leadership positions to women, creating rituals that include women in the category of human being, formulating rituals that affirm girls and women, and highlighting important foremothers. Women and men are also creating new religious movements that affirm women, promote women's religious leadership, and imagine the divine as female, androgynous, or impersonal.[8]

We live in challenging times as more women and men make choices and work to create egalitarian families, religions, and societies. Others work against greater inclusiveness and equality of women, while even more people are not in social contexts where they are able to make choices concerning the empowerment of girls and women. The status of women in religions and societies will continue to be contested, but in particular areas and religious organizations improvement can be discerned.

QUESTIONS FOR DISCUSSION

INTRODUCTION: WHY STUDY WOMEN IN RELIGIONS?

1. How do you think education and economic empowerment of women might influence the status of women in religions?
2. The text argues that technology, economy, and gender roles influence characteristics of religion, and that characteristics of religion influence socially constructed gender roles. When technology, economy, and gender roles change, there is pressure on the religion to change. What are examples that might illustrate this thesis?
3. What are some other challenges facing women in religions that you have seen in the news or experienced firsthand?

CHAPTER 1: FOUNDATIONS, METHODOLOGY, AND RELEVANT TERMS

1. Would you call yourself a feminist? Why or why not?
2. What contributions to women's equality have been made by people who have considered themselves feminists?
3. How have feminism and religion been connected in the past? Do feminism and religion go together?
4. What is "intersectionality" and how might it contribute to understanding women in religions?
5. What does historian of religions Rita M. Gross mean by "quadruple androcentrism," and how does it relate to women in religions?
6. What are some important questions to explore in relation to the study of women in religions?
7. How is feminism relevant to the study of women in religions?
8. What do feminist scholars mean by the terms *sex*, *sexuality*, and *gender*?
9. What are some of the ways that we "do gender" in our lives? How is "doing gender" related to women in religions?
10. What is classical patriarchy and how is it related to women in religions?

11. What does historian Gerda Lerner mean by "paternalistic dominance"? Is paternalistic dominance necessarily related to the mistreatment of daughters and wives? How do you think paternalistic dominance might be manifested in religions?

12. Why do you think women might collude with men to perpetuate patriarchy in families, societies, and religions?

CHAPTER 2: THE ECONOMIC THEORY OF THE EMERGENCE
AND TRANSFORMATION OF PATRIARCHY

1. What are the shortcomings of the invasion theory of the origin of patriarchy? What purpose has the invasion theory of the origin of patriarchy served for feminist women and men?

2. What are your views on the economic theory of the emergence and transformation of patriarchy? Does it make sense to you? Why or why not?

3. According to the economic theory presented, what are the factors that support the emergence and perpetuation of patriarchy and ultimately the transformation of patriarchal society?

4. What do you think the female figurines from the Paleolithic and the Neolithic indicate about prehistoric religion and actual women?

5. What were women's likely roles and statuses at the beginning of the Neolithic? What were women's roles and statuses by the end of the Neolithic? What socioeconomic factors contributed to this change?

6. What does archaeology tell us about women and men, gender roles, and religion at the Neolithic town of Çatalhöyük? What do you think were women's roles in the religion and society at Çatalhöyük?

7. What were the economic contributions of Apache women when the Apaches were egalitarian foragers, and how did the Apache religion reflect women's gender roles?

8. In the Yorùbá culture in southwest Nigeria, what are the gender roles and traditional economic activities of women and men, and how are these reflected in the indigenous Yorùbá religion?

9. What did archaeologist Jeannine Davis-Kimball learn about women's roles in the pastoral cultures of the Eurasian Steppe, where the dead were buried in *kurgans*? Do you think women were equal or subordinated in the steppe societies and their religions? What types

of work, including religious work, did women do, and how is it known to archaeologists?

10. What is the economic basis of society in the North Indian village of Karimpur, and what are the roles for women and men in that society? What is the significance of *vratas* (vows) for the Hindu women living in Karimpur?

CHAPTER 3: PSYCHOLOGICAL THEORIES OF GENDER ROLES AND WOMEN'S SELF-ESTEEM

1. According to feminist psychological theories, what are the factors that support the emergence and perpetuation of patriarchy? What psychological factors contribute to the transformation of patriarchy toward egalitarian families, societies, and religions?

2. What is your opinion of the psychoanalytic theories of Nancy Chodorow and Dorothy Dinnerstein of why people resist having women in positions of authority? What sorts of evidence supports or contradicts these theories? What sorts of changes do Chodorow and Dinnerstein suggest are needed to end the social and psychological reproduction of patriarchy? What is your opinion of their proposed changes?

3. According to psychologist Linda E. Olds, what is the problem with dichotomous thinking? How does she describe a *feminine-identified woman*, a *masculine-identified man*, and *androgynous women and men*? How do these different types of individuals "do gender"? What are the social advantages and disadvantages of each way of "doing gender"? How do these different ways of "doing gender" relate to women in religions?

4. Feminist activist Gloria Steinem argues that there is need for women to experience a "revolution from within" in regard to their personal self-esteem in addition to social revolution toward equality. What is your opinion of Steinem's thesis? How does her stress on the need for women's self-esteem and ways to accomplish it relate to religions?

CHAPTER 4: ISSUES FOR WOMEN IN RELIGIONS

1. What are factors that support equality and subordination of women in religions? How might factors supporting equality be optimized in a religious tradition?

2. What are your opinions of the examples given of issues affecting women in religions? Do any other issues need to be considered when assessing the status of women in a religious culture?

3. How are *distinct gender roles* manifested and reinforced in religions? What is your opinion of strongly distinct gender roles? What are the ways they affect women's lives?

4. What does *complementarity* mean in relation to gender roles? How might this view of gender manifest in religions?

5. What does *mutuality* mean when discussing gender roles? How might this view of gender manifest in religions and religious practice?

6. What are the various religious specialist roles that might be available to women?

7. What are the social circumstances that make different types of religious leadership roles available to women?

8. How is *charisma* defined in the text? What is the significance of *charisma* to women's religious leadership?

9. What are the different expressions of *shamanism*, and how do they relate to women in religions?

10. What are the different ways that a woman may gain *credentials* to be a religious leader?

11. What can the study of goddesses reveal about how real women are viewed in a religious culture? Do goddesses necessarily promote the equality of women?

12. What are examples of rituals that tell us something about women's religious lives? Do you think these rituals benefit women in some way, or do they disempower women religiously and socially? How?

13. What is the relevance of LGBTQ studies and queer theory to the study of women in religions?

14. What are the factors that are needed to move women in religions beyond patriarchy toward equality?

CONCLUSION

1. What kinds of changes are we seeing in societies and religions today? Where is continued resistance to women's equality manifested and what form is it taking? What are women and men doing to try to overcome the resistance to women's equality in society and religions?

2. What changes are needed in religious societies or organizations that oppress women? What are the types of factors that will support those changes?
3. What do you think will be the most strategic approach to enhancing the status of women: work to improve women's status in society, or work to improve women's status in religion?
4. Where do you think we are going in terms of women and gender roles in society and in religions?

FOR FURTHER READING

Anderson, Leona M., and Pamela Dickey Young, eds. *Women and Religious Traditions*, 3rd ed. Oxford: Oxford University Press, 2015.

Bednarowski, Mary Farrell. *The Religious Imagination of American Women*. Bloomington: Indiana University Press, 1999.

De-Gaia, Susan, ed. *Encyclopedia of Women in World Religions: Faith and Culture*, 2 vols. Santa Barbara: CA: ABC-CLIO, 2019.

Falk, Nancy Auer, and Rita M. Gross, eds. *Unspoken Worlds: Women's Religious Lives*, 3rd ed. Belmont, CA: Wadsworth/Thomson Learning, 2001.

Gross, Rita M. *Feminism and Religion: An Introduction*. Boston: Beacon Press, 1996.

Holm, Jean, with John Bowker, eds. *Women in Religion*. New York: Pinter, 1994.

Keller, Rosemary Skinner, and Rosemary Radford Ruether, eds., with Marie Cantlon, assoc. ed. *Encyclopedia of Women and Religion in North America*, 3 vols. Bloomington: Indiana University Press, 2006.

Machacek, David W., and Melissa M. Wilcox, eds. *Sexuality and the World's Religions*. Santa Barbara, CA: ABC-CLIO, 2003.

Moore, Rebecca, and Catherine Wessinger, eds. *Women in the World's Religions and Spirituality Project*. https://wrldrels.org. Accessed April 8, 2020.

Sered, Susan Starr. *Priestess, Mother, Sacred Sister: Religions Dominated by Women*. New York: Oxford University Press, 1994.

Sharma, Arvind, ed. *Religion and Women*. Albany: State University of New York Press, 1994.

———, ed. *Women in World Religions*. Albany: State University of New York Press, 1987.

Sharma, Arvind, and Katherine K. Young, eds. *Her Voice, Her Faith: Women Speak on World Religions*. Cambridge, MA: Westview Press, 2003.

Vance, Laura. *Women in New Religions*. New York: New York University Press, 2015.

Wessinger, Catherine, ed. *Religious Institutions and Women's Leadership: New Roles Inside the Mainstream*. Columbia: University of South Carolina Press, 1996.

———, ed. *Women's Leadership in Marginal Religions: Explorations outside the Mainstream*. Urbana: University of Illinois Press, 1993.

NOTES

INTRODUCTION

1 By "history of religions" I am not referring to the "history of religions" formulated by Mircea Eliade. See Baird, *Category Formation and the History of Religions*. The history of religions approach taken here is generally termed "religious studies" to refer to the academic study of religions, their histories, development, scriptures, beliefs, practices, cultures, artistic expressions, and social organizations.

2 This was first demonstrated to me very clearly by Ruether's "Christianity."

3 I thank my colleague Elizabeth Goodine, Loyola University New Orleans, for emphasizing this point in a conversation.

4 *Catechism of the Catholic Church*, 2nd ed., paragraph 2357, states: "Homosexual acts are contrary to the natural law. They close the sexual act to the gift of life. They do not proceed from a genuine affective and sexual complementarity. Under no circumstances can they be approved." Paragraph 2359 says, "Homosexual persons are called to chastity." Paragraph 2358 states that while the homosexual "inclination" is "objectively disordered," men and women with this inclination are to be treated with "respect, compassion, and sensitivity," and not subjected to "unjust discrimination." Available at http://www.scborromeo.org/ccc (accessed June 19, 2019).

5 Many of the sisters' communities have founded and operate hospitals and other healthcare facilities.

6 Congregatio pro Doctrina Fidei, "Doctrinal Assessment, 1, 8.

7 Sartain et al., "Joint Final Report."

8 Sanders, "Leadership Conference of Women Religious (LCWR)."

9 Holland et al., "Statement of the LCWR Officers."

10 Welker, "Mormon Women Knock at the Door."

11 See Wessinger, "Seeking Equality in the LDS Church."

12 Equality Now, website.

13 Ordain Women, website.

14 Notably, according to Rita Banerjee, "The 2011 census of India shows that the highest rates of elimination of girls through sex-selection and infanticide is not in the poorest states of India, but in the wealthiest states and cities, such as in Punjab and Haryana, and the cities of Delhi and Chandigarh." "Why Education and Economics Are Not the Solution."

15 Sanghavi, Bhalla, and Das, "Fire-Related Deaths in India in 2001."

16 Sirohi, *Sita's Curse*.

17 "Advice on How to Protect Yourself from Dowry Extortion and Violence."

18 Filkins, "Afghan Girls."

19 Yousafzai and Lamb, *I Am Malala*.

20 Tsomo, "Is the Bhikṣuṇī Vinaya Sexist?" See also Tsomo, *Women in Buddhist Traditions*.

21 Sakyadhita: International Association of Buddhist Women, website.

22 Lee and Han, "Mother and Moral Activist." In this book, in East Asian names, the family name is put in upper and lower case small caps the first time it is mentioned in a chapter. Thereafter in the same chapter, the small caps are not used.

23 Tsomo, "Khunying Kanitha."

24 de Silva, "Reclaiming the Robe."

25 Observe the different views of laypeople toward the Thai nuns in the Al Jazeera report "Everywoman—Buddhist Nun and Hijab Fashion," from :00 to 6:04 minutes: Laypeople are donating food to the nuns, which indicates acceptance.

26 Samten, "Historic Moment for Buddhist Women"; "Geshema Degree."

27 See Lipscomb, *Battle for the Minds*; Central Baptist Theological Seminary, website.

28 Marshall, "The Peril of Selective Inerrancy."

29 Nadell, "Rabbi, Rabba, Maharat, Rabbanit."

30 Dolsten, "10 Years after the Founding of the First Orthodox School to Train Female Clergy."

31 Seedat, "An Intellectual Mentor"; Elewa and Silvers, "'I Am One of the People."

32 The Women's Mosque of America, website.

33 Gross, *Feminism and Religion*, 94.

34 Crenshaw, "Mapping the Margins."

35 I coined the term "classical patriarchy" in the 1980s for use in my women and religions courses. An anonymous reviewer of the manuscript for this book called to my attention that Deniz Kandiyoti used the term "classic patriarchy" in "Bargaining with Patriarchy," an article published in 1988.

1. FOUNDATIONS, METHODOLOGY, AND KEY TERMS

1 Gross, *Feminism and Religion*, 45–48, discusses the beginnings of feminist religious studies scholarship.

2 My continued use of the phrase "women's religious lives" is a reference to Falk and Gross, *Unspoken Worlds*. The first edition of this groundbreaking collection of studies was published in 1980.

3 Gross, *Feminism and Religion*, 72.

4 Gross, *Feminism and Religion*. See also her *Beyond Androcentrism*.

5 Baird, *Category Formation and the History of Religions*, 18.

6 Gross, *Feminism and Religion*, 9.

7 Gross, *Feminism and Religion*, 9.

8 Allik, "Sex and Finitude."

9 See Wessinger, *The Oxford Handbook of Millennialism*.

10 Brodd et al., *Invitation to World Religions*, 9. I have replaced the word "transcendent" in the definition with "ultimate."

11 Gross, *Feminism and Religion*, 16–17.

12 Aquinas, "Question XCII. The Production of the Woman. (In Four Articles.)," Reply Obj. 1, in Young, *An Anthology of Sacred Texts by and about Women*, 68–69.

13 Part 1, question 6, in Uyl, *Malleus Maleficarum*, 39.

14 Eller, *The Myth of Matriarchal Prehistory*, 15–20, discusses the broad categories of feminism in the second wave.

15 I thank my former colleague at Loyola University New Orleans, Dr. Tiina Allik, for pointing this out many years ago in our feminist conversations.

16 Gross, *Feminism and Religion*, 24.

17 Bem, *The Lenses of Gender*.

18 Gross, *Feminism and Religion*, 17.

19 See the Sojourner Truth Project, website, for historical explanation of the problematic features of the famous account of Sojourner Truth's speech composed twelve years later by Frances Dana Barker Gage, and why the most authentic report of Sojourner Truth's speech is found in the account given by Rev. Marius Robinson, with a digital image of the *Anti-Slavery Bugle* page on which it appeared in 1851.

20 MacHaffie, *Her Story*; Moore, *Women in Christian Traditions*; Bacon, *Mothers of Feminism*.

21 Friedan, *The Feminine Mystique*.

22 Gillis, Howie, and Munford, *Third Wave Feminism*.

23 Walker, *In Search of Our Mothers' Gardens*.

24 Mitchem, *Introducing Womanist Theology*.

25 Isasi-Díaz, *Mujerista Theology*.

26 Aquino and Rosado-Nunes, *Feminist Intercultural Theology*.

27 Sollee, "6 Things to Know about 4th Wave Feminism."

28 See, for example, Sharma and Young, *Her Voice, Her Faith*.

29 Hassan, "Islam"; Badran, *Feminism in Islam*.

30 Oduyoye, *Introducing African Women's Theology*.

31 Kyung, *Struggle to Be the Sun Again*; Lee and Han, "Mother and Moral Activist."

32 Crenshaw, "Mapping the Margins," 1245.

33 Joyce, *Ancient Bodies, Ancient Lives*; Fausto-Sterling, "The Five Sexes." The medical condition known as Klinefelter syndrome, which has various symptoms, is identified when a boy is born with an extra copy of the x chromosome

34 Nanda, *Gender Diversity*, 2.

35 West and Zimmerman, "Doing Gender," 127.

36 West and Zimmerman, "Doing Gender," 137.

37 West and Zimmerman, "Doing Gender," 141.

38 West and Zimmerman, "Doing Gender," 147.

39 Welter, "The Cult of True Womanhood: 1820–1860."

40 Lee and Han, "Mothers and Moral Activists," 54–77; Buddhist Compassion Relief Tzu Chi Foundation, website; Tzu Chi USA, website.

41 Lerner, *The Creation of Patriarchy*, 239.

42 Friedl, *Women and Men*, 7.

43 On the worship of expressions of Durgā in India to support kingship, see Fuller, *The Camphor Flame*, 108–19.

44 Lerner, *Creation of Patriarchy*, 239–40.

45 Lerner, *Creation of Patriarchy*, 240.

46 Eller, *The Myth of Matriarchal Prehistory*.

47 Sanday, *Women in the Center*.

48 Goettner-Abendroth, *Matriarchal Societies*, xxvi.

49 For example, see anthropologist Joan P. Mencher's description of landowning Nayar family organization in the south Malabar region in Kerala, India, prior to increasing division of the Nayar matrilineal family (*taravad*) during late nineteenth and early twentieth centuries, in "The Nayars of South Malabar," 183–85.

50 Ehrenberg, *Women in Prehistory*, 84.

2. THE ECONOMIC THEORY OF THE EMERGENCE AND TRANSFORMATION OF PATRIARCHY

1 The following discussion relies on Friedl, *Women and Men*.

2 Aberle, "Matrilineal Descent in Cross-Cultural Perspective," 661, 665 Table 17-2, 666 Table 17-3, 670–76, 677 Table 17-4, 726.

3 Friedl, *Women and Men*, 8.

4 Kelly, *The Lifeways of Hunter-Gatherers*, 220–22, 224.

5 Renfrew, *Archaeology and Language*, 39.

6 Renfrew, *Archaeology and Language*, 37–39.

7 Renfrew, *Archaeology and Language*, 4.

8 "Before Present" is terminology used by archaeologists to refer to large periods of time.

9 Gimbutas, "Women and Culture in Goddess-Oriented Old Europe"; Gimbutas, *The Language of the Goddess*; Gimbutas, *The Civilization of the Goddess*.

10 Gimbutas, "Women and Culture," 23.

11 Gimbutas, "Women and Culture," 30.

12 Eisler, *The Chalice and the Blade*.

13 Ellwood and McGraw, *Many Peoples, Many Faiths*, 8–9.

14 Eller, "Relativizing the Patriarchy"; Eller, *The Myth of Matriarchal Prehistory*, thoroughly critiques the faulty logic of the invasion theory of the origin of patriarchy articulated in various popular books.

15 For example, see Meskell, "Goddesses, Gimbutas and 'New Age' Archaeology," 76.

16 Tringham and Conkey, "Rethinking Figurines," 39.

17 Renfrew, "Marija Redivivia."

18 Renfrew, *Archaeology and Language*, 182.

19 In 2017 geneticist David Reich presented a lecture in which he concluded that ge-
    netic studies have demonstrated that males with steppe ancestry of the Yamnaya
    people in Eastern Europe near the Ural mountain range spread throughout Eu-
    rope and also into the Indian subcontinent 4,500 years ago. Since the steppe DNA
    of different populations of Europeans and South Asians corresponds strongly with
    Indo-European languages, he believes that this migration of Yamnaya males is
    the source of this large language family. See Reich, "Ancient DNA Suggests Steppe
    Migrations Spread Indo-European Languages." I find it implausible that steppe
    pastoralist males would have migrated without their wives and other women in
    their families. Perhaps as they traveled, steppe pastoralist males, or their male off-
    spring, took wives or concubines from indigenous populations, thus accounting
    for the genetic traces of the male steppe pastoralist line in European and South
    Asian populations.
20 Balter, "Mysterious Indo-European Homeland." See Omrak et al. "Genomic
    Evidence," and Racimo et al., "The Spatiotemporal Spread," for discussions of ge-
    netic studies that support the theory of the movement of Neolithic farmers from
    Anatolia to Europe, as well as the movement of steppe peoples into Europe during
    the Bronze Age.
21 Renfrew, *Archaeology and Language.*
22 Renfrew, *Archaeology and Language,* 96.
23 On division of labor in rice cultivation in India, see Mencher, "Women, Agricul-
    ture and the Sexual Division of Labor."
24 Tringham and Conkey, "Rethinking Figurines," 39.
25 Gross, *Feminism and Religion,* 94.
26 Ehrenberg, *Women in Prehistory.*
27 Adovasio, Soffer, and Page, *The Invisible Sex,* 86, 161–62, 173, 177, 181–82, 185,
    188–92.
28 Kelly, *Lifeways of Hunter-Gatherers.*
29 Friedl, "Society and Sex Roles," 128. This section of the text relies on the anthropo-
    logical analysis in this essay and on Friedl, *Women and Men.*
30 Ehrenberg, *Women in Prehistory,* 54.
31 Lupo and Schmitt, "Upper Paleolithic Net-Hunting," 159.
32 Ehrenberg, *Women in Prehistory,* 41–50.
33 Adovasio, Soffer, and Page, *The Invisible Sex,* 111–13.
34 Nelson, "Diversity of the Upper Palaeolithic 'Venus' Figurines."
35 Ehrenberg, *Women in Prehistory,* 66–69, 74–75.
36 McCoid and McDermott, "Toward Decolonizing Gender."
37 Ehrenberg, *Women in Prehistory,* 74–76.
38 Ochre is pigmented clay, which comes in white, yellow, red, purple, and brown
    colors. Ochres have been used on living and dead bodies and on objects for
    many millennia. Neanderthals, who appeared out of *Homo erectus* populations
    about 230,000 years ago in Europe during the Ice Age, used red ochre in burials.
    Anatomically modern humans emerged in East Africa about 200,000 to 100,000

years ago, and approximately 60,000 years ago started moving out of Africa eastward around the coastline of the Indian Ocean to further points, and northward to Central Asia, although recent archaeological discoveries indicate that humans may have left Africa thousands of years earlier. Ochre has been used by human populations throughout the world, including in some burials. Ehrenberg reports that among the European Paleolithic burials with skeletons that have been identified as male, nearly all the men were buried with stone or bone implements or animal bones and were covered in ochre, while the female burials did not include ochre or grave goods. In the Mesolithic in Europe men and especially older men were more likely to be buried with antlers or stone artifacts and ochre. Women's grave goods may have been made of organic materials that disintegrated, but the use of ochre in male burials is notable, especially compared to the woman that Barbara Tedlock identifies as a shaman. See Tedlock, *The Woman in the Shaman's Body*; Ehrenberg, *Women in Prehistory*, 61–62; Adovasio, Soffer, and Page, *The Invisible Sex*, 190–91; Randolph-Quinney, "The Discovery of Stone Tools in India."

39 Tedlock, *The Woman in the Shaman's Body*, 3–4, 33.

40 Tedlock, *The Woman in the Shaman's Body*, 4.

41 Opler, *An Apache Life-Way*; Opler, *Myths and Tales*; Hoijer, *Chiricahua and Mescalero Apache Texts*; Ball, *In the Days of Victorio*; Boyer and Gayton, *Apache Mothers and Daughters*; Robinson, *Apache Voices*; Stockel, *Chiricahua Apache Women and Children*.

42 Jones, "The Matrilocal Tribe."

43 Stockel, *Chiricahua Apache Women and Children*; Boyer and Gayton, *Apache Mothers and Daughters*; Farrer, *Living Life's Circle*; Farrer, *Thunder Rides a Black Horse*; Talamantez, "Images of the Feminine."

44 Farrer, *Thunder Rides a Black Horse*, 49. For the White Mountain Apaches' version of the girl's puberty ceremony, see the video directed by Gianfranco Norelli, *The Sunrise Dance*; and Jay Cravath and Rick Ench, prod. and dir., *1000 Years of Song: The Apache*.

45 Kelly, *Lifeways of Hunter-Gatherers*, 241–68, quotations on 241, 248, 266.

46 Friedl, *Women and Men*, 53–60, quotation on 57.

47 Adovasio, Soffer, and Page, *The Invisible Sex*, 249.

48 Friedl, *Women and Men*, 63–64.

49 Friedl, *Women and Men*, 61.

50 Adovasio, Soffer, and Page, *The Invisible Sex*, 257–61.

51 Ehrenberg, *Women in Prehistory*, 99–101.

52 Mellaart, *Çatal Hüyük*; Mellaart, *Çatal Hüyük and Anatolian Kilims*; Barstow, "The Prehistoric Goddess."

53 The following information is taken from Hodder, *The Leopard's Tale*; and Hodder, *Religion in the Emergence of Civilization*.

54 Hodder, *The Leopard's Tale*, 7–20.

55 Hodder and Pels, "History Houses"; Whitehouse and Hodder, "Modes of Religiosity at Çatalhöyük."

56 Hodder, *The Leopard's Tale*, 14–15, 17.

57 Meskell, "Twin Peaks," 60.

58 Ehrenberg, *Women in Prehistory*, 70; Mellaart, *Çatal Hüyük*; Mellaart, *Çatal Hüyük and Anatolian Kilims*.

59 Barstow, "The Prehistoric Goddess."

60 Hodder, *The Leopard's Tale*, 39–40; Rountree, "Archaeologists and Goddess Feminists at Çatalhöyük."

61 Pilloud et al., "A Bioarchaeological and Forensic Re-Assessment."

62 Hodder, "Women and Men at Çayalhöyük"; Larsen et al., "Bioarchaeology of Çayalhöyük."

63 Türkcan, "Is It a Goddess or Bear?"

64 Hodder, *The Leopard's Tale*, 50–51, 62, 91–92, 106, 114, 117, 125, 137–39, 141–42, 152, 190–91, 201, 216–17.

65 Hodder, *The Leopard's Tale*, 56–57, 79, 172–75.

66 Hodder, *The Leopard's Tale*, 185, 198–201, 203.

67 Hodder and Meskell, "The Symbolism of Catalhöyük in Its Regional Context," 32–72.

68 Whitehouse and Hodder, "Modes of Religiosity at Çatalhöyük," 129.

69 Whitehouse and Hodder, "Modes of Religiosity at Çatalhöyük," 129.

70 Hodder, *The Leopard's Tale*, 148, 209–10, 259–61.

71 Meskell, "Refiguring the Corpus at Catalhöyük," 152.

72 Hodder, *The Leopard's Tale*, 148–49.

73 Hodder, *The Leopard's Tale*, 207–08, 254–55; Hodder and Meskell, "The Symbolism of Catalhöyük in Its Regional Context," 65.

74 Hodder, *The Leopard's Tale*, 191, 194–97.

75 Hodder, *The Leopard's Tale*, 214, 236, 258.

76 Hodder, *The Leopard's Tale*, 251, 254.

77 Hodder, *The Leopard's Tale*, 237.

78 See Matory, *Sex and the Empire That Is No More*; Bascom, *The Yoruba of Southwestern Nigeria*; Drewal, *Yoruba Ritual*; Olajubu, *Women in the Yoruba Religious Sphere*. See also Olademo, *Women in Yorùbá Religions*.

79 Barber, *I Could Speak until Tomorrow*.

80 Drewal, *Yoruba Ritual*, 184, 190.

81 Drewal, *Yoruba Ritual*, 177–78.

82 Lawal, *The Gèlèdé Spectacle*, 36, 71–82; see also Drewal and Drewal, *Gèlèdè*; and Drewal, "Art and the Perception of Women."

83 McIntosh, *Yoruba Women*; Olademo, *Women in Yorùbá Religions*.

84 Olademo, *Women in Yorùbá Religions*.

85 Davis-Kimball, *Warrior Women*, xiii–xiv, 9, 21–25, 35–45, 45–49, 98–107.

86 Wood, "Shamans at the Centre of the World."

87 Penkala-Gawęcka, "The Way of the Shaman," 42.

88 Vejas, "My Strange Winter"; Osipova, "Washed in Blood."

89 Kelly, *Lifeways of Hunter-Gatherers*, 186–97, discusses the evidence that forag- ers space children by practicing infanticide and that among egalitarian foragers infanticide is not strongly linked to sex selection of children. The exception is among foragers in the Arctic, where there is a preference for sons, because of dependence on the hunting and fishing of men. Kelly points out that it can no longer be argued that lengthy breastfeeding provides effective birth control in spacing children among foragers.

90 Friedl, *Women and Men*, 64–65.

91 Erndl, "Is Shakti Empowering for Women?"; Wessinger, "Woman Guru, Woman Roshi."

92 Wiser and Wiser, *Behind Mud Walls*; Wadley, "No Longer a Wife"; Wadley, "Hindu Women's Family and Household Rites."

93 Wadley, "Hindu Women's Family and Household Rites," 111–12.

94 The Brahman class is given the highest social ranking in the Hindu hierarchical class categorization. In Karimpur, Brahman families are more likely to own farm- land. Wadley, *Struggling with Destiny in Karimpur*, 132–34, 234–42; Wadley, "The Village in 1998," in *Behind Mud Walls*, 324–26, 328, 330–31, 334.

95 Wadley, "The Village in 1998," 335.

96 Lerner, *Creation of Patriarchy*.

97 This and subsequent points on the creation of patriarchy rely on Lerner, *Creation of Patriarchy*.

98 Lerner, *Creation of Patriarchy*, 215.

99 Hodder, *The Leopard's Tale*, 258.

100 Kinsley, *Hindu Goddesses*, 202–03.

101 Welter, "The Cult of True Womanhood"; MacHaffie, *Her Story*; Moore, *Women in Christian Traditions*.

102 The term "re-imagining" is derived from a Christian feminist theology conference held in Minneapolis in 1993, "Re-Imagining: A Global Theological Conference by Women: For Men and Women."

103 Ruether, "Christianity."

3. PSYCHOLOGICAL THEORIES OF GENDER ROLES AND WOMEN'S SELF-ESTEEM

1 Chodorow, *The Reproduction of Mothering*; Chodorow, *Feminism and Psychoana- lytic Theory*.

2 Chodorow cites Karen Horney, "The Dread of Women," *International Journal of Psycho-Analysis* 13 (1932): 348–60.

3 Dinnerstein, *The Mermaid and the Minotaur*.

4 Wessinger, "Charismatic Leaders."

5 Stanley, "The Promise Fulfilled." See also Marder, "Are Women Changing the Rab- binate? A Reform Perspective," who argues that women rabbis often prefer small congregations as being more compatible with their childrearing commitments, and that more male rabbis are making similar career choices.

6 "Women in the U.S. Congress 2020," https://www.cawp.rutgers.edu; and "Women in Statewide Elective Executive Office 2020," Center for American Women and Politics, website.
7 Laughlin, "Who's Minding the Kids?"; Liu, "Who's Minding the Kids? Not Dads."
8 Olds, *Fully Human.*
9 Silsby, "Sociology."
10 American Sociological Association, "ASA Press Release."
11 Steinem, *Revolution from Within.*
12 Quotation from *UNICEF Pakistan News* (May 1990) in Gross, *Wasted Resources, Diminished Lives*, 34.
13 Quotation from *Manushi, A Journal about Women and Society* 33 (1986): 2–3, in Gross, *Wasted Resources, Diminished Lives*, 34.

4. ISSUES FOR WOMEN IN RELIGIONS
1 Nanda, *Gender Diversity*, 11–26.
2 See the Bhagavad Gita.
3 Xu, "Poststructuralist Feminism," 52, 62.
4 Xu, "Poststructuralist Feminism," 63.
5 Xu, "Poststructuralist Feminism," 64.
6 "The Laws of Manu," in Young, *An Anthology of Sacred Texts*, 277–78.
7 Gerhard Cardinal Müller, Preface, in Lopes and Alvaré, *Not Just Good, but Beautiful*, vii.
8 Müller, "Preface," viii.
9 Pope Francis, "Not Just Good, but Beautiful," in Lopes and Alvaré, *Not Just Good, but Beautiful*, 2–5.
10 Farley, "Feminist Consciousness," 53.
11 Novak, "Jewish Marriage."
12 Weiss and Gross-Horowitz, *Marriage and Divorce in the Jewish State.*
13 Lawler, *Marriage and the Catholic Church*, 1–2, 94, 99–101, 105–11; quotation from Pope John Paul II on 109; quotation from Lawler on 111.
14 Ali, *Sexual Ethics and Islam*, 4–5.
15 Ali, *Sexual Ethics and Islam*, 5.
16 Ali, *Sexual Ethics and Islam*, 4, 25.
17 Majeed, *Polygyny*, 132.
18 Harun, "SIS: Islam Recognises Women's Roles"; Sisters in Islam: Empowering Voices for Change, website.
19 Ali, *Sexual Ethics and Islam*, 28.
20 Ali, *Sexual Ethics and Islam*, 28–31.
21 Ali, *Sexual Ethics and Islam*, 41.
22 Bhalotra et al., "The Price of Gold," 1–2.
23 Kishwar, "Destined to Fail."
24 Smith, "Women in Islam," 237, 239.
25 Wessinger, "Woman Guru, Woman Roshi," 128–29.

26 Hoijer, *Chiricahua and Mescalero Apache Texts*, 25–27; see also Opler, *Myths and Tales of the Chiricahua Apache Indians*, 28–73.

27 Also, "respect" avoidance taboos between in-laws meant the father had to avoid his mother-in-law and/or grandmother-in-law who attended the birth. Opler, *An Apache Life-Way*, 6–7, 80–81, 154.

28 Wadley, *Struggling with Destiny in Karimpur*, 37–38.

29 White, *Kiss of the Yoginī*. See Biernacki, "Sex Talk and Gender Rites," for a discussion of *tantra*s (texts) that enjoin the male practitioner to acknowledge the subjectivity of women and to treat all women with respect.

30 Ali, *Sexual Ethics and Islam*, 131.

31 Quoted in Ali, *Sexual Ethics and Islam*, 134.

32 Ali, *Sexual Ethics and Islam*, 135.

33 Gruenbaum, *The Female Circumcision Controversy*, 2–3.

34 Gruenbaum, *The Female Circumcision Controversy*, 3.

35 Toubia, *Female Genital Mutilation*, 32.

36 Toubia, *Female Genital Mutilation*, 21–32; Stop FGM in Kurdistan, website. See information and statistics on FGM provided by UNICEF at "Female Genital Mutilation (FGM)."

37 Boddy, *Wombs and Alien Spirits*.

38 Boddy, "The Normal and the Aberrant," 57.

39 Boddy, "The Normal and the Aberrant," 58.

40 Boddy, "The Normal and the Aberrant," 60.

41 Boddy, "The Normal and the Aberrant," 49.

42 Boddy, "The Normal and the Aberrant," 61–62.

43 Sudan Ministry of Cabinet, Central Bureau of Statistics, "Multiple Indicator Cluster Survey 2014," ix.

44 Walsh, "In a Victory for Women in Sudan."

45 See the various views articulated in Shell-Duncan and Hernlund, *Female Circumcision in Africa*.

46 Ali, *Sexual Ethics and Islam*, 140–41.

47 Barstow, *Witchcraze*, 23–25, 61–62.

48 Barstow, *Witchcraze*, 143–45.

49 Joyce, "Biblical Battered Wife Syndrome"; Sayer et al., "She Left, He Left."

50 Quoted in Aslan, *No God but God*, 70.

51 Osborne, "Saudi Family Therapist Offers Advice." In August 2019, Saudi Arabia's Council of Ministers approved a royal decree issued by Crown Prince Mohammed bin Salman that permits women over age twenty-one to obtain a passport and go out of the country without first obtaining permission from their male guardians. Additionally, employment discrimination protections will extend to women. The extent to which these changes will be implemented remains to be seen, since the male guardianship system remains in place. See van Wagtendonk, "Saudi Arabia Changed Its Guardianship Laws."

52 "About Us," Musawah: For Equality in the Muslim Family, website.

53 Wadud, "The Ethics of *Tawhid* over the Ethics of *Qiwamah*," 273.

54 Sen, "More Than 100 Million Women Are Missing."

55 Toubia, *Female Genital Mutilation*, 32.

56 Wessinger, "Charismatic Leaders in New Religious Movements."

57 Wessinger, "Charisma and Credentials"; Wessinger, "Going Beyond and Retaining Charisma"; Wessinger, "Women's Religious Leadership in the United States."

58 Hopfe and Woodward, "Characteristics of Basic Religions."

59 Marvin and Ingle, *Blood Sacrifice and the Nation*.

60 Tedlock, *The Woman in the Shaman's Body*, 24.

61 Wessinger, "Charismatic Leaders in New Religious Movements."

62 Wessinger, "Going Beyond and Retaining Charisma," 17n12.

63 Ellwood and McGraw, *Many Peoples, Many Faiths*, 37.

64 Bourguignon, *Possession*.

65 Sered, *Priestess, Mother, Sacred Sister*, 185.

66 Boddy, *Wombs and Alien Spirits*.

67 Personal communication from Janice Boddy, October 23, 2018; Kenyon, "Zar Spirit Possession in Central Sudan."

68 See Conner, *Queering Creole Spiritual Traditions*.

69 Sered, *Priestess, Mother, Sacred Sister*, 188–90.

70 Harvey, "Possession Sickness and Women Shamans in Korea."

71 Kendall, "When the Shaman Becomes a Cultural Icon," 200; personal communication from Jorge Mañes Rubio, December 15, 2019.

72 Harvey, "Possession Sickness and Women Shamans in Korea," 65.

73 Blacker, *The Catalpa Bow*, 244.

74 Blacker, *The Catalpa Bow*, 244.

75 Sered, *Priestess, Mother, Sacred Sister*, 260–62.

76 Braude, "The Perils of Passivity," 57.

77 Sered, *Priestess, Mother, Sacred Sister*, 268–78, quotations on 274 and 277.

78 Dorman, *Celebrity Gods*, 6.

79 Nakamura, "No Women's Liberation."

80 Hackett, "Sacred Paradoxes."

81 Aamodt, Land, and Numbers, *Ellen Harmon White*; Vance, "Field Notes: Rejecting Women's Ordination."

82 Hiatt, "Women's Ordination in the Anglican Communion"; Thompsett, "Women in the American Episcopal Church."

83 Merritt, "The Selective Outrage of the Anglican Church." For a broader perspective on the relationships within the Anglican Communion, see Kirkpatrick, "No, the Anglican Communion Did Not Suspend the Episcopal Church."

84 Daigler, *Incompatible with God's Design*.

85 For a discussion of the various Vatican documents against women's ordinations, see Halter, *The Papal "No."*

86 Beauchesne, "The Flawed Nuptial Analogy."

87 New Testament scholars judge that the gospels of Matthew and Luke were written ca. 80–85 C.E. The gospel of John, which does not mention the term "apostle," is judged to have been written ca. 90–110 C.E.

88 Via, "Roman Catholic Women Priests (RCWP)."

89 "Meet the Ordained Members," Roman Catholic Womenpriests, website.

90 Personal communication from Bishop Jane Via and Bishop Suzanne Thiel of Roman Catholic Womenpriests-USA, April 7, 2020.

91 Moon, "Womenpriests."

92 "Declaration for Our Daughters," A Church for Our Daughters, website; Miller, "Do Women Have a Future in the Catholic Church?"

93 Christ, "Why Women Need the Goddess," 276.

94 Kinsley, *Hindu Goddesses*, 19, 28–29, 34.

95 Bailly, "Śrī-Lakṣmī."

96 Narayan, "Śrī."

97 Fuller, *The Camphor Flame*, 111–14.

98 Kinsley, *Hindu Goddesses*; Hawley and Wulff, *Devī: Goddesses of India*; Pintchman, *Seeking Mahādevī*.

99 Erndl, "Is Shakti Empowering for Women?"; Wessinger, "Woman Guru, Woman Roshi."

100 "Adiparasakthi: Learn about Adiparasakthi and the Temple," Supreme Sakthi: Melmaruvathur Adhiparasakthi Spiritual Movement, website.

101 Pechilis, "Karaikkal Ammaiyar."

102 Spina, "Women in Hinduism"; Spina, *Women's Authority and Leadership*.

103 Wessinger, "Going Beyond and Retaining Charisma"; Bednarowski, "Outside the Mainstream."

104 Pearson, *"Because It Gives Me Peace of Mind,"* 81, 208.

105 Pearson, *"Because It Gives Me Peace of Mind,"* 193–221.

106 Description of the ceremony on Mescalero Apache Reservation is found in Farrer, *Living Life's Circle*, 128–83; Farrer, *Thunder Rides a Black Horse*; Stockel, *Chiricahua Apache Women and Children*, chap. 4; Talamantez, "Images of the Feminine in Apache Religious Tradition," 131–45; Opler, *An Apache Life-Way*, 82–134. Several descriptions of Chiricahua ceremonies are found in Boyer and Gayton, *Apache Mothers and Daughters*. National Geographic provides a short video depiction of the Fourth of July girls' puberty ceremony at Mescalero Apache Reservation: "Apache Girl's Rite of Passage." Norelli, *The Sunrise Dance*, depicts the ceremony for a White Mountain Apache girl living on Fort Apache Reservation in Arizona.

107 Hyman, "Bat Mitzvah."

108 See Starhawk, *The Spiral Dance*.

109 Berger surveyed over 8,000 Pagans in 59 nations, with over 6,000 responses from the United States. See Berger, *Solitary Pagans*, xiii, 1.

110 Ruether, *Women-Church*; Hunt, "Women-Church."

111 Steinfels, "After a Long Delay, a New Catechism." Clifford provides reasons for the use of inclusive language in "The Bishops, the Bible and Liturgical Language."

112 Wilcox, "Outlaws or In-Laws?," 76.

113 Wilcox, "Innovation in Exile," 325.

114 "The Lies and Dangers of Efforts to Change Sexual Orientation or Gender Identity."

115 "Conversion Therapy Laws," MAP: Movement Advancement Project, website.

116 "Global Presence," Metropolitan Community Churches, website.

117 Burke, "Reaction Mixed."

118 Lee and Han, "Mothers and Moral Activists."

119 Hunt, "Did Ireland Just Bury the Catholic Church?"

120 Jacobs, Thomas, and Lang, Introduction, in Jacobs, Thomas, and Lang, *Two-Spirit People*, 3; see Williams, "The 'Two-Spirit' People of Indigenous North Americans."

121 See video embedded in Baker, "Love Is Love Is Love Is . . . Cut the Mike."

122 Dehlin, "Mormon Story #759."

123 Versaldi and Zani, "'Male and Female He Created Them,'" 4–5, 8, 30, 31.

124 Held, "Vatican Issues Document during Pride Month."

125 Wilcox, "Innovation in Exile," 335; see Wilcox, *Queer Women and Religious Individualism*.

126 Faludi, *Backlash*.

127 Concerning heart-breaking economic exploitation of the bodies of girls and women and the efforts to turn it back, see Kristof and WuDunn, *Half the Sky*.

128 Joyce, *Quiverfull*.

CONCLUSION

1 Friedl, "Society and Sex Roles," 131.

2 Friedl, "Society and Sex Roles," 131.

3 Wessinger, "Going Beyond and Retaining Charisma."

4 Vance, *Women in New Religions*; Wessinger, *Women's Leadership in Marginal Religions*.

5 See the report of the Pew Research Center, "Executive Summary: 'Nones' on the Rise," on the situation in the United States. See also Alper, "Why America's 'Nones' Don't Identify with a Religion."

6 Wessinger, "An Outsider's View," 211–13.

7 Friedl, "Society and Sex Roles," 131.

8 Bednarowski, "Outside the Mainstream"; Wessinger, *Women's Leadership in Marginal Religions*; Bednarowski, *The Religious Imagination of American Women*.

BIBLIOGRAPHY

Aamodt, Terrie Dopp, Gary Land, and Ronald L. Numbers, eds. *Ellen Harmon White: American Prophet*. New York: Oxford University Press, 2014.

Aberle, David F. "Matrilineal Descent in Cross-Cultural Perspective." In *Matrilineal Kinship*, edited by David M. Schneider and Kathleen Gough, 655–727. Berkeley: University of California Press, 1961.

"Adiparasakthi: Learn about Adiparasakthi and the Temple." Supreme Sakthi: Melmaruvathur Adhiparasakthi Spiritual Movement. http://supremesakthi.com. Accessed December 1, 2019.

Adovasio, J. M., Olga Soffer, and Jake Page. *The Invisible Sex: Uncovering the True Roles of Women in Prehistory*. Walnut Creek, CA: Left Coast Press, 2007.

"Advice on How to Protect Yourself from Dowry Extortion and Violence." December 5, 2011. 50 Million Missing: The Fight to End Female Genocide in India. http://genderbytes.wordpress.com.

Ali, Kecia. *Sexual Ethics and Islam: Feminist Reflections on Qur'an, Hadith, and Jurisprudence*, exp. and rev. ed. London: Oneworld Publications, 2016.

Allik, Tiina. "Sex and Finitude: The Social Construction of Women's Experience." Loyola Lectures in Religion, Fall 1991. Loyola University New Orleans. http://cas.loyno.edu.

Alper, Becka A. "Why America's 'Nones' Don't Identify with a Religion." *FACT TANK: News in the Numbers*, August 8, 2018. Pew Research Center. https://www.pewresearch.org

American Sociological Association. "ASA Press Release: ASA Files Amicus Brief with U.S. Supreme Court in Same-Sex Marriage Cases." February 28, 2013. https://www.asanet.org.

Aquino, María Pilar, and Maria José Rosado-Nunes, eds. *Feminist Intercultural Theology: Latina Explorations for a Just World*. Maryknoll, NY: Orbis Books, 2007.

Bacon, Margaret Hope. *Mothers of Feminism: The Story of Quaker Women in America*. New York: HarperCollins, 1989.

Badran, Margot. *Feminism in Islam: Secular and Religious Convergences*. Oxford: Oneworld Publications, 2009.

Bailly, Constantina Rhodes. "Śrī-Lakṣmī: Majesty of the Hindu King." In *Goddesses Who Rule*, edited by Elisabeth Benard and Beverly Moon, 133–45. New York: Oxford University Press, 2000.

Baird, Robert D. *Category Formation and the History of Religions*. The Hague: Mouton, 1971.

Baker, Elna. "Love Is Love Is Love Is . . . Cut the Mike." *New York Times*, June 24, 2017. https://www.nytimes.com

Ball, Eve. *In the Days of Victorio: Recollections of a Warm Springs Apache*. Tucson: University of Arizona Press, 1970.

Balter, Michael. "Mysterious Indo-European Homeland May Have Been in the Steppes of Ukraine and Russia." *Science*, February 13, 2015. http://www.sciencemag.org.

Banerjee, Rita. "Why Education and Economics Are Not the Solution to India's Female Genocide." June 12, 2011. 50 Million Missing: The Fight to End Female Genocide in India. http://genderbytes.wordpress.com.

Barber, Karin. *I Could Speak until Tomorrow: Oriki, Women, and the Past in a Yoruba Town*. Edinburgh: Edinburgh University Press, 1991.

Barstow, Anne Llewellyn. *Witchcraze: A New History of the European Witch Hunts*. New York: HarperOne, 1994.

———. "The Prehistoric Goddess." In *The Book of the Goddess Past and Present: An Introduction to Her Religion*, edited by Carl Olson, 7–15. New York: Crossroad, 1986.

Bartholomeusz, Tessa. *Women under the Bō Tree: Buddhist Nuns in Sri Lanka*. Cambridge: Cambridge University Press, 1994.

Bascom, William. *The Yoruba of Southwestern Nigeria*. Prospect Heights, IL: Waveland Press, 1969.

Bhalotra, Sonia, Abhishek Chakravarty, and Selim Gulesci. "The Price of Gold: Dowry and Death in India." *Journal of Development Economics* 143 (2020): 1–16.

Biernacki, Loriliai. "Sex Talk and Gender Rites: Women and the Tantric Sex Rite." *Hindu Studies* 10 (2006): 185–206.

Beauchesne, Richard J. "The Flawed Nuptial Analogy (Christ Relates to the Church as a Husband Relates to His Wife) Used as the Theological Argument against Women's Ordination." Paper presented at the College Theology Society, Loyola University New Orleans, 1990. Available at https://www.academia.edu.

Bednarowski, Mary Farrell. *The Religious Imagination of American Women*. Bloomington: Indiana University Press, 1999.

———. "Outside the Mainstream: Women's Religion and Women's Religious Leaders in Nineteenth-Century America." *Journal of the American Academy of Religion* 48, no 2 (June 1980): 207–31.

Bem, Sandra Lipsitz. *The Lenses of Gender: Transforming the Debate on Sexual Inequality*. New Haven, CT: Yale University Press, 1993.

Berger, Helen A. *Solitary Pagans: Contemporary Witches, Wiccans, and Others Who Practice Alone*. Columbia: University of South Carolina Press, 2019.

Blacker, Carmen. *The Catalpa Bow: A Study of Shamanistic Practices in Japan*. London: George Allen & Unwin, 1975.

Blevins, Carolyn D. "Baptist Women." In *Encyclopedia of Women and Religion in North America*, edited by Rosemary Skinner Keller and Rosemary Radford Ruether, assoc. ed., Marie Cantlon, 1:285–96. Bloomington: Indiana University Press, 2006.

Boddy, Janice. "The Normal and the Aberrant in Female Genital Cutting: Shifting Paradigms." *Hau: Journal of Ethnographic Theory* 6, no. 2 (2016): 41–69.

———. *Wombs and Alien Spirits: Women, Men, and the Zar Cult in Northern Sudan.* Madison: University of Wisconsin Press, 1989.

Bourguignon, Erika. *Possession.* San Francisco: Chandler & Sharp Publishers, 1976.

Boyer, Ruth McDonald, and Narcissus Duffy Gayton. *Apache Mothers and Daughters: Four Generations of a Family.* Norman: University of Oklahoma Press, 1992.

Braude, Ann. "The Perils of Passivity: Women's Leadership in Spiritualism and Christian Science." In *Women's Leadership in Marginal Religions: Explorations Outside the Mainstream,* edited by Catherine Wessinger, 55–67. Urbana: University of Illinois Press, 1993.

Brodd, Jeffrey, Layne Little, Bradley Nystrom, Robert Platzner, Richard Shek, and Erin Stiles. *Invitation to World Religions.* New York: Oxford University Press, 2013.

Brooks, Joanna. "The Real Mormon Moment." *Religion Dispatches,* June 24, 2014. http://religiondispatches.org.

Bruning, Karla. "Islam's Gender Boundaries Being Pushed." Columbia News Service, December 2, 2006.

Buchanan, Kimberly Moore. *Apache Women Warriors.* El Paso: Texas Western Press, University of Texas at El Paso, 1986.

Childe, V. Gordon. *Prehistoric Migrations in Europe.* Oslo: Aschehoug, 1950.

———. *The Aryans: A Study of Indo-European Origins.* London: Kegan Paul, Trench & Trubner, 1926.

Chodorow, Nancy. *Feminism and Psychoanalytic Theory.* New Haven, CT: Yale University Press, 1989.

———. *The Reproduction of Mothering: Psychoanalysis and the Sociology of Gender.* Berkeley: University of California Press, 1978.

Christ, Carol P. "Why Women Need the Goddess." In *Womanspirit Rising: A Feminist Reader on Religion,* edited by Carol P. Christ and Judith Plaskow, 273–87. San Francisco: Harper & Row, 1979.

Clifford, Richard J., S.J. "The Bishops, the Bible and Liturgical Language." *America,* May 27, 1995, 12–16. Available at the Catholic Biblical Association of America, cba.cua.edu/clif.htm.

Cole, D. C. *The Chiricahua Apache 1846–1876: From War to Reservation.* Albuquerque: University of New Mexico Press, 1988.

Congregatio pro Doctrina Fidei (Congregation for the Doctrine of the Faith). "Doctrinal Assessment of the Leadership Conference of Women Religious." April 18, 2012. Available at http://www.usccb.org.

Conner, Randy P., with David Hatfield Sparks. *Queering Creole Spiritual Traditions: Lesbian, Gay, Bisexual, and Transgender Participation in African-Inspired Traditions in the Americas.* Binghamton, NY: Haworth Press, 2004.

Crenshaw, Kimberlé. "Mapping the Margins: Intersectionality, Identity Politics, and Violence against Women of Color." *Stanford Law Review* 43, no. 6 (1991): 1241–99.

Daigler, Mary Jeremy. *Incompatible with God's Design: A History of the Women's Ordination Movement in the U.S. Roman Catholic Church*. Lanham, MD: Rowman & Littlefield, 2012.

Davis-Kimball, Jeannine, with Mona Behan. *Warrior Women: An Archaeologist's Search for History's Hidden Heroines*. New York: Warner Books, 2002.

de Silva, Ranjani. "Reclaiming the Robe: Reviving the Bhikkhunī Order in Sri Lanka." In *Buddhist Women and Social Justice*, edited by Karma Lekshe Tsomo, 119–35. Albany: State University of New York Press, 2004.

Dinnerstein, Dorothy. *The Mermaid and the Minotaur*. New York: Harper & Row, 1976.

Dolsten, Josefin. "10 Years after the Founding of the First Orthodox School to Train Female Clergy, What's Actually Changed?" *Jewish Telegraphic Agency*, December 17, 2019. https://www.jta.org.

Dorman, Benjamin. *Celebrity Gods: New Religions, Media, and Authority in Occupied Japan*. Honolulu: University of Hawai'i Press, 2012.

Drewal, Henry. "Art and the Perception of Women in Yorùbá Culture." *Cahiers d'Etudes africaines* 17, no. 4 (1977): 545–67.

Drewal, Henry John, and Margaret Thompson Drewal. *Gẹlẹdẹ: Art and Female Power among the Yoruba*. Bloomington: Indiana University Press, 1983.

Drewal, Margaret Thompson. *Yoruba Ritual: Performers, Play, Agency*. Bloomington: Indiana University Press, 1992.

Ehrenberg, Margaret. *Women in Prehistory*. Norman: University of Oklahoma Press, 1989.

Eisler, Riane. *The Chalice and the Blade: Our History, Our Future*. San Francisco: Harper & Row, 1988.

Elewa, Ahmed, and Laury Silvers. "'I *Am* One of the People: A Survey and Analysis of Legal Arguments on Woman-Led Prayer in Islam." *Journal of Law and Religion* 26, no. 1 (2010–2011): 141–71.

Eller, Cynthia. *The Myth of Matriarchal Prehistory: Why an Invented Past Won't Give Women a Future*. Boston: Beacon Press, 2000.

———. "Relativizing the Patriarchy: The Sacred History of the Feminist Spirituality Movement." *History of Religions* 30, no. 3 (1991): 279–95.

Ellwood, Robert S., and Barbara A. McGraw. *Many Peoples, Many Faiths: Women and Men in the World Religions*, 7th ed. Englewood Cliffs, NJ: Prentice Hall, 2002.

Erndl, Kathleen M. "Is Shakti Empowering for Women? Reflections on Feminism and the Hindu Goddess." In *Is the Goddess a Feminist? The Politics of South Asian Goddesses*, edited by Alf Hiltebeitel and Kathleen M. Erndl, 91–103. New York: New York University Press, 2000.

Evans, Whitney. "Women Seeking Priesthood March Again to Temple Square." *Deseret News*, April 5, 2014. http://www.deseretnews.com.

Falk, Nancy Auer, and Rita M. Gross, eds. *Unspoken Worlds: Women's Religious Lives*, 3rd ed. Belmont, CA.: Wadsworth/Thomson Learning, 2001.

Faludi, Susan. *Backlash: The Undeclared War Against American Women*, 15th anniversary ed. New York: Three Rivers Press, 2006.

Farley, Margaret A. "Feminist Consciousness and the Interpretation of Scripture." In *From Christ to the World: Introductory Readings in Christian Ethics*, edited by Wayne G. Boulton, Thomas D. Kennedy, and Allen Verhey, 51–57. Grand Rapids, MI: Wm. B. Eerdmans, 1994.

Farrer, Claire R. *Thunder Rides a Black Horse: Mescalero Apaches and the Mythic Present*. Prospect Heights, IL: Waveland Press, 2011.

———. *Living Life's Circle: Mescalero Apache Cosmovision*. Albuquerque: University of New Mexico Press, 1991.

Fausto-Sterling, Anne. "The Five Sexes: Why Male and Female Are Not Enough." In *The Meaning of Difference: American Constructions of Race, Sex and Gender, Social Class, and Sexual Orientation*, edited by Karen E. Rosenblum and Toni-Michelle C. Travis, 68–73. New York: McGraw-Hill, 1996.

Filkins, Dexter. "Afghan Girls, Scarred by Acid, Defy Terror, Embracing School." *New York Times*, January 13, 2009. http://www.nytimes.com.

Friedan, Betty. *The Feminine Mystique*. New York: W. W. Norton, 1963.

Friedl, Ernestine. "Society and Sex Roles." *Human Nature*, April 1978, 127–32.

———. *Women and Men: An Anthropologist's View*. Prospect Heights, IL: Waveland Press, 1975.

Fuller, C. J. *The Camphor Flame: Popular Hinduism and Society in India*. Princeton, NJ: Princeton University Press, 1992.

"Geshema Degree." Tibetan Nuns Project. https://tnp.org. Accessed December 8, 2019.

Gillis, Stacy, Gillian Howie, and Rebecca Munford. *Third Wave Feminism*, exp. 2nd ed. New York: Palgrave MacMillan, 2007.

Gimbutas, Marija. *The Civilization of the Goddess: The World of Old Europe*, edited by Joan Marler. San Francisco: HarperSanFrancisco, 1991.

———. *The Language of the Goddess*. San Francisco: Harper & Row, 1989.

———. "Women and Culture in Goddess-Oriented Old Europe." In *The Politics of Women's Spirituality: Essays on the Rise of Spiritual Power within the Feminist Movement*, edited by Charlene Spretnak, 22–31. New York: Doubleday, 1982.

Goettner-Abendroth, Heide. *Matriarchal Societies: Studies on Indigenous Cultures across the Globe*, translated by Karen Smith. New York: Peter Lang, 2012.

Gross, Rita M. *Feminism and Religion: An Introduction*. Boston: Beacon Press, 1996.

———. *Beyond Androcentrism: New Essays on Women and Religion*. Missoula, MT: Scholar's Press, 1977.

Gross, Susan Hill. *Wasted Resources, Diminished Lives: The Impact of Boy Preference on the Lives of Girls and Women*. St. Louis Park, MN: Upper Midwest Women's History Center, 1992.

Gruenbaum, Ellen. *The Female Circumcision Controversy: An Anthropological Controversy*. Philadelphia: University of Pennsylvania Press, 2001.

Hackett, Rosalind I. J. "Sacred Paradoxes: Women and Religious Plurality in Nigeria." In *Women, Religion, and Social Change*, edited by Yvonne Y. Haddad and Ellison B. Findly, 247–71. Albany: State University of New York Press, 1985.

Haley, James L. *Apaches: A History and Culture Portrait.* Garden City, NY: Doubleday & Company, 1981.

Halter, Deborah. *The Papal "No": A Comprehensive Guide to the Vatican's Rejection of Women's Ordination.* New York: Crossroad, 2004.

Harun, Hana Naz. "SIS: Islam Recognises Women's Roles." *Kuala Lumpur New Straits Times,* July 26, 2019. https://www.nst.com.

Harvey, Youngsook Kim. "Possession Sickness and Women Shamans in Korea." In *Unspoken Worlds: Women's Religious Lives,* 3rd ed., edited by Nancy Auer Falk and Rita M. Gross, 59–65. Belmont, CA: Wadsworth/Thomson Learning, 2001.

Hassan, Riffat. "Islam." In *Her Voice, Her Faith: Women Speak on World Religions,* edited by Arvind Sharma and Katherine K. Young, 215–42. Cambridge, MA: Westview Press, 2003.

Hawley, John Stratton, and Donna Marie Wulff, eds. *Devī: Goddesses of India.* Berkeley: University of California Press, 1996.

Heilman, Uriel. "Rabbi Lila Kagedan Poised to Make History at Orthodox Shul." Jewish Telegraphic Agency, January 13, 2016. http://www.jta.org.

Held, Amy. "Vatican Issues Document during Pride Month Denying Concept of Gender Identity." National Public Radio, June 10, 2019. https://www.npr.org.

Hiatt, Suzanne Radley. "Women's Ordination in the Anglican Communion: Can This Church Be Saved?" In *Religious Institutions and Women's Leadership: New Roles inside the Mainstream,* edited by Catherine Wessinger, 211–27. Columbia: University of South Carolina Press, 1996.

Hodder, Ian. *The Leopard's Tale: Revealing the Mysteries of Çatalhöyük.* London: Thames & Hudson, 2006.

———. "Women and Men at Çayalhöyük." *Scientific American,* January 1, 2005. https://www.scientificamerican.com.

Hodder, Ian, ed. *Religion in the Emergence of Civilization: Çatalhöyük as a Case Study.* Cambridge: Cambridge University Press, 2010.

Hodder, Ian, and Lynn Meskell. "The Symbolism of Catalhöyük in Its Regional Context." In *Religion in the Emergence of Civilization: Çatalhöyük as a Case Study,* edited by Ian Hodder, 32–72. Cambridge: Cambridge University Press, 2010.

Hodder, Ian, and Peter Pels. "History Houses: A New Interpretation of Architectural Elaboration at Çatalhöyük." In *Religion in the Emergence of Civilization: Çatalhöyük as a Case Study,* edited by Ian Hodder, 163–86. Cambridge: Cambridge University Press, 2010.

Hoijer, Harry. *Chiricahua and Mescalero Apache Texts, with Ethnological Notes by Morris Edward Opler.* Chicago: University of Chicago Press, 1938.

Holland, Sharon, IHM, Marcia Allen, CSJ, Carol Zinn, SSJ, and Joan Marie Steadman, CSC. "Statement of the LCWR Officers on the CDF Doctrinal Assessment and Conclusion of the Mandate." Leadership Conference of Women Religious. https://lcwr.org. Accessed December 19, 2019.

Hopfe, Lewis M., and Mark W. Woodward. "Characteristics of Basic Religions." In *Religions of the World,* 9th ed., 14–28. Upper Saddle River, NJ: Pearson/Prentice Hall, 2004.

Hunt, Mary E. "Did Ireland Just Bury the Catholic Church?" *Religion Dispatches*, May 26, 2015. http://religiondispatches.org.

———. "Women-Church: Feminist Concept, Religious Commitment, Women's Movement." *Journal of Feminist Studies in Religion* 25, no. 1 (2009): 85–98.

Hyman, Paula E. "Bat Mitzvah: American Jewish Women." *Jewish Women's Archive Encyclopedia*. http://jwa.org. Accessed June 19, 2019.

Isasi-Díaz, Ada Maria. *Mujerista Theology: A Theology for the Twenty-First Century.* Maryknoll, NY: Orbis Books, 1996.

Jacobs, Sue-Ellen, Wesley Thomas, and Sabine Lang. Introduction. In *Two-Spirit People: Native American Gender Identity, Sexuality, and Spirituality*, edited by Sue-Ellen Jacobs, Wesley Thomas, and Sabine Lang, 1–18. Urbana: University of Illinois Press, 1997.

Jha, Prabhat, Maya A. Kesler, Rajesh Kumar, Faujdar Ram, Usha Ram, Lukasz Aleksandrowicz, Diego B. Bassani, Shailaja Chandra, and Jayant K. Banthia. "Trends in Selective Abortions of Girls in India: Analysis of Nationally Representative Birth Histories from 1990 to 2005 and Census Dates from 1991 to 2011." *The Lancet* 377, no. 9781 (2011): 1921–28. http://www.thelancet.com.

Jones, Doug. "The Matrilocal Tribe: An Organization of Demic Expansion." *Human Nature* 22, nos. 1–2 (2011): 177–200.

Joyce, Kathryn. "Biblical Battered Wife Syndrome: Christian Women and Domestic Violence." *Religion Dispatches*, January 22, 2009. http://www.religiondispatches.org.

———. *Quiverfull: Inside the Christian Patriarchy Movement.* Boston: Beacon Press, 2009.

Joyce, Rosemary A. *Ancient Bodies, Ancient Lives: Sex, Gender, and Archaeology.* New York: Thames & Hudson, 2008.

Kandiyoti, Deniz. "Bargaining with Patriarchy." *Gender and Society* 2, no. 3 (1988): 274–90.

Kelly, Robert L. *The Lifeways of Hunter-Gatherers: The Foraging Spectrum*, 2nd ed. Cambridge: Cambridge University Press, 2013.

Kendall, Laurel. "When the Shaman Becomes a Cultural Icon, What Happens to Efficacy? Some Observations from Korea." In *Ritual and Identity: Performative Practices as Effective Transformations of Social Reality*, edited by Klaus-Peter Köpping, Bernhard Leistle, and Michael Rudolph, 195–218. Berlin: Lit Verlag, 2006.

Kenyon, Susan M. "Zar Spirit Possession in Central Sudan." *Women in the World's Religions and Spirituality Project*, November 20, 2019. https://wrldrels.org.

Kinsley, David R. *Hindu Goddesses: Visions of the Divine Feminine in the Hindu Religious Tradition.* Berkeley: University of California Press, 1986.

Kirkpatrick, Frank. "No, The Anglican Communion Did Not Suspend the Episcopal Church." *Religion in the News*, February 5, 2016. http://religioninthenews.org.

Kishwar, Madhu Purnima. "Destined to Fail: Inherent Flaws in the Anti Dowry Legislation." *Manushi* 148 (May–June 2005): 3. http://manushi.in.

Kristof, Nicholas D., and Sheryl WuDunn. *Half the Sky: Turning Oppression into Opportunity for Women Worldwide.* New York: Vintage Books, 2009.

Kyung, Chung Hyun. *Struggle to Be the Sun Again: Introducing Asian Women's Theology.* Maryknoll, NY: Orbis Books, 1990.

Larsen, Clark Spencer, Simon W. Hillson, Başak Boz, Marin A. Pilloud, Joshua W. Sadvari, Sabrina C. Agarwal, Bonnie Glencross, Patrick Beauchesne, Jessica Pearson, Christopher B. Ruff, Evan M. Garofalo, Lori D. Hager, Scott D. Haddow, and Christopher J. Knüsel. "Bioarchaeology of Çatalhöyük: Lives and Lifestyles of an Early Farming Society in Transition." *Journal of World Prehistory* 28 (2015): 27–68.

Laughlin, Lynda. "Who's Minding the Kids? Childcare Arrangements: Spring 2005/ Summer 2006." US Census Bureau, 2010. http://www.census.gov.

Lawal, Babatunde. *The Gẹ̀lẹ̀dẹ́ Spectacle: Art, Gender, and Social Harmony in an African Culture.* Seattle: University of Washington Press, 1996.

Lawler, Michael G. *Marriage and the Catholic Church.* Collegeville, MN: Liturgical Press, 2002.

Lee, Chengpang, and Ling Han. "Mothers and Moral Activists: Two Models of Women's Social Engagement in Contemporary Taiwanese Buddhism." *Nova Religio: The Journal of Alternative and Emergent Religions* 19, no. 3 (2016): 54–77.

Lerner, Gerda. *The Creation of Patriarchy.* New York: Oxford University Press, 1986.

"The Lies and Dangers of Efforts to Change Sexual Orientation or Gender Identity." Human Rights Campaign. http://www.hrc.org. Accessed June 14, 2016.

Liu, Jonathan H. "Who's Minding the Kids? Not Dads." *Wired,* February 10, 2010. http://www.wired.com.

Lopes, Steven, and Helen Alvaré, eds. *Not Just Good, but Beautiful: The Complementary Relationship between Man and Woman.* Walden, NY: Plough Publishing House, 2015.

Lupo, Karen D., and Dave N. Schmitt. "Upper Paleolithic Net-Hunting, Small Prey Exploitation, and Women's Work Effort: A View from the Ethnographic and Ethnoarchaeological Record of the Congo Basin." *Journal of Archaeological Method and Theory* 9, no. 2 (June 2002): 147–79.

MacHaffie, Barbara J. *Her Story: Women in Christian Tradition,* 2nd ed. Minneapolis, MN: Fortress Press, 2006.

Majeed, Debra. *Polygyny: What It Means When African American Muslim Women Share Their Husbands.* Gainesville: University Press of Florida, 2015.

Marder, Janet R. "Are Women Changing the Rabbinate? A Reform Perspective." In *Religious Institutions and Women's Leadership: New Roles inside the Mainstream,* edited by Catherine Wessinger, 271–90. Columbia: University of South Carolina Press, 1996.

Marshall, Molly T. "The Peril of Selective Inerrancy." *Baptist News Global,* May 29, 2018. https://baptistnews.com.

Marvin, Carolyn, and David W. Ingle. *Blood Sacrifice and the Nation: Totem Rituals and the American Flag.* Cambridge: Cambridge University Press, 1999.

Matory, J. Lorand. *Sex and the Empire That Is No More: Gender and the Politics of Metaphor in Oyo Yoruba Religion.* N.p.: Berghahn Books, 2005 [1994].

McCoid, Catherine Hodge, and Leroy D. McDermott. "Toward Decolonizing Gender: Female Vision in the Upper Paleolithic." *American Anthropologist* 98, no. 2 (1996): 319–26.

McIntosh, Marjorie Keniston. *Yoruba Women, Work, and Social Change*. Bloomington: Indiana University Press, 2009.

Mellaart, James. *Çatal Hüyük and Anatolian Kilims*. Vol. 2 of *The Goddess from Anatolia*, by James Mellaart, Udo Hirsch, and Belkis Balpinar. 4 vols. Adenau, West Germany: Eskenazi, 1989.

———. *Çatal Hüyük: A Neolithic Town in Anatolia*. New York: McGraw-Hill, 1967.

Mencher, Joan P. "Women, Agriculture and the Sexual Division of Labor: A Three-State Comparison." 1993. Unpublished paper. Available at https://www.academia .edu.

———. "The Nayars of South Malabar." In *Comparative Family Systems*, edited by M. F. Nimkoff, 163–91. Boston: Houghton Mifflin Company, 1965.

Merritt, Jonathan. "The Selective Outrage of the Anglican Church." *The Atlantic*, January 18, 2016. http://www.theatlantic.com.

Meskell, Lynn. "Refiguring the Corpus at Catalhöyük." In *Image and Imagination: A Global Prehistory of Figurative Representation*, edited by Colin Renfrew and Iain Morley, 143–56. Cambridge: McDonald Institute for Archaeological Research, University of Cambridge, 2007.

———. "Twin Peaks: The Archaeologies of Çatalhöyük." In *Ancient Goddesses*, edited by Lucy Goodison and Christine Morris, 46–62. Madison: University of Wisconsin Press, 1998.

———. "Goddesses, Gimbutas and 'New Age' Archaeology." *Antiquity* 69, no. 262 (March 1995): 74–86.

Miller, Patricia. "Do Women Have a Future in the Catholic Church? Social Justice Orgs Petition Bishops This Week." *Religion Dispatches*, June 14, 2016. http://religiondis patches.org.

Mitchem, Stephanie Y. *Introducing Womanist Theology*. Maryknoll, NY: Orbis Books, 2002.

Moon, Hellena. "Womenpriests: Radical Change or More of the Same?" *Journal of Feminist Studies in Religion* 24, no. 2 (2008): 115–34.

Moore, Rebecca. *Women in Christian Traditions*. New York: New York University Press, 2015.

Müller, Cardinal Gerhard. "Meeting of the Superiors of the Congregation for the Doctrine of the Faith with the Presidency of the Leadership Conference of Women Religious (LCWR): Opening Remarks." Rome, Italy, April 30, 2014. http://www .vatican.va.

Nadell, Pamela S. "Rabbi, Rabba, Maharat, Rabbanit: For Orthodox Jewish Women, What's in a Title?" Sightings: Religion in Public Life. January 28, 2016. https://divin ity.uchicago.edu.

Nakamura, Kyoko Motomochi. "No Women's Liberation: The Heritage of a Woman Prophet in Modern Japan." In *Unspoken Worlds: Women's Religious Lives*, 3rd ed., edited by Nancy Auer Falk and Rita M. Gross, 168–78. Belmont, CA: Wadsworth/ Thomson Learning, 2001.

Nanda, Serena. *Gender Diversity: Crosscultural Variations*. Long Grove, IL: Waveland Press, 2000.

Narayan, Vasudha. "Śrī: Giver of Fortune, Bestower of Grace." In *Devī: Goddesses of India*, edited by John Stratton Hawley and Donna Marie Wulff, 87–108. Berkeley: University of California Press, 1996.

Neal, Marie Augusta, SND de Namur. "Ministry of American Catholic Sisters: The Vowed Life in Church Renewal." In *Religious Institutions and Women's Leadership: New Roles inside the Mainstream*, edited by Catherine Wessinger, 231–43. Columbia: University of South Carolina Press, 1996.

Nelson, Sarah M. "Diversity of the Upper Paleolithic 'Venus' Figurines and Archeological Mythology." In *Archeological Papers of the American Anthropological Association* 2, no. 1 (June 2008): 11–22.

Novak, David. "Jewish Marriage: Nature, Covenant, and Contract." In *Marriage, Sex, and Family in Judaism*, edited by Michael J. Broyde and Michael Ausubel, 61–87. Lanham, MD: Rowman & Littlefield, 2005.

Oduyoye, Mercy. *Introducing African Women's Theology*. Sheffield: Sheffield Academic Press, 2001.

Olademo, Oyeronke. *Women in Yorùbá Religions*. New York: New York University Press, forthcoming.

Olds, Linda E. *Fully Human: How Everyone Can Integrate the Benefits of Masculine and Feminine Sex Roles*. Englewood Cliffs, NJ: Prentice-Hall, 1981.

Omrak, Ayça, Torsten Günther, Cristina Valdiosera, Emma M. Svensson, Helena Malmström, Henrike Kiesewetter, William Aylward, Jan Storå, Mattias Jokobsson, and Anders Güntherström. "Genomic Evidence Establishes Anatolia as the Source of the European Neolithic Gene Pool." *Current Biology* 26, no. 2 (2016): 270–75.

Opler, Morris Edward. *Myths and Tales of the Chiricahua Apache Indians*. Lincoln: University of Nebraska Press, 1994.

———. *An Apache Life-Way: The Economic, Social, and Religious Institutions of the Chiricahua Indians*. New York: Cooper Square Publishers, 1965.

Osborne, Samuel. "Saudi Family Therapist Offers Advice on How to 'Beat Your Wife.'" *The Independent*, May 11, 2016. https://www.independent.co.uk.

Osipova, Olga. "Washed in Blood: A Guest of the Shaman Bifatima." Bird in Flight, April 8, 2015. https://birdinflight.com.

Parker, Kim, and Wendy Wang. "Modern Parenthood: Roles of Moms and Dads Converge as They Balance Work and Family." Pew Research, Social and Demographic Trends, March 14, 2013. http://www.pewsocialtrends.org.

Pearson, Anne MacKenzie. *"Because It Gives Me Peace of Mind": Ritual Fasts in the Religious Lives of Hindu Women*. Albany: State University of New York Press, 1996.

Pechilis, Karen. "Karaikkal Ammaiyar." *Women in the World's Religions and Spirituality Project*, April 13, 2016. https://wrldrels.org.

Penkala-Gawęcka, Danuta. "The Way of the Shaman and the Revival of Spiritual Healing in Post-Soviet Kazakhstan and Kyrgyzstan." *Shamanism* 22, nos. 1–2 (2014): 35–59.

Pew Research Center. "Executive Summary: 'Nones' on the Rise: One-in-Five Adults Have No Religious Affiliation." The Pew Forum on Religion and Public Life, October 9, 2012. http://www.pewforum.org.

Pilloud, Marin A., and Scott D. Haddow, Christopher J. Knüsel, and Clark Spencer Larsen. "A Bioarchaeological and Forensic Re-Assessment of Vulture Defleshing and Mortuary Practices at Neolithic Çayalhöyük." *Journal of Archaeological Science: Reports* 10 (2016): 735–43.

Pinksy, Mark I. "American Nuns Respond to Vatican Rebuke with Conciliatory Statement." *Huffington Post*, August 20, 2013. http://www.huffingtonpost.com.

Pintchman, Tracy, ed. *Seeking Mahādevī: Constructing the Identities of the Hindu Great Goddess*. Albany: State University of New York Press, 2001.

Pogrebin, Abigail. "The Rabbi and the Rabba." *New York Magazine*, July 11, 2010. http://nymag.com.

Randolph-Quinney, Patrick. "The Discovery of Stone Tools in India Suggests Humans May Have Left Africa Earlier Than We Thought." *Quartz India*, January 31, 2018. https://qz.com.

Racimo, Fernando, Jessie Woodbridge, Ralph M. Fyfe, Martin Sikora, Karl-Göran Sjögren, Kristian Kristiansen, and Marc Vander Linden. "The Spatiotemporal Spread of Human Migrations during the European Holocene." *PNAS Latest Articles*, April 1, 2020. https://www.pnas.org/.

Ravitz, Jessica. "Mormon Feminist Excommunicated for Apostasy." CNN Belief Blog, June 24, 2014. http://religion.blogs.cnn.com.

Reich, David. "Ancient DNA Suggests Steppe Migrations Spread Indo-European Languages." *Proceedings of the American Philosophical Society* 162, no. 1 (2018): 39–55.

Renfrew, Colin. "Marija Redivivia: DNA and Indo-European Origins." Marija Gimbutas Memorial Lecture. The Oriental Institute, University of Chicago, November 8, 2017. https://www.youtube.com.

———. *Archaeology and Language: The Puzzle of Indo-European Origins*. New York: Cambridge University Press, 1987.

Robinson, Sherry. *Apache Voices: Their Stories of Survival as Told to Eve Ball*. Albuquerque: University of New Mexico Press, 2000.

Rountree, Kathryn. "Archaeologists and Goddess Feminists at Çatalhöyük: An Experiment in Multivocality." *Journal of Feminist Studies in Religion* 23, no. 2 (2007): 7–26.

Ruether, Rosemary Radford. "Christianity." In *Women in World Religions*, edited by Arvind Sharma, 207–33. Albany: State University of New York Press, 1987.

———. *Women-Church: Theology and Practice of Feminist Liturgical Communities*. San Francisco: Harper and Row, 1985.

Sales, Ben. "Orthodox Union Asks Women Clergy to Change Their Titles." Jewish Telegraph Agency, May 19, 2017. http://www.jta.org.

Sanday, Peggy Reeves. *Women in the Center: Life in a Modern Matriarchy*. Ithaca, NY: Cornell University Press, 2002.

Sanders, Sister Annmarie, IHM. "Leadership Conference of Women Religious (LCWR)." *Women in the World's Religions and Spirituality Project*, December 7, 2019. https://wrldrels.org.

——. "LCWR Statement on Meeting with CDF." April 15, 2013. https://lcwr.org.

Sanghavi, Prachi, Kavi Bhalla, and Veena Das. "Fire-Related Deaths in India in 2001: A Retrospective Analysis of Data." *The Lancet* 373, no. 9671 (2009): 1282–88. http://www.thelancet.com.

Sartain, Most Rev. J. Peter, Most Rev. Leonard P. Blair, Most Rev. Thomas J. Paprocki, Sr. Sharon Holland, IMH, Sr. Marcia Allen, CSJ, Sr. Carol Zinn, SSJ, and Sr. Joan Marie Steadman, CSC. "Joint Final Report." April 16, 2015. https://lcwr.org.

Sayer, Liana C., Paula England, Paul Allison, and Nicole Kangas. "She Left, He Left: How Employment and Satisfaction Affect Men's and Women's Decisions to Leave Marriages." *American Journal of Sociology* 116, no. 6 (2011): 1982–2018.

Seedat, Fatima. "An Intellectual Mentor." In *A Jihad for Justice: Honoring the Work and Life of Amina Wadud*, edited by Kecia Ali, Juliane Hammer, and Laury Silvers, 191–95. N.p.: Kecia Ali, Juliane Hammer, and Laury Silvers, 2012. Available at https://www.bu.edu.

Sen, Amartya. "More Than 100 Million Women Are Missing." *New York Review of Books*, December 1990. http://www.nybooks.com.

Sered, Susan Starr. *Priestess, Mother, Sacred Sister: Religions Dominated by Women*. New York: Oxford University Press, 1994.

Sharma, Arvind, and Katherine K. Young, eds. *Her Voice, Her Faith: Women Speak on World Religions*. Cambridge, MA: Westview Press, 2003.

Shell-Duncan, Bettina, and Ylva Hernlund, eds. *Female Circumcision in Africa: Culture, Controversy, and Change*. Boulder, CO: Lynne Rienner, 2000.

Silsby, Gilien. "Sociology: Study Examines Gender Roles of Children with Gay Parents." *USC News*, May 30, 2001. https://news.usc.edu.

Sirohi, Seema. *Sita's Curse: Stories of Dowry Victims*. New Delhi: HarperCollins India, 2003.

Smith, Jane I. "Women in Islam." In *Women in World Religions*, edited by Arvind Sharma, 235–50. Albany: State University of New York Press, 1987.

Sollee, Kristen. "6 Things to Know about 4th Wave Feminism." *Bustle*, October 30, 2015. https://www.bustle.com.

Spina, Nanette R. *Women's Authority and Leadership in a Hindu Goddess Tradition*. New York: Palgrave Macmillan, 2017.

——. "Women in Hinduism: Ritual Leadership in the Adhi Parasakthi Temple Society of Canada." In *Canadian Women Shaping Diasporic Religious Identities*, edited by Becky R. Lee and Terry Tak-ling Woo, 301–35. Waterloo, Ontario: Wilfrid Laurier University Press, 2016.

Stanley, Susie C. "The Promise Fulfilled: Women's Ministries in the Wesleyan/Holiness Movement." In *Religious Institutions and Women's Leadership: New Roles inside the*

Mainstream, edited by Catherine Wessinger, 139–57. Columbia: University of South Carolina Press, 1996.

Starhawk. *The Spiral Dance: A Rebirth of the Ancient Religion of the Goddess: 20th Anniversary Edition*. New York: HarperOne, 1999.

Steinem, Gloria. *Revolution from Within: A Book of Self-Esteem with a New Afterword by the Author*. Boston: Little, Brown and Company, 1993.

Steinfels, Peter. "After a Long Delay, a New Catechism Appears in English." *New York Times*, May 28, 1994. https://www.nytimes.com.

Stockel, H. Henrietta. *Chiricahua Apache Women and Children: Safekeepers of the Heritage*. College Station: Texas A&M University Press, 2000. ebook.

Sudan Ministry of Cabinet, Central Bureau of Statistics. "Multiple Indicator Cluster Survey 2014: Final Report." UNICEF/MICS. http://mics.unicef.org/.

Sweas, Megan. "Pope Francis Loves Nuns, but Can the Divide between Sisters and Vatican Be Healed?" *Religion Dispatches*, September 14, 2015. http://religiondispatches.org.

Talamantez, Ines. "Images of the Feminine in Apache Religious Tradition." In *After Patriarchy: Feminist Transformations of the World Religions*, edited by Paula M. Cooey, William R. Eakin, and Jay B. McDaniel, 131–45. Maryknoll, NY: Orbis Books, 1991.

Tedlock, Barbara. *The Woman in the Shaman's Body: Reclaiming the Feminine in Religion and Medicine*. New York: Bantam Books, 2005.

Tenzin Samten. "Historic Moment for Buddhist Women." *Contact*, May 16, 2016. http://www.contactmagazine.net.

Thompsett, Fredrica Harris. "Women in the American Episcopal Church." In *Encyclopedia of Women and Religion in North America*, edited by Rosemary Skinner Keller and Rosemary Radford Ruether, 1:269–79. Bloomington: Indiana University Press, 2006.

Toubia, Nahid. *Female Genital Mutilation: A Call for Global Action*. New York: Women, Ink, 1993.

Tringham, Ruth, and Margaret Conkey. "Rethinking Figurines: A Critical View from Archaeology of Gimbutas, the 'Goddess' and Popular Culture." In *Ancient Goddesses*, edited by Lucy Goodison and Christine Morris, 22–45. Madison: University of Wisconsin, 1998.

Tsomo, Karma Lekshe. *Women in Buddhist Traditions*. New York: New York University Press, 2020.

———. "Is the Bhikṣuṇī Vinaya Sexist?" In *Buddhist Women and Social Justice: Ideals, Challenges, and Achievements*, edited by Karma Lekshe Tsomo, 45–72. Albany: State University of New York Press, 2004.

———. "Khunying Kanitha: Thailand's Advocate for Women." In *Buddhist Women and Social Justice: Ideals, Challenges, and Achievements*, edited by Karma Lekshe Tsomo, 173–91. Albany: State University of New York Press, 2004.

Türkcan, Ali Umut. "Is It a Goddess or Bear? The Role of Çatalhöyük Animal Seals in Neolithic Symbolism." *Documenta Praehistorica* 34 (2007): 257–66.

Uyl, Anthony, ed. *Malleus Maleficarum of Heinrich Kramer and James Sprenger.* Woodstock, ON: Devoted Publishing, 2016.

UNICEF. "Female Genital Mutilation (FGM)." UNICEF Data, February 2020. https://data.unicef.org.

Vance, Laura. "Field Notes: Rejecting Women's Ordination: The Sixtieth General Conference Session of the Seventh-day Adventist Church." *Nova Religio: The Journal of Alternative and Emergent Religions* 21, no. 1 (2017): 85–99.

———. *Women in New Religions.* New York: New York University Press, 2015.

van Wagtendonk, Anya. "Saudi Arabia Changed Its Guardianship Laws, but Activists Who Fought Them Remain Imprisoned." *Vox,* August 3, 2019. https://www.vox.com.

Vejas, Denis. "My Strange Winter with a Shaman in Kazakhstan." *Vice,* November 30, 2016. https://www.vice.com.

Versaldi, Giuseppe Cardinal, and Archbishop Angelo Vincenzo Zani. "'Male and Female He Created Them': Towards a Path of Dialogue on the Question of Gender Theory." Congregation for Catholic Education, February 2, 2019. http://www.educatio.va.

Via, Jane. "Roman Catholic Women Priests (RCWP)." *Women in the World's Religions and Spirituality Project,* May 26, 2020. http://wrldrels.org.

Wadley, Susan S. "Hindu Women's Family and Household Rites in a North Indian Village." In *Unspoken Worlds: Women's Religious Lives,* 3rd ed., edited by Nancy Auer Falk and Rita M. Gross, 103–13. Belmont, CA: Wadsworth/Thomson Learning, 2001.

———. "The Village in 1998." In *Behind Mud Walls: Seventy-Five Years in a North Indian Village with Chapters by Susan S. Wadley,* updated and exp. ed., by William Wiser and Charlotte Wiser, 317–38. Berkeley: University of California Press, 2000.

———. "No Longer a Wife: Widows in Rural North India." In *From the Margins of Hindu Marriage: Essays on Gender, Religion, and Culture,* edited by Lindsey Harlan and Paul B. Courtright, 92–118. New York: Oxford University Press, 1995.

———. *Struggling with Destiny in Karimpur, 1925–1984.* Berkeley: University of California Press, 1994.

Wadud, Amina. "The Ethics of *Tawhid* over the Ethics of *Qiwamah.*" In *Men in Charge? Rethinking Authority in Muslim Legal Tradition,* edited by Ziba Mir-Hosseini, Mulki Al-Sharmani, and Jana Rumminger, 256–74. London: Oneworld Publications, 2015.

Walker, Alice. *In Search of Our Mothers' Gardens: Womanist Prose.* San Diego: Harcourt Brace Jovanovich, 1983.

Walsh, Decian. "In a Victory for Women in Sudan, Female Genital Mutilation Is Outlawed." *New York Times,* April 30, 2020. https://www.nytimes.com.

Welker, Holly. "Mormon Women Knock at the Door, Are Turned Away." *Religion Dispatches,* October 6, 2013. http://www.religiondispatches.org.

Welter, Barbara. "The Cult of True Womanhood: 1820–1860," *American Quarterly* 18, no. 2, part 1 (1966): 151–74.

Weiss, Susan M., and Netty C. Gross-Horowitz. *Marriage and Divorce in the Jewish State: Israel's Civil War*. Waltham, MA: Brandeis University Press, 2013.

Wessinger, Catherine. "Seeking Equality in the LDS Church: Activism for Women's Ordination: Interview with Kate Kelly." *World Religions and Spirituality Project*, October 27, 2014. http://wrldrels.org.

———. "Charismatic Leaders in New Religious Movements." In *The Cambridge Companion to New Religious Movements*, edited by Olav Hammer and Mikael Rothstein, 80–96. New York: Cambridge University Press, 2012.

———. "Charisma and Credentials: Women's Religious Leadership in America." H. James Yamauchi, S.J., Lecture in Religion, Fall 2007. Loyola University New Orleans. http://chn.loyno.edu.

———. "Women's Religious Leadership in the United States." In *Religious Institutions and Women's Leadership: New Roles inside the Mainstream*, edited by Catherine Wessinger, 3–36. Columbia: University of South Carolina Press, 1996.

———. "An Outsider's View." In *Re-Membering and Re-Imagining*, edited by Nancy J. Berneking and Pamela Carter Joern, 211–13. Cleveland, OH: Pilgrim Press, 1995.

———. "Going Beyond and Retaining Charisma: Women's Leadership in Marginal Religions." In *Women's Leadership in Marginal Religions: Explorations Outside the Mainstream*, edited by Catherine Wessinger, 1–19. Urbana: University of Illinois Press, 1993.

———. "Woman Guru, Woman Roshi: The Legitimation of Women's Religious Leadership in Hindu and Buddhist Groups in America." In *Women's Leadership in Marginal Religions: Explorations Outside the Mainstream*, edited by Catherine Wessinger, 125–46. Urbana: University of Illinois Press, 1993.

———, ed. *The Oxford Handbook of Millennialism*. New York: Oxford University Press, 2011.

———, ed. *Religious Institutions and Women's Leadership: New Roles inside the Mainstream*. Columbia: University of South Carolina Press, 1996.

———, ed. *Women's Leadership in Marginal Religions: Explorations Outside the Mainstream*. Urbana: University of Illinois Press, 1993.

West, Candace, and Don H. Zimmerman. "Doing Gender." *Gender and Society* 1, no. 2 (1987): 125–51.

White, David Gordon. *Kiss of the Yoginī: "Tantric Sex" in Its South Asian Contexts*. Chicago: University of Chicago Press, 2003.

Whitehouse, Harvey, and Ian Hodder. "Modes of Religiosity at Çatalhöyük." In *Religion in the Emergence of Civilization: Çatalhöyük as a Case Study*, edited by Ian Hodder, 122–45. Cambridge: Cambridge University Press, 2010.

Wilcox, Melissa M. *Queer Women and Religious Individualism*. Bloomington: Indiana University Press, 2009.

———. "Outlaws or In-Laws? Queer Theory, LGBT Studies, and Religious Studies." *Journal of Homosexuality* 52, nos. 1–2 (2006): 73–100.

———. "Innovation in Exile: Religion and Spirituality in Lesbian, Gay, Bisexual, and Transgender Communities." In *Sexuality and the World's Religions*, edited by David W. Machacek and Melissa M. Wilcox, 323–57. Santa Barbara, CA: ABC-CLIO, 2003.

Williams, Walter L. "The 'Two-Spirit' People of Indigenous North Americans." First People. http://www.firstpeople.us. Accessed June 19, 2019.

Wiser, William, and Charlotte Wiser. *Behind Mud Walls: Seventy-Five Years in a North Indian Village with Chapters by Susan S. Wadley*, updated and exp. ed. Berkeley: University of California Press, 2000.

Wood, Nicholas Breeze. "Shamans at the Centre of the World: A Brief Introduction to the Shamanism of Kazakhstan and Central Asia." *Sacred Hoop* 91 (2006): 36–43. http://www.3worlds.co.uk.

Xu, Judith Chuan. "Poststructuralist Feminism and the Problem of Femininity in the *Daodejing*." *Journal of Feminist Studies in Religion* 19, no. 1 (2003): 47–64.

Young, Serinity, ed. *An Anthology of Sacred Texts by and about Women*. New York: Crossroad, 1993.

Yousafzai, Malala. "Our Books and Our Pens Are the Most Powerful Weapons." Transcription of address to United Nations Youth Assembly. *The Guardian*, July 12, 2013. http://www.guardian.co.uk.

Yousafzai, Malala, and Christina Lamb. *I Am Malala: The Girl Who Stood Up for Education and Was Shot by the Taliban*. Boston: Little, Brown, 2013.

MOVIES AND VIDEOS

Al Jazeera English. "Everywoman—Buddhist Nun and Hijab Fashion." https://www.youtube.com. Uploaded August 28, 2007.

Cravath, Jay, and Rick Ench, prod. and dir. *1000 Years of Song: The Apache*. Jay Cravath and Rick Ench, 1996 (19:37 min.). https://www.youtube.com.

Dehlin, John. "Mormon Story #759: The Courage of Savannah." June 19, 2017 (1:05 min.). https://www.youtube.com.

Lipscomb, Steven, prod. and dir. *Battle for the Minds*. New Day Films, 1997.

National Geographic. "Apache Girl's Rite of Passage." (4:39 mins.) https://video.nationalgeographic.com/. Accessed May 3, 2020.

Norelli, Gianfranco, prod. and dir. *The Sunrise Dance*. Documentary Educational Resources, 1994 (28 mins.).

WEBSITES

A Church for Our Daughters. http://achurchforourdaughters.org. Accessed June 19, 2019.

Buddhist Compassion Relief Tzu Chi Foundation. http://www.tzuchi.org/. Accessed June 19, 2019.

Center for American Women and Politics. https://www.cawp.rutgers.edu/. Accessed March 30, 2020.

Central Baptist Theological Seminary. https://www.cbts.edu/. Accessed June 19, 2019.

Equality Now. https://www.equalitynow.org/. Accessed November 29, 2019.

Human Rights Campaign. https://hrc.org/. Accessed June 19, 2019.

The Malala Fund. http://www.malala.org. Accessed June 19, 2019.

MAP: Movement Advancement Project. http://www.lgbtmap.org/. Accessed June 19, 2019.

Metropolitan Community Churches. https://www.mcchurch.org/. Accessed April 7, 2020.

Musawah: For Equality in the Muslim Family. http://www.musawah.org/. Accessed June 19, 2019.

Ordain Women: Mormon Women Seeking Equality and Ordination to the Priesthood. http://ordainwomen.org/. Accessed June 19, 2019.

Pew Research Center. https://www.pewresearch.org/. Accessed June 19, 2019.

Roman Catholic Womenpriests. http://romancatholicwomenpriests.org/. Accessed April 5, 2020.

Sakyadhita: International Association of Buddhist Women. http://www.sakyadhita.org/. Accessed June 19, 2019.

Sisters in Islam: Empowering Voices for Change. https://www.sistersinislam.org.my/. Accessed July 26, 2019.

Sojourner Truth Memorial Committee. https://sojournertruthmemorial.org/. Accessed June 19, 2019.

Stop FGM in Kurdistan. http://www.stopfgmkurdistan.org/. Accessed June 19, 2019.

The 50 Million Missing: The Fight to End Female Genocide in India. https://50millionmissing.wordpress.com/. Accessed June 19, 2019.

The Women's Mosque of America. http://womensmosque.com/. Accessed December 16, 2019.

Tibetan Nuns Project. https://tnp.org/. Accessed December 8, 2019.

Tzu Chi USA. https://tzuchi.us/. Accessed June 19, 2019.

UNICEF Data. https://data.unicef.org/. Accessed April 8, 2020.

Yeshivat Maharat. http://www.yeshivatmaharat.org/. Accessed June 19, 2019.

INDEX

Adam and Eve. *See also* Eve
Adam, Eve, and the Serpent (Genesis 2–3),
    45, 84, 112, 120, 139
Adhi Parasakthi Temple Society of
    Canada, 145
Adhiparashakthi (Ādi Parāśakti), 144–
    45
Adigalar, Bangaru, 145
Adovasio, J. M., 49, 52, 54, 58
agunah (plural, *agunot*), 106–7
"Ain't I a Woman?" speech. *See* Truth,
    Sojourner
àjẹ, 71
Ali, Kecia, 109, 110, 111, 115, 118
Amaterasu, 34, 134
American Psychological Association
    (APA), 152
American Society of Muslims, 109
American Sociological Association, 95
ancestor veneration, 126
androcentrism, 19–20; quadruple andro-
    centrism, 19–20
androgynous women and men, 16, 94
androgyny, 94
Anglican Church of New Zealand, 139
Anglican Communion, 136, 139, 140, 152,
    185n83
animism, 124
annulment of marriage in Catholic
    Church, 108
Apache, 80, 147–48, 184n27; Chiricahua
    and Mescalero, 55–57, 113, 147–48,
    186n106; Lipan, 55; White Mountain,
    180n44, 186n106

Apache boy's puberty ritual, 55
Apache girl's puberty ritual, 55–57, 119,
    147–48, 180n44, 186n106
Apache "respect" taboos, 184n27
apostle, meaning of, 137–38, 186n87
apostolic succession, 141, 142
Aquinas, Thomas, 24–25
Aristotelian biology, 25
Aristotle, 24
art as practical science, 69
Aryans, 42–44
àṣẹ, 71
Association of Roman Catholic Women
    Priests (ARCWP), 141, 142

backlash, 14, 24, 27, 155, 157
Baird, Robert D., 21
Banerji, Rita, 7
bar mitzvah, 149
basic religion, 124–26
bat mitzvah, 148–50
Benedict XVI, Pope, 3
Beta Israel. *See* Ethiopian Jews
bhikkhuni. *See* Buddhist nuns
bhikṣuṇī. *See* Buddhist nuns
biblical inerrancy, 11
blood, of women, 113–14
brit milah, 148
Bronze Age, 46
Buddha, Gautama, 8
Buddhist Compassion Tzu Chi Founda-
    tion, 32
Buddhist nuns, 8–10
Burning Times, 25, 119–20, 150

ABOUT THE AUTHOR

Catherine Wessinger is the Rev. H. James Yamauchi, S.J. Professor in the History of Religions in the Religious Studies Department at Loyola University New Orleans. She is the editor of *Women's Leadership in Marginal Religions: Explorations outside the Mainstream* and of *Religious Institutions and Women's Leadership: New Roles inside the Mainstream.* She is co-editor of *Women in the World's Religions and Spirituality Project,* which is part of the online *World Religions and Spirituality Project.* She is the editor of the *Women in Religions* series at New York University Press.

Lightning Source UK Ltd.
Milton Keynes UK
UKHW012100081120
372905UK00015B/242